AF234664

MR MOONLIGHT

MR MOONLIGHT

BRIAN EPSTEIN AND
THE MAKING OF THE BEATLES

PHILIP NORMAN

**SIMON &
SCHUSTER**

London · New York · Amsterdam/Antwerp · Sydney/Melbourne · Toronto · New Delhi

First published in Great Britain by Simon & Schuster UK Ltd, 2026

Copyright © Philip Norman, 2026

The right of Philip Norman to be identified as the author of this work has been asserted in accordance with the Copyright, Designs and Patents Act, 1988.

1 3 5 7 9 10 8 6 4 2

Simon & Schuster UK Ltd, 1st Floor
222 Gray's Inn Road, London WC1X 8HB

www.simonandschuster.co.uk
www.simonandschuster.com.au
www.simonandschuster.co.in

Simon & Schuster Australia, Sydney
Simon & Schuster India, New Delhi

The authorised representative in the EEA is Simon & Schuster Netherlands BV, Herculesplein 96, 3584 AA Utrecht, Netherlands. info@simonandschuster.nl

A CIP catalogue record for this book is available from the British Library

Hardback ISBN: 978-1-3985-4226-6
Trade Paperback ISBN: 978-1-3985-4227-3
eBook ISBN: 978-1-3985-4228-0

Typeset in Bembo by M Rules
Printed and Bound in the UK using 100% Renewable Electricity
at CPI Group (UK) Ltd

MIX
Paper | Supporting
responsible forestry
FSC® C013604

CONTENTS

Prologue

RONNIE KRAY'S BIG IDEA

One day in January 1985, the *Liverpool Echo*'s crime reporter Peter Trollope set out on an assignment far outside the *Echo*'s circulation area, driving 250 miles south to Parkhurst maximum security prison on the Isle of Wight to interview Reggie Kray.

Reggie and his identical twin Ronnie were crime bosses who once ruled London's East End like Al Capone did the Chicago of the 1920s. As well as the most ruthless and cruel, they were the scariest of thugs with their barely distinguishable fleshy faces, genteel Cockney accents and fixed expressions of outrage that they could ever be suspected of wrongdoing.

Throughout the 1960s, their so-called 'Firm' carried on its multifarious trade of murder, armed robbery, extortion, arson and money-laundering with minimal interference from the police. The collapsing class barriers of that era allowed them to mingle with politicians and the aristocracy, be photographed by David Bailey and appear on television talk shows.

In 1969, the twins were finally collared for the murder of two of their own associates – Jack 'The Hat' McVitie, disembowelled with a carving knife, and George Cornell, shot down in a Bethnal Green pub called the Blind Beggar – and given identical

1

life sentences. The schizophrenic sexual predator Ronnie was sent to Broadmoor psychiatric hospital, the marginally saner Reggie to Parkhurst, whose island location makes it Britain's nearest equivalent to Alcatraz.

Peter Trollope had recently written a series of articles about heroin abuse on Merseyside, then so rife that babies were becoming addicted in the womb. An underworld contact of Trollope's had sent the articles to Reggie Kray, who'd shown great interest in them and requested a meeting with their author.

It turned out that he'd been deeply stirred to read of Merseyside's heroin problem and its prevalence among unemployed young men. Like many old-school villains, the Krays had abhorred drugs despite the vast profits to be made. 'Anyone we caught dealing on our territory we would run out of London,' he told Trollope. 'Or break their legs or *remove* them.'

What was more, he had a plan to save those young Merseysiders from addiction. It was to get them into boxing as he and Ronnie had been as boys, creating the matching pair of lethal lightweights who'd preceded the criminal heavyweights.

With the resources available to him even as a 'lifer', he proposed to finance a boxing gym in Birkenhead, one of the worst addiction areas, and was offering the story to Trollope as an exclusive. 'I want to show these kids another way,' said this most unlikely of social reformers. 'Boxing teaches you respect and discipline. You don't need drugs. It keeps you fit and you're able to take care of yourself.'

Far from showing reticence about his past, he looked back nostalgically to the Firm's years as a branch office of the American Mafia and the dependability of its services, whether shooting, knifing or garrotting. 'For us, the Mob were always in the background. They knew that if they wanted anything done in England, they could do it through the Krays.'

His outside contact had told him that as well as covering crime for the *Liverpool Echo*, his visitor wrote a weekly pop music column. It was in this context that he suddenly mentioned a name Trollope least expected to hear within the walls of Britain's Alcatraz: Brian Epstein.

The Beatles' manager, he said, had been a frequent guest at the lavish parties he and Ronnie used to throw in the Swinging Sixties for showbusiness chums like Frank Sinatra, Liza Minnelli, Dusty Springfield and Peter Sellers. And with their talent for sniffing out human frailty, the twins had recognised a victim as defenceless as any paying them protection in the East End.

They had first intended to exploit Brian's homosexuality, then in its last days as a criminal offence. They'd acquired some photographs of him with another man that, if made public, would have destroyed him and irreparably tainted his cherished Beatles. Then Ronnie had come up with a more elaborate scenario designed to burnish their lustre as celebrities.

'We ruled London, but we were looking for ways to expand,' Reggie told Peter Trollope. 'We'd heard that Epstein was in trouble. Ronnie had this idea that if we could get him to sign The Beatles over to us, that would have been a passport to worldwide fame.'

The plot was – for the Krays – unusually subtle. As they knew, Brian had a gambling addiction that had greatly worsened since The Beatles had stopped touring in order to concentrate on making albums, and so no longer needed his obsessive day-to-day care and attention.

3

To fill this void in his life, he haunted the chemin-de-fer table at Mayfair's plush Clermont Club, regularly losing thousands of pounds in a sitting. The Clermont's owner, John Aspinall, who was in the Krays' pocket, had agreed to rig the 'chemmy' until Brian was so deeply in debt that he'd have no choice but to sell them John, Paul, George and Ringo.

In the end, though, they'd decided not to add Britain's greatest national treasure to their portfolio of murder and mayhem, but to stick to what they knew. 'We were just going to blackmail Epstein over the photographs,' Reggie said, 'but then he goes and dies . . .'

'Going and dying' sounded like something Brian had chosen to do solely to inconvenience them. But then came an elliptical reference to his particular way of going and dying: from an overdose of barbiturates, all alone at the seeming apogee of his success.

Reggie came as near as a Kray twin could to smiling over the inquest verdict of accidental death from an 'incautious self-overdose', observing sagely that 'It's easy to kill someone and make it look like an overdose.'

As he'd hinted earlier, when the twins were plotting to move in on The Beatles they'd known about Brian's one great managerial misstep. Three years on, he still seemed to be trying to dull the memory of it with ever-increasing doses of drugs and alcohol.

The band's conquest of America in 1964 had created a demand for themed merchandise that should have earned them millions. But Brian had failed to realise its potential and delegated the issuing of manufacturing licences to a group of young British entrepreneurs based in New York. Ninety per cent of the proceeds were to go to them and 10 per cent to him and The Beatles when it should have been the other way round.

Realising his blunder, he'd started bypassing his New York partners and doing merchandising deals of his own from London for a more realistic percentage. Major US customers like the Macy and J. C. Penney department stores had been unable to tell whether his or the partners' licences were the valid ones and, fearing legal repercussions if they made the wrong choice, had cancelled millions of dollars' worth of orders.

As a result, some smaller manufacturers who'd turned over their whole production lines to Beatle guitars or cushions or bubblegum had faced financial ruin. The stress had given one of them a fatal heart attack and his son had publicly sworn revenge by taking out a contract on Brian.

Given the Krays' Mafia connection, the job might well have been delegated to them. 'But it wasn't us,' Reggie told Trollope, clearly signalling that it *had* been someone – and he knew who.

Sadly for the *Liverpool Echo*'s crime reporter, his reminiscing ended there, never to be continued in his wildly scrawled letters to Trollope about the boxing gym until the project faded away, nor with anyone else. He still had not named Brian's supposed killer or killers when he died from cancer in 2000.

1

'EPPY'

There never was nor could be another pop manager like Brian Samuel Epstein, the young record-retailer from Liverpool with the uncertain smile who spun what has truly been called 'the twentieth century's greatest romance'.

Partly this is because there never could be other clients quite like The Beatles. When Brian took them on in 1962, his much-derided aim was to make them 'bigger than Elvis Presley', at that time the supreme pop superstar. It proved an uncharacteristic understatement: after only two years in his hands, they'd be bigger than any earthly instrument could measure.

Pop artists' managers in Britain thus far had been a seedy bunch known to the public, if at all, for their ruthless exploitation and the defrauding of their naïve young charges. Brian was of an utterly different stamp, with his educated accent, punctilious good manners and belief in honouring agreements and giving value for money.

His achievement in a profession of which he had no previous experience, and for which no rulebook existed, remains jaw-dropping. A devout classical music fan, he was nonetheless solely responsible for a new genre of pop that was to change its course, and Britain's international image, for ever – yet, disgracefully, earn him no public honour, nor even thanks.

After The Beatles, he signed up further young Liverpool talent, enough to constitute a 'Mersey Sound' and elevate him, aged twenty-nine, from manager into mogul: Gerry and the Pacemakers, Billy J. Kramer, Cilla Black, The Fourmost. At the Mersey Sound's high-water mark, around 1963–64, there was seldom a week without one or more of his discoveries in the UK singles or album charts.

British pop during the class-bound early '60s had been overwhelmingly blue collar, its name still besmirched by the antisocial behaviour its rowdier parent, rock 'n' roll, had visited on the mid-'50s. Without adulterating the Beatles' sound or their personalities in the slightest, Brian gave them an air of refinement they would keep even after prematurely losing him.

The cover of their debut album, *Please Please Me*, showed four hard-boiled Scousers whom the camera didn't much love, grinning down from an anonymous balcony; on that of their second, *With The Beatles*, eight months later they'd become polo-necked, subtly lit and solemn like art students or denizens of the Parisian Left Bank. From then on, middle- and upper-class teenagers, the aristocracy, finally even royalty could be Beatlemaniacs too.

But to Brian The Beatles were always more than just a licence to print money; they were the children a homosexual man in the 1960s otherwise couldn't hope for. Though less than six years older than Ringo, the eldest, he always referred to them collectively as 'the boys'.

To them he was 'Eppy', a very Liverpool subversion of his executive airs (at times varied by crushing cruelty on John's part). But their belief and trust in him were almost child-like; from first to last, they would sign any piece of paper he put in front of them usually without reading it.

His peak as what nowadays would be called an 'influencer' came in February 1964 when he took them to America to play to a nationwide television audience of 73 million. In that moment, a decade whose youthful creativity thus far had mainly been about cinema, the theatre and art, finally began to 'swing'.

The numerous British bands fashioned in The Beatles' image (i.e., the bespoke-suited, pixie-booted look decreed by Brian) poured across the Atlantic after them, a literal invasion that wiped out the whole existing generation of American popstars at a plectrum-stroke. Young musicians from coast to coast discarded their crewcuts and Bermuda shorts to form foursomes with Beatle fringes and Beatle suits, singing tough-tender Beatle harmonies in faux-Liverpudlian accents. Without ever knowing it, all of them, too, were Brian's boys.

His vision was not all-encompassing. The master plan for the Beatles that he drew up initially took no account of John and Paul's prolific songwriting genius – the sphere in which they were always bigger than Elvis – nor the speed at which it evolved from the simple crayoning of 'Love Me Do' and 'She Loves You' to masterpieces in oils like 'Penny Lane' and 'A Day in the Life'.

Indeed, in that later period he became semi-detached from their music, leaving their inspirational producer, George Martin, to oversee its creative quantum leaps. Rather, he focused on what he felt was an almost sacred duty to supply their every need, gratify their slightest whims and otherwise maintain the invisible shield with which he prevented their terrifying fame from tearing them to pieces.

The pity was, he could never construct a similar shield around himself. For even at his golden zenith he had to endure the anti-Semitism that was then commonplace, sometimes naked but more often the stealthy British variety unnoticeable to anyone but the victim. And until the last weeks of his short life, he was forced to live outside the law in a lingering dark age where consensual sex between men, however private, was deemed 'an act of gross indecency' and punished by indecently long prison sentences with a maximum of life.

The neutral term 'gay' had yet to come into general use. Most Britons employed the taunts of the homophobe: 'pouf', 'nonce', 'pansy', 'arse-bandit', 'shirt-lifter', but none so ubiquitous and venomous as 'queer', both as noun and adjective. Brian would have been amazed to see today's LGBTQ community embrace the adjective as a proud cultural and artistic validation.

Him it condemned to a furtive parallel existence, racked by the dual guilt of betraying his old-school Jewish parents, as he saw it, and offending against the religion that always meant much to him. Adding immeasurably to that burden, a streak of masochism in an otherwise gentle and sensitive nature made him seek out younger straight men, usually in public spaces after dark, courting arrest, humiliation, robbery, beatings-up and blackmail.

John's way of repudiating a middle-class suburban background was to pretend to be just the kind of street-corner hoodlum Brian found most fatally attractive. It was what had first drawn him to The Beatles and his obsession with John never went away, like scar tissue that could bleed afresh at any moment.

As he rose higher in the entertainment business, he met many major figures with discreet permanent gay relationships but, aside from a short-lived one during his teens, Brian was never so fortunate: the greater his success, the more reckless and joyless were his casual affairs and the more entrenched his delusion that his precious boys knew nothing about them.

Few twenty-first-century Beatles fans appreciate how short was their time together at the top – barely six years. By two thirds of the way through, they'd very obviously stopped being boys in any eyes but Brian's.

In August 1967, his management contract with them was about to expire and, he believed, would not be renewed. He put on a brave show of acceptance that sooner or later they were bound to fly the steel-reinforced nest he had built for them.

When he died, mysteriously and alone, aged only thirty-two and at the height of the so-called Summer of Love, they had seemingly declared their independence by adopting a very different mentor, the Indian guru Maharishi Mahesh Yogi.

'Then we're fucked,' John said when told the news – and they were.

2

'HELP ME, I AM LOST'

But for the whim of a racist mob, Brian would not have been born in Liverpool, to find his marvellous and tragic destiny there.

His paternal grandfather Isaac Epstein came to Britain from Lithuania in 1894, an 18-year-old Ashkenazi Jew, alone, penniless and speaking only Yiddish, but with a highly developed work ethic and iron determination to succeed.

Isaac found his way to Manchester's Jewish quarter, where he worked in a draper's shop owned by a couple named Joseph and Esther Hyman, in due course marrying their daughter, Dinah, with whom he had six children. By the age of twenty-three he'd moved his family thirty-four miles west to Liverpool and opened his own furniture shop at 80 Walton Road in the city's Kirkdale district.

Before the Great War, Kirkdale's mixed Irish, Welsh, German, Jewish and West Indian population had coexisted in harmony. All that changed in May 1915 when the Cunard liner *Lusitania*, en route from New York to Liverpool, was sighted by a German U-boat lurking off the Irish coast. A single torpedo sent the ship to the bottom in eighteen minutes and 1,198 of the 1,962 on board were lost.

The crew had included many Liverpudlians with relatives in Kirkdale and the tragedy set off a wave of violence against its German residents and looting of their businesses. The onslaught soon extended to any person or shop with a foreign-sounding name and there was widespread malicious rumour-mongering that this or that blameless tradesperson was a covert 'Hun'. Many such victims were forced to place advertisements in the *Liverpool Echo*, protesting their Britishness to the marrow.

Although Isaac Epstein had held British nationality since 1904, he soon found his family and business threatened in this way. His pre-emptive *Echo* advert stood out from the others by offering a £50 reward – in those days the price of a small house – to 'anyone giving information that will lead to the conviction of any person or persons who have circulated the untrue and slanderous statement that we are Germans'.

Whether or not anyone collected or was sued for slander is not recorded. However, not long afterwards, a furniture shop in Russian-Jewish ownership only a few doors from Isaac's was attacked and looted but then the mob dispersed without so much as cracking a window pane on his premises.

None of Kirkdale's traders received a penny in compensation for the damage to their property. Those who'd been burnt out were sent to temporary accommodation in Hawick, Scotland, where many chose to settle. Others moved elsewhere in England, sickened by the way their former neighbours and customers had treated them.

But as Isaac's business was still intact, he stayed on – and so the grandson of whom he didn't yet dream would one day be in exactly the right place at the right time.

* * *

Staying on didn't mean standing still. After the war, Isaac purchased the shops on either side of him to create a continuous frontage, and expanded his stock from own-brand furniture to upholstery, household goods and 'baby cars' – Liverpool-ese for children's strollers.

His further acquisition of numbers 70 to 72 Walton Road in 1929 brought him a small musical instrument dealer's called North End Music Stores, known locally as 'Nems'. In advertising his copious wares, Isaac could now list 'pianos' after 'sideboards'.

His sons, Leslie and Harry Wolf, joined him in the business as was expected, although only the younger, Harry, showed any affinity with it and could tolerate their father's despotic grip on its every department.

In 1933, the 29-year-old Harry married 18-year-old Malka Hyman, who coincidentally had the same surname as his mother, Dinah. These Hymans were also in furniture, a chisel-notch above the Epsteins as owners of the Sheffield Veneering Company, which manufactured living-room 'suites' of couch and twin armchairs with impressive titles such as 'The Clarendon'.

Harry's bride was a young woman more suggestive of Delft china than teak or mahogany. The Hebrew word *malka* means queen, so from childhood she'd been called Queenie, in Britain a nickname usually connoting dig-in-the ribs cheeriness and gin on the breath. Nothing could have been further from her shy, fastidious nature.

Harry and Queenie's first child was born in a private clinic in Rodney Street, Liverpool, on 19 September 1934. It being

Yom Kippur, the Jewish Day of Atonement, added further to the joy and high expectations due a male firstborn.

Nineteen thirty-four was the height of the Depression, nowhere crueller than in Liverpool's docks, where grey multitudes of cloth-capped men surrounded each 'spike' or hiring-point with the hopelessness of cattle in an abattoir and hungry children played barefoot in the streets.

But at 27 Anfield Road, Harry and Queenie's substantial terrace house close to Liverpool FC's Anfield stadium, all was comfort and security. There Brian spent his infancy in a glow of parental admiration and praise. The birth of a brother, Clive John, in 1936 did little to dim his lustre.

Physically he was like his father, dark-eyed and snub-nosed with wavy light-brown hair, but his temperament was his mother's, especially in his love of refinement and innate sense of style. When I interviewed Queenie during the 1970s, she recalled how he'd come to her room as she got ready to go out for the evening and gravely confer with her about the dress and accessories she should choose.

In that pre-television age, he shared her passion for the cinema, Hollywood musicals above all. When she took him to see *The Wizard of Oz*, its theme song 'Somewhere Over the Rainbow' performed by the 17-year-old Judy Garland, so entranced him that for hours afterwards he could barely speak.

Isaac's sister Stella, Brian's great-aunt who regularly came to the house to look after him and Clive if their parents were going out, noticed how he'd try to make conversion appealing to her. '"Tell me, Auntie," he'd say, "How is Mrs So-and-so?" He was like a little old man.'

He was generally even-tempered but abnormally sensitive: if anything upset him, a deep blush would herald a furious tantrum for which, more often than not, he'd humbly apologise later.

Harry and Queenie were prominent and popular members of the largest Jewish community outside London, unfailing attendees at their local synagogue, Greenbank Park, and generous donors to its associated charities. Queenie maintained a kosher household, never serving meat with milk, keeping a separate set of plates, glasses and cutlery for festivals and high holidays like Passover and Rosh Hashana and cherishing the pre-Sabbath family ritual of Friday night dinner.

Harry was a man of strong faith but equally strong principles. Offered various prestigious honorary posts at Greenbank Park, he declined them on the grounds of not being 'hundred per cent observant' because he worked at the shop on Saturdays.

Socially sensitive Queenie preferred Brian not to mix with the children of I. Epstein employees but in Joe Flannery's case it was unavoidable. Joe's Liverpool-Irish father, Christopher, designed and made the bespoke furniture that remained Epstein's core business. Isaac was a stickler for quality, demanding that the drawers in a chest of drawers open and close just as smoothly if inserted upside-down. Chris Flannery's handiwork never failed this test.

Away from his workbench, the meticulous craftsman was a monster to his wife, Agnes, and their six children, a drunken wastrel, pub brawler, philanderer and wife-beater even during Agnes's pregnancies. He was especially vile to Joe, his mild, serious third son, whom he derided as 'a wet Nellie' for not kicking a football around like other boys and requesting dancing shoes

17

as a Christmas present. 'He'd say, "We're going to have to buy you a *dress*",' Joe told me in our many talks together. 'And he'd make out that I wanted to molest my little brother, Peter, who I loved. "Don't look at your brother like that!" he used to shout.'

There was something more than a business relationship between Harry Epstein and Flannery, with whom he'd occasionally sneak off to boxing-matches in central Liverpool without Queenie's knowledge. And Agnes Flannery knew Queenie, by then the firm's bookkeeper, since payments to her husband often fell into arrears and to keep her children fed she had to pursue them in person, feeling it more effective to do so at Queenie's home than the shop. Joe would sometimes go with her and, while the two women conducted their business, he would act as three-years-younger Brian's playmate-cum-minder.

He was dazzled by the quantity and expensiveness of Brian's toys, all of lead or tin rather than the crude wooden ones his joiner father turned for him and his siblings. The latest was a model of the gold-encrusted State Coach recently seen passing through London in King George VI's Coronation procession, with eight white horses ridden by four liveried grooms and an escort of mounted trumpeters and beplumed Household Cavalry.

'It was like a piece of crown jewellery to me,' Joe recalled, 'but when I tried to play with it, Brian threw a moody and stamped on the horses' legs until he'd broken them.'

One far-distant day, he would possess a still more wondrous toy that the whole world longed to play with. Only then, he'd be the one to get broken.

* * *

This roseate existence was interrupted by the outbreak of the Second World War in 1939 and Liverpool's transformation from obscure north-western metropolis to frontline combatant. Its docks handled 90 per cent of the war materials and desperately needed food supplies coming into Britain from the US and was the main base for warships fighting the Battle of the Atlantic. In consequence it suffered German air raids second only to London's with around 4,000 civilians killed and 10,000 homes reduced to rubble.

Brian and Clive were spared any such trauma for their father rented houses in the relative safety of North Wales first, and then Southport on the west Lancashire coast, where the family remained until the Liverpool Blitz was over.

Being thus uprooted then moved from one temporary junior school to another inevitably had a destabilising effect on Brian's education. It would have mattered less if he'd made use of the intelligence and quick wits he clearly possessed. But by the age of ten he'd attended four nursery or prep schools, settled down at none of them and been expelled from two for inattentiveness and poor results.

That year, 1944, Harry brought his family back to Liverpool, to the handsome five-bedroom house he'd had built on Queens Drive in the upmarket Childwall district. Brian was enrolled at Liverpool College, the city's top fee-paying school.

At the end of his first year, the headmaster asked his parents to remove him for surreptitiously doing 'a dirty drawing' during a mathematics class. According to Brian it had been a design for a pretend-theatre programme, legitimately adorned with the

19

figures of dancing girls. But privately the head told Queenie he'd turned out to be 'a problem child' without giving any further detail.

Some fathers might have protested this was grossly unfair but Harry Epstein had too much respect for authority in any form. Brian was never to forget the cheek-burning shame of sitting on the sofa in the living-room of his new family home and hearing angry words from his father that seemed to write him off for ever: 'I don't know *what* we're going to do with you.'

He told his mother the real problem at Liverpool College had been anti-Semitism – a bizarre notion just after a war that had been fought at huge cost to save Europe's Jews from annihilation by Hitler. Even so, most British people saw nothing wrong in using epithets like 'Jewboy' and 'Yid' or telling jokes about rabbis and circumcision in supposedly Jewish accents ('Vat you vant?') or mimicking supposed Jewish avarice by waving their fingers as if counting money. Queenie guessed it must have been the same at previous schools where he'd seemed to do so badly.

The only solution seemed to be a school that catered for Jewish boys yet provided a secular education approximating to Liverpool College's. The nearest his parents could find was a boarding school named Beaconsfield in Kent, more than 200 miles to the south. Still chastened by the scene with Harry, Brian agreed to give it a try.

Beaconsfield's Judaism was in the lowest possible key: learning Hebrew was not on the curriculum, most of the staff were Christian and the school synagogue's services were conducted half in English. Brian was not to be completely isolated there. His brother Clive insisted on following him – much to

Queenie's distress at having both of them so far away – and they soon made friends with another Liverpool boy named Malcolm Shifrin, likewise the son of furniture dealers.

In mid-twentieth-century Britain, no institution was unhealthier than the average boys' private boarding school whose pupils could quite legally be kept starving, freezing and terrified on the Victorian principle that it was character-building. With many of them at the onset of puberty, claustrophobically confined together for months on end, homoeroticism was almost an extra school rule: big boys molested small ones while housemasters predated as they pleased.

Thanks to Beaconsfield's religious underpinning, it practised zero-tolerance of boy-on-boy sex, albeit by methods somewhat recalling the French Revolution. In Brian's first term, two who had been caught masturbating each other were ritualistically paraded in the headmaster's study in front of their dormitorymates, Brian included, as the head caned them on their bare behinds.

Corporal punishment for the most trivial offences was a part of everyday life, but there was a weird culture of boys showing off and comparing their welts and bruises – even a certain prestige in possessing the bloodiest examples.

The majority passed through this seedy vestibule to sex, where punishment coexisted with titillation, and shame and bravado were one, without serious long-term effects. Clive Epstein was to do so, but not his brother.

* * *

Brian's two years at Beaconsfield brought out talents that had previously gone unnoticed, especially for art and design and acting. Although indifferent to games, he asked Harry and Queenie if he could have horse-riding lessons, a costly 'extra' of which they expected he would soon tire. Instead, it became such a passion that when he won a prize for art, he chose a book called *Equitation*. His indulgent parents bought him a horse named Amber, which was stabled in Liverpool (no easy matter) while he was away at school.

He also joined the school choir, much to Clive's surprise as he'd never heard him sing other than in synagogue. In fact, he had an attractive tenor voice, though he was never to do anything further with it.

However, his previous disrupted school career meant that his marks in class and examinations remained consistently poor whereas his studious, hard-working younger brother invariably did well. It deepened the feeling that gnawed at him of being, in his own words, 'a failure, dullard and inferior person'.

What might be termed his horsey period did not affect his precocious love of grown-up luxury and glamour. During the school holidays, his greatest treat was to be taken out to dinner at Liverpool's splendiferous Adelphi Hotel in Ranelagh Place with its Art Nouveau vestibule and pillared Palm Court modelled on the one that had gone down with the *Titanic*.

One such evening at the Adelphi, he unexpectedly met an old acquaintance but not as another diner. His former playmate-cum-minder Joe Flannery, now a very tall sixteen-year-old, was training to be a commis waiter in the hotel's French restaurant and one of the team serving the Epsteins.

Joe was so excited to see them that he forgot his professional formality, but was brought up short by Brian's guarded response. '[He] said, "Please don't stand at the table talking to me because my mother doesn't like it." I was so *embarrassed*,' Joe told me in the 1980s, still wincing at the memory.

Harry and Queenie could easily have afforded continental holidays but preferred old-fashioned British seaside resorts like Llandudno in North Wales or St Annes on Lancashire's Fylde coast despite their chronically unpredictable weather. One summer in Llandudno when the rain poured down, Queenie took Brian to a matinee concert by the Liverpool Philharmonic Orchestra. From that moment, he loved and wanted to learn about classical music.

Another year in St Annes, his parents struck up a friendship with Geraldo, one of that era's most famous big band leaders and radio celebrities. During the Epsteins' visit, Geraldo had to make a record in Blackpool and invited them along to watch.

Queenie told how Brian sat spellbound as the red light went on for silence – doubtless supposing this would be his one and only visit to a recording-studio and that he'd better make the most of it.

By now he had embarked on the long preparation for his bar mitzvah, the ceremony in which every 13-year-old Jewish boy officially becomes a man. He was deep into it before he realised he was studying the wrong section of the Torah, from which he'd have to read aloud on the big day. He went to a rabbi in Liverpool for catch-up coaching and was soon on the right page, showing that he could do anything if he put his mind to it. His bar mitzvah service at Greenbank Park synagogue went off without a hitch: he was word-perfect in all his responses and read immaculately from the Torah.

Afterwards there was a lavish reception for a hundred people back at 197 Queens Drive, Brian using his flair for acting in his speech of thanks to Harry and Queenie. His aunt Stella's husband, Meier – a lawyer, so no pushover – thought his performance 'very competent ... I got the strong impression that he had a degree of refinement and culture which was unusual in a boy of his age, and a good deal of self-assurance. It did occur to me that he was going places even then.'

* * *

With the end of his time at Beaconsfield approaching, he sat the Common Entrance, the examination necessary to complete his schooling at one of Britain's historic academies that are not 'common' any more than they merit their designation as 'public'.

The three leading public schools in his parents' sights were Repton, Rugby or Clifton, but a mediocre exam result got him only to Clayesmore, a much smaller and less exalted one near Blandford Forum in Dorset.

His first term did not go well. Although there was no anti-Semitism, overtly at least, he was subjected to merciless bullying by his schoolfellows, and what set him apart was not his Jewishness but his dislike of sports. 'As soon as he got there, he started grumbling,' Queenie said. 'Oh, those grumbles of his were *enormous*.'

Yet he soon found himself warming to the place. Its ideas were progressive for that era and it allowed its pupils an unusual degree of freedom and nonconformity. Its alumnae included impressive names from the two fields that most interested Brian, the painter and war artist Edward Ardizzone, and George Devine, the director and founder of London's Old Vic Theatre School.

Brian's interest in art was encouraged, his paintings were praised and he sold several to members of the teaching staff.

24

This implanted a new feeling of confidence, reflected in his much-improved classwork. He even got into football and long-distance running, which did wonders for his standing in the school community. He would later call this 'perhaps the only content period in my life'.

It was not to last. His parents had never been comfortable with Clayesmore's being a 'minor' public school and in his third term his father persuaded the headmaster of an indisputably major one, Wrekin College in Shropshire, to grant him an interview. Deploying his usual maturity and charm, he was admitted on the spot.

Yet this first real success of his life brought him no satisfaction. 'Now for Wrekin I hate,' he wrote in his diary. 'I go there only for my parents' pleasure.'

However Wrekin offered a range of activities and facilities he found impossible to resist. He continued to paint in oils and watercolour, to general acclaim, and branched out into sculpture. There was a theatre group which he joined and soon effectively took over by producing the school play, a costume drama about Christopher Columbus. In its small, cardboard-daggered way, it exhibited all the qualities of the impresario to come: painstaking organisation, meticulous attention to detail, skill in motivating and handling people.

His mother recalled how he also took the lead role, although a fit of bashfulness prevented him from letting her and Harry know beforehand or even when they arrived at the school to see it. 'We had no idea,' Queenie said, 'until we saw him up there on the stage.'

Like Beaconsfield, Wrekin maintained a ceaseless watch for 'funny business' among the boys, albeit without the same ritual

25

chastising of offenders. Throughout Brian's two years there, he never fell under the slightest suspicion of such behaviour, in fact he was one of the ostentatiously macho set, to be seen at mealtimes ogling the younger women on the catering staff. 'He never struck me as being anything other than someone interested in the female body,' a fellow ogler recalls.

His days were filled with wholesome activity of every kind. He joined the school's Combined Cadet Force, which conditioned boys for a career in one or other of the armed services, took an interest in Roman Catholicism, with which Judaism has much in common, and played rugby well enough to get into the First XV. In a team photograph after the winning of some clearly important trophy, he is the tallest and toughest-looking one. When in due course Clive came to join him, he was a significant enough figure to prevent his 'minor', in public school jargon, from being bullied or baited.

Yet he would recall this as the time when 'loneliness entered my life to stick' and it became a daily ordeal to walk to the refectory to tea by himself 'while the other boys passed by laughing and joking in twos and fours'.

His parents were hugely relieved that he seemed to have settled down at last and be reconciled to his proper future as a first son, which was to complete his education, then join his grandfather and father in the family firm, get married and have children. Meanwhile he was writing in his diary: 'Help me, I am lost. Help me, I am lost.'

Harry and Queenie were used to his letters from Wrekin being hearteningly about scoring tries or drilling with the CCF, so were dumbfounded by the one that arrived during the summer term of 1950. It informed them that he'd come top of his class in art and design and wanted to leave school and become a dress designer.

That the usual term was 'couturier' brought Harry little consolation. To him it suggested everything that was frilly, perfumed and precious and he shuddered to think what the furniture trade and Greenbank Park synagogue would make of this terrible metamorphosis in his rugger-playing son.

Queenie was more sympathetic, recalling how even as a toddler Brian had had an instinctive sense of which clothes and accessories suited her best. But Harry's flat refusal to underwrite such folly was final. His alternative plea to be allowed to go to art college received equally short shrift from his father.

He was allowed to leave Wrekin with no academic qualifications; otherwise, filial duty was unrelenting. That September, just after his sixteenth birthday, he started work at I. Epstein and Sons.

3

'FORWARD, BRIAN'

On his first morning, a woman came into the shop in search of a cheap mirror. He was told to serve her – 'Forward, Brian', the traditional command that would have been used – and in a few minutes convinced her that what she really needed was a table costing £12, equivalent to about £200 today.

He proved himself a born salesman, courteous without being crawly, persistent without being pushy, somehow able to make every sale feel like the most laudable good sense on the purchaser's part. Even as a sixteen-year-old, he gave tone to the place with his faultless attire and grooming and a voice that after three public schools was as cultured as a BBC newsreader's with the faintest touch of Liverpool around the edges.

Nor was the job such a blow to his proud artistic spirit. It was in its way as satisfying as painting a picture or moulding a piece of sculpture to arrange goods to look their most enticing around the shop or in its windows along Walton Road. And at long last, he was doing something that didn't disappoint or puzzle or exasperate but actually pleased his father.

His grandfather less so. At the age of seventy-four, Isaac Epstein still exerted absolute control over the business he'd

29

founded at the turn of the century and still ran in much the same way. But Brian had all kinds of new ideas about presentation, culled from glossy magazines and Liverpool's three major department stores, and began putting them into effect with all the impatience and tactlessness of youth.

When dressing a window with a dining table and matching chairs, he arranged the chairs as if for a dinner party with some of their backs facing the street. Isaac was outraged by this casual disregard of a tradition dating back before the Great War: in I. Epstein windows, chairs of whatever kind had always stood in a row, all facing forward. Brian argued that his way was 'more natural', doubtless with the furious blush that always came at moments of stress.

Such aesthetic clashes became so frequent that Harry thought it best to get him out of Isaac's way for a while and arranged for him to spend six months with a national retailer, the Times Furnishing Company, based at its Lord Street branch in the city centre.

There his efficiency and people skills soon made an impression and the reports back to his father were consistently favourable. When his time there ended, the management presented him with an expensive Parker pen and pencil set (the same pen he would one day lend Paul McCartney to sign The Beatles' first contract with him).

His standing in the family firm greatly improved when Harry persuaded Isaac to open a new shop in Hoylake on the Cheshire Wirral aimed at a more sophisticated clientele than Walton Road's. It was named Clarendon Furnishing, a subtle upgrading from mere 'furniture'; Brian was made its manager and allowed to order the very latest in conical basketwork chairs, pastel-coloured tables with splayed legs and curtains patterned with Picasso-esque faces.

He decided it must have a grand celebrity opening and, rather than the usual civic dignitary, he chose Muriel Levy, aka 'Auntie Muriel', one of the presenters of BBC Radio's *Children's Hour*, fondly remembered from his own wartime childhood. His tracing of her agent, negotiation of her fee, arrangement of her journey to Liverpool and assiduous care of her during her stay were his first steps as an impresario, every one sure-footed. And under his management, the new venture was a huge success.

He'd never paid much attention to North End Music Stores – aka 'Nems' – the little musical instrument dealership his grandfather had taken over during the expansionist 1920s. But in 1951, the decision was taken to extend its stock from pianos and the occasional triangle to gramophones and records. Brian was the obvious choice to manage it in tandem with Clarendon Furnishings.

He dutifully stocked it with all the current, predominantly American pop hits like Nat 'King' Cole's 'Too Young', Patti Page's 'Tennessee Waltz', Johnnie Ray's 'Cry', Rosemary Clooney's 'Come-On-A-My House' and Frankie Laine's 'Jezebel'.

But his heart belonged to classical music. He had an extensive collection of recordings by the world's greatest opera singers and many symphonies, all housed in a cabinet specially made for him by his Sheffield Veneering Company relations, that none of his family was allowed to touch. With his former Beaconsfield classmate Malcolm Shifrin, he was an ardent supporter of the Liverpool Philharmonic Orchestra, an ensemble then – and still – equal to London's best.

'Brian's knowledge of music really was impressive,' Shifrin recalled. 'So it was too of related arts, like ballet. And he always seemed to know people behind the scenes – John Pritchard, the Phil's conductor, was a personal friend of his.'

Outwardly he personified what used to be called 'an eligible bachelor' with his good looks, elegance, intelligence and charm. Knowing his shyness, Queenie steered him towards a succession of suitable young women from her wide social circle with marriage and grandchildren ever in mind. He asked them out willingly enough, but never sought to repeat the date.

Some consolation was that he showed no sign of wanting to leave home as most young men his age would have done, but seemed content to remain at 197 Queens Drive, seemingly now at peace with his father and, as ever, his mother's trusty adviser on clothes and accessories.

One day in Walton Road he bumped into Joe Flannery, whom he'd last encountered as an over-talkative waiter in the Adelphi Hotel's French restaurant and whose family home turned out to be in City Road, only a few minutes' walk from I. Epstein's. With the social barrier of the Adelphi removed, the two began what was at first a casual friendship, meeting for coffee, going to the cinema, their common obsession, or browsing in Crease's record shop, Nems's chief local competitor, in County Road.

To three-years-older Joe, Brian was still the boy whose pampered existence he'd once briefly shared. As he told me, 'I used to lie awake at night, thinking about that lovely Coronation coach he'd trodden to bits rather than let me play with it.'

Joe's home life was still unremittingly hard, under the sway of a brutal father – I. Epstein's star cabinetmaker – who constantly mocked and reviled him for being 'different' from other young men without ever giving it its terrible name.

In fact he was deeply confused about his sexuality, and now discovered he wasn't the only one. 'Brian was obviously desperate to talk to someone and he started telling me about some of the things he'd gone through at school that his parents had no idea about.'

Joe Flannery was the first to realise that Brian's poise and sophistication went no deeper than the veneers on the furniture he sold. 'He was a very unhappy boy and I could see he needed a kind of affection he couldn't get from his family.'

* * *

In 1952, aged eighteen, Brian began the two years' compulsory national service that continued long after the Second World War with adolescence on one side and adulthood on the other, the 'teenager' a species as yet unknown.

He hoped to join the Royal Air Force for its lingering Battle of Britain glamour but was absorbed into the vast standing army whose main function by this time seemed to be providing radio comedians with easy laughs.

For most new 'squaddies' the weeks of basic training, designed to eradicate every trace of individualism and instil zombie-like obedience, were a living nightmare. Brian had already experienced some of their rigours in the Combined Cadet Force, to say nothing of three boarding schools, so couldn't have been as traumatised as some of his fellow inductees.

He applied for training as an officer, which would have entitled him to private living quarters and a batman (i.e., valet) but was turned down without taking the exhaustive leadership tests.

33

Instead, he was put into the 100 per cent glamour-free Royal Army Service Corps, which generally organises and supplies military operations rather than participating in them.

The British army of that era was notorious for giving its personnel jobs for which they were laughably unfitted, but Brian's as a 'documentation clerk', dealing with reams of paperwork, suited him perfectly and would prove to be useful training for the future he didn't dream of.

He might have been posted to Kenya or Cyprus, the two chronic trouble spots in Britain's fading empire, but was sent first to a camp near Taunton – not far from his alma mater, Clayesmore School – then to Regents Park Barracks in London.

It seemed in every way what soldiers called 'a cushy billet'. Work in the clerical office ended at 6 p.m. and after that his time was his own. The stark Victorian barracks in Albany Street were within walking distance or the West End's cinemas and theatres and, since his clerical duties included the issuing of leave-passes, he could authorise himself to get back to Liverpool whenever he chose.

He was required to spend only minimal time on the parade ground, much to his drill sergeant's relief for he seemed unable to tell right from left and several times wrecked otherwise perfect marching displays by wheeling in the wrong direction. Once, he managed to fall over while standing on parade, a spectacle usually associated with busby-wearing Grenadier Guardsmen in the summer heat of a royal Trooping the Colour ceremony.

His higher social class than most of his fellow recruits mattered little in his office environment and only once did his well-to-do background stand out. Queenie kept him so well supplied with pocket money that he didn't bother to draw his army pay until an irate regimental sergeant major ordered him to do so on pain of being put 'on a charge'.

Soldiering in London brought homosexuality into the open as much as it dared to be. Around the barracks Brian continually heard talk of 'queers' or 'arse-bandits', always in tones of deepest revulsion, and how there were pubs and clubs where they congregated in defiance of the law and common decency, but it never occurred to him to investigate the matter for himself.

At nineteen, he'd not yet had any kind of sexual encounter with another male – indeed, he would later claim to have still been ignorant of the facts of life. However, London taught him that, far from being isolated rarities, there were homosexuals everywhere and special signs by which one could recognise them, of which the hating hetero world remained totally unaware.

He learned, too, that the law's retribution made no allowance for a person's value to society. In the year of his enlistment, Alan Turing, the Second World War's codebreaking genius, was convicted of the same 'gross indecency' as Oscar Wilde half a century earlier. Opting for so-called chemical castration rather than prison, Turing was subjected to the same hormonal 'cure' with its horrible side-effects that the Nazis had been developing in Buchenwald concentration camp. Two years later, in the midst of pioneering work on computers, he would take his own life.

Brian soon came to loathe the army for its sclerotic bureaucracy and the nonsensical activities it invented for its men in the absence of any real purpose, such as scrubbing floors with toothbrushes or whitewashing coal.

Once, aboard a late train back from Liverpool, the prospect

of returning to duty so horrified him that he paced its corridors fretfully for almost the entire journey, only returning to his (first class) compartment just before arrival at Euston, to find that all the personal possessions he'd left there had been stolen.

Off-duty and freed from drab khaki, he adopted the civilian look favoured by junior lieutenants: a camelhair 'British Warm' topcoat and a pinstriped suit from Gieves, the military tailor, narrow-trousered, slant-pocketed, set off by a tightly rolled umbrella and a bowler hat. In this guise he regularly made use of the Naval and Military Club in Piccadilly – nicknamed 'The In and Out' after the gateposts to its driveway –without ever being challenged.

One day he returned to Albany Barracks from an outing, wearing his posh civvies and in a chauffeur-driven car. A sentry who didn't know him came to attention and saluted while a sergeant who did was standing nearby. With that, the game of looking like an officer turned into the serious military crime of impersonating one.

Normally he could have expected to be court-martialled and spend some time in an army 'glasshouse', but instead he was confined to barracks for a week, then put through a series of medical and psychiatric tests suggesting something rather more serious than receiving undeserved salutes.

All three of Britain's armed services in those days banned homosexuals as morally corrupting as well as too feeble to do any real fighting. Brian was evidently thought to have sneaked in under the net. He was pronounced 'psychologically unfit' for soldiering and discharged after serving less than half of his two-year term without being shown the medical report that had damned him.

36

In a surreal postscript, the army provided a glowing reference, describing him as 'a conscientious and hard-working clerk who uses his initiative and can in every respect be depended on to see a job through satisfactorily without supervision. Of smart appearance and sober habits at all times, he is utterly trustworthy.'

His appearance would always be unimpeachable but not necessarily the sober habits.

* * *

Now that the army had outed Brian – if only to himself – he felt obligated to share the revelation at the first family Friday night dinner after his return home.

His father and brother were astounded, Clive especially, for at the boarding schools they'd attended together Brian had given no sign of the turmoil he was going through. But with a mother's instinct Queenie had long had her suspicions.

In the early 1950s, being gay wasn't easy anywhere but in a tough northern seaport like Liverpool it could get you killed. The statue of Queen Victoria in Derby Square was a reminder of how little attitudes had changed here since she'd signed the Act of Parliament criminalising homosexuality in 1885, as was the ferociously macho culture of the docks.

The police hunted offenders like game, with entrapment by agents provocateurs their weapon of choice. Magistrates seldom imposed lesser penalties than the incarceration allowed by law. At night, dedicated 'queer-bashing' gangs patrolled the dockland roads, ready to fall on anyone who inadvertently betrayed himself in clothes, hairstyle or way of walking.

Only a small minority were exempted from this perpetual manhunt by wealth and influence. The Epsteins' next-door neighbour in Queens Drive was a prominent local lawyer named E. Rex Makin, a family friend and president of the Stapley Jewish care home for which Harry acted as treasurer.

Although married with children, Makin was a sexual predator whose cosy relationship with the police allowed him to cruise the city in his big car after dark, forcing young men to get into the back with him on pain of being reported for some non-existent offence.

At that time, homosexuality was regarded as a mental disorder capable of being 'cured'. Brian's parents initially clung to that hope – as he did himself – and when Harry offered to pay for him to see a psychoanalyst, he readily agreed.

The sessions took place two or three times a week, delving deep into his psyche and far back in his life. Under questioning, he recalled it had been during his brief time at Liverpool College, aged eight, that he'd first been aware of 'my feeling for other male persons' and a longing for 'a close and intimate friend on an entirely platonic and emotional level'. And how once at Wrekin when another boy called him 'a yid', he'd felt a sudden sexual attraction to his persecutor.

But midway through the treatment he broke it off. The shame of asking his father for the three guineas per session was too much for him. After this he confided in no one else and took inordinate care not to give himself away, for instance by throwing out anything in his wardrobe that might betray him such as yellow socks or too decorative a lining in a jacket.

The only person to guess the truth was his old schoolfriend Malcolm Shifrin who like himself had gone into the family furniture business. When the two travelled down to London together for an interior decor exhibition, Brian persuaded

Malcolm to accompany him to a club named the Mandrake whose clientele were exclusively male.

Despite that shocking revelation at Friday night dinner, Queenie refused to give up hope of grandchildren and went on propelling him towards her friends' daughters or nieces.

The only one to make any impression on him was Sonia Seligson whom he met when they were having tea with their respective mothers in the Adelphi Hotel lounge. The daughter of a leading Liverpool jeweller, 16-year-old Sonia had a Jewish background similar to his but was more extrovert than Queenie's usual choices, glamorous and stylish and known for her dashing hats.

The clincher for Brian was a passion for the theatre even greater than his. Sonia had studied drama at Liverpool's Crane Theatre, belonged to a prestigious am-dram group, the Green Room Players, and was currently learning stage management at a theatre in Southport on her way to becoming a successful actress under the name Sonia Stevens.

Brian was her first boyfriend and she would recall being 'absolutely fascinated by him . . . his manners were immaculate and he made a girl feel good. He opened doors ahead of me, knew how to behave and dressed perfectly, usually in a pinstriped suit. He took a great interest in my clothes and loved me to wear black dresses. He could be quite critical of the way I looked but usually it was "Oh, you look good tonight."'

They seemed a perfect match: Sonia's parents, Frank and Ethel, both adored Brian and she became close to Queenie, who was overjoyed at the way things had turned out and already thinking about wedding caterers.

As was customary for a teenage boy and girlfriend in that era,

39

they went no further than petting, yet Sonia never doubted that Brian was entirely heterosexual. Several of her girlfriends – including some he'd previously dated – thought otherwise, but she put that down to jealousy. Her only concern was the amount he drank, albeit as a rule with no loss of self-control.

Then one night during a party at Malcolm Shifrin's, he got very drunk and proposed to her. She accepted at once, but she couldn't help regretting he hadn't been able to do it sober. However, the next day he backtracked, saying they ought not to rush things, and soon afterwards told her there was 'no future' in their relationship.

'You're obviously going with another woman,' Sonia sobbed.

'No,' Brian said. 'I've got to tell you the truth. I'm going with another man.'

*   *   *

The man was Joe Flannery, whom he'd known on and off since they were children without any such thing ever crossing his mind.

They had drifted apart when Joe was conscripted into the army ahead of Brian, although with no question mark over his 'psychological fitness'. Quite the opposite, he'd regularly won the title of Stick Man as the outstandingly immaculate soldier in his hut. At the end of his two years, he'd been pressed to sign up again with a guarantee of promotion to sergeant but had decided he'd had enough.

Since returning to civilian life, he'd tried working as a joiner in his father's cabinet-making business, still hoping to win the love that the drunken, brutal Chris Flannery had always withheld. 'There was a record out then called "O Mein Papa" by

Eddie Fisher that I decided to buy for him,' Joe told me. 'It was one of those big old shellac ones we used to call seventy-eights. But when I gave it to him, he broke it over my head.'

Like Brian, Joe had long been in a state of total confusion – or, rather, indecision – concerning his own sexuality. While working at the Adelphi, he'd been separately propositioned by two celebrity guests, the playwright Noël Coward and the musical comedy star Ivor Novello, and had very nearly been flattered into saying 'yes'.

Yet for a long time he'd had a steady girlfriend and in the army had once participated in a heterosexual orgy for which, as a devout Catholic, he'd rushed to Confession the next day.

His only other encounter with homosexuality had had none of the glamour of Coward or Novello. One night when he was walking home, a large car had pulled up and the predatory lawyer (and next-door neighbour of the Epsteins) Rex Makin had told him to get in if he didn't want trouble with the police. 'I just turned and ran for my life,' he recalled.

He'd finally escaped his father's homophobic taunts by leaving the family home and opening a small bric-à-brac shop in Kirkdale Road that had basic living accommodation at the rear. This now became a safe space where he and Brian could meet.

It would always be on a Wednesday, half-day closing for their respective businesses. 'Just after one o'clock, I'd hear the tell-tale light rap on the frosted glass of the door.'

For the other half of the day, Brian could pour out the full story of his self-discovery without eliciting shock or incredulity or revulsion. He had found that 'close and intimate friend on an entirely platonic and emotional level' he had been seeking since he was eight. Before long, it seemed no more than natural

41

that he should stay the night and the platonic part become non-applicable.

To make the back room more comfortable, Joe bought a sofa bed on an instalment plan. 'But I didn't think it was right somehow to get it from Epstein's,' he said, 'so I went to a place up the road named Gerrard Kelly.'

He would treasure the book in which the weekly payments were recorded for the rest of his life.

4

'THE IMMACULATE DECEPTION'

For a time, Joe seemed the one more likely to find a career in popular music. He had a pleasing baritone voice and strong stage-presence and in 1955 successfully auditioned for one of Britain's foremost big-band leaders, Joe Loss. He spent the rest of that year on a national tour with his namesake, ending at the famous Hammersmith Palais ballroom in London.

Returning to his family home for New Year's Eve, he found his father Chris, as ever, drunk and abusive to his long-suffering mother, Agnes. When Joe tried to intervene, Chris seized him by the throat with both hands and, like a Rottweiler, refused to let go. The resulting damage to his larynx put paid to any future on the bandstand.

His relationship with Brian wasn't a hugely passionate one; as he said years later, 'I was always rather afraid of sex.' For him the surpassing thrill was the sophisticated lifestyle he found himself sharing with Brian; the former waiter now greeted deferentially in Liverpool's plushest restaurants and having dinner with wine at eight rather than tea at six – in the north of England, a heavy early evening meal as well as a hot drink.

Brian introduced him to the theatre, about which he soon

became equally passionate. It was a rare week that didn't find them at the Liverpool Playhouse, a former Victorian music hall, or the Art Deco Royal Court or both.

To someone who only just scraped a living from his little bric-a-brac shop, Brian's carelessness with money and possessions was at first horrifying, then amusing. 'He'd just passed his driving-test after four tries. Trying to get out of a parking space, he'd usually hit the car behind or in front. He'd just laugh and say, "What are bumpers for?"'

When the Royal Court put on Tennessee Williams's *A Streetcar Named Desire* with Vivian Leigh in the role of Blanche DuBois she'd recently played on screen, they booked front-row seats for every night of its week-long run and attended every performance in their best clothes, Brian's of course the very best.

He had to miss one because of family Friday night dinner, but Joe went anyway. At the curtain as the star took her bow, she noticed the empty seat and mouthed at Joe, 'Where's your friend?'

Brian's gift for knowing the right people gave them unlimited backstage access, occasionally even dressing-room access. Having the kind of patrician voice all actors did then, he was often mistaken for a cast member and, in an echo of his army imposture, took to handing out signed photographs of himself.

He clung to the theatre not just for the wonderful plays and performances he saw but as the one sphere where homosexuality seemed to be completely accepted.

Two years earlier, the great Shakespearean actor John Gielgud had been prosecuted for 'cottaging' – loitering with intent outside public men's toilets. The next week he had appeared at Liverpool's Royal Court in the pre-London run of a new play,

N. C. Hunter's *A Day by the Sea*, expecting to be booed off the stage but his first entrance received a standing ovation.

Around the theatre district were several pubs which daringly reflected that tolerance by serving people irrespective of their sexuality. The best-known were the small, unassuming Stork Hotel behind the Playhouse and a faux-Tudor pub across the road from the Royal Court named the Magic Clock. Inevitably, they became known to their shared clientele as the Stalk Hotel and the Magic Cock, their atmosphere rather like that of a French Resistance cell under Nazi occupation.

Brian and Joe frequented the Stork's Aintree Bar and the Magic Clock but always made clear they were uninterested in anyone but themselves. This strictly maintained hands-off rule earned them the nickname 'The Untouchables'. Brian always worried that a report of his visit might get back to his parents and so kept such a beautifully tailored low profile that some fellow habitués began to wonder if he really was one of them and dubbed him 'the Immaculate Deception'.

But that fastidious, cautious Brian lasted only so long. 'At a certain time of night, he turned into someone else,' Joe recalled. 'He'd drive off by himself without telling me where he was going and I never liked to ask.'

The mystery was solved when he turned up at Joe's in the early hours with a cut and bruised face and his expensive Peter England shirt torn open at the front and soaked in blood.

He said that at a pub outside the theatre district's charmed circle named The Lisbon he'd got talking to a friendly young docker whom he'd offered 'a lift home'. This had been mutually understood to mean oral sex in Liverpool's great municipal open space, Sefton Park. Afterwards the docker, no longer friendly, had demanded his wallet and threatened to kill him if he didn't hand it over.

As he clearly couldn't go home to his parents in this state, Joe cleaned him up and lent him a fresh (though much less costly) shirt. 'And that was to happen again, time after time.'

It was possibly with the young docker's death threat still on his mind that in February 1956 Brian drew up 'THE LAST WILL AND TESTAMENT OF THE WRITER BRIAN SAMUEL EPSTEIN' and put it in a drawer in his bedroom together with his most treasured small possessions as if it might be needed sooner rather than later.

He left everything to his immediate family 'or issue' apart from his clothes, which he wanted donated to the fledgling state of Israel, and his collections of records, theatre programmes and magazines, which were to go to 'my great and dear friend Brendan H. Garry' (of whom nothing further would ever be heard) after his family had had their pick of them.

Attentive to detail as always, he stipulated that no Kaddish prayers should be said for him and his Shiva, the mourning period observed by his family, should last no longer than a week. Touchingly, the final clause was a 'desire that my mother, father and brother know of my eternal love for them'.

It was to be the only will he would ever make.

* * *

In those bountiful times for the arts in Britain, the Liverpool Playhouse had its own repertory company which put on a new production, classical or modern, every three weeks.

The star of its 1955–56 season was Brian Bedford who'd come straight from the Royal Academy of Dramatic Art in London

(RADA) to play Hamlet. Like his fellow graduate Albert Finney, he made no attempt to hide his northern working-class roots, starting a trend that would reach its height with a befringed pop group five years later.

At the Playhouse's stage-door bar, The Basnett, Brian soon got to know Bedford and the Ophelia to his Prince of Denmark, Helen Lindsay. After weeks together offstage as well as on, the two were thoroughly bored with each other and their fellow players and glad of such a charming and cultivated new acquaintance.

Soon afterwards, Helen was puzzled to receive a note from Brian inviting her to meet for a drink on their own. He was five years younger, she reasoned, so his intentions could hardly be romantic. (Even in the 'safe' company of stage people, he hadn't mentioned his sexual preference and, as usual in daylight hours, none had suspected it.)

She found him to be less a theatre buff than a fanatic who could quote from every one of the Playhouse's productions so far that season. He was as fascinated by the craft of acting itself and how it was possible 'to think oneself into the skin of another person'.

Another skin or, at least, a thicker one was just what he felt he needed at that moment. His grandfather had recently stepped back from the family business at last and Harry had taken over control. The precept that fathers and sons shouldn't work together was never truer than with Brian and him: their rows had become more or less continuous, father always prevailing and son's fragile self-esteem plummeting anew.

Now he told Helen Lindsay that acting had always been what he really wanted to do, but had left too late to try. She firmly contradicted this, pointing to several much later starters

47

in the profession, and offered to coach him for an audition at RADA.

The coaching took place at Helen's rented flat several times a week without the knowledge of his parents or even Joe Flannery. At the outset she realised that, despite Brian's poise in social situations, he was physically awkward; her first bit of guidance therefore was to choose roles in which he didn't have to be too active. On the credit side she thought he had 'a maturity beyond his years and a kind of natural dignity'.

Choosing an audition piece for RADA took some thought. They worked for a time on Mark Antony's 'Friends, Romans, Countrymen ...' from Shakespeare's *Julius Caesar*, then Brian asked if he was too recognisably Jewish to deliver one of the young soldier king's rousing speeches from *Henry V*.

Helen replied that just about every male auditioner would make the same choice and that she didn't see him as a soldier, a view the British army would wholeheartedly have endorsed. Instead, she steered him to the much smaller yet crucial role of the Duke of Burgundy, who isn't seen until the end of the play – and just stands there – yet makes peace between the warring kingdoms of England and France.

He wrote away for RADA's prospectus and application form early in 1956, but months passed as his mother and father tried to talk him out of what seemed yet another crazily impractical idea and he himself had several changes of heart.

He didn't go to London for his audition until 19 September, his twenty-second birthday. The ordeal proved to have two parts, the first in front of a panel, the second less formally with RADA's principal John Fernald, who'd previously run the Liverpool Playhouse.

The Duke of Burgundy having been dropped along the way, he read two poems by T. S. Eliot and a section of Eliot's new verse play *The Confidential Clerk*. 'He didn't have a spectacular talent,' Fernald recalled a quarter of a century later, 'but it was a pleasing one. If you think in terms of typecasting, he would have played the second male lead – the best friend in whom the hero can always confide.'

To his astonishment, he got in. There wasn't the stampede for places at drama schools there would be in the 1960s and Fernald's good opinion – and, perhaps, lingering nostalgia for Liverpool – carried the day.

His mother made a last attempt to reason with him but in vain. 'He'd made up his mind he wanted to be a duffle-coated student,' she said. 'He wouldn't even take his car with him. We'd given it to him for his twenty-first birthday, a beautiful little cream and maroon Hillman Continental.'

He therefore exchanged his comfortable quarters at 197 Queens Drive for a bedsitting-room in Inverness Terrace, Bayswater, the heart of west London's 'bedsit' subcontinent. It proved so horrific that Queenie stepped in, scouring the *Jewish Chronicle*'s small-ads section until she found something far better in suburban Finchley whose landlady was reassuringly Jewish. Her sister, Freda, living in Hampstead just to the south, promised to keep an eye on him and ensure he never lacked an invitation to Friday night dinner.

He adopted a student-like persona to the extent of getting part-time jobs even though his father was paying his tuition fees and expenses through gritted teeth. During vacations, he worked alternately at Ashcroft and Dawes, London's first all-paperbacks bookshop, and at a second-hand one in Moorgate.

But the pose never fitted him nearly as well as that of an army subaltern had done. At twenty-two, he was four years older than almost all his fellow students and no amount of determined duffle-coat-wearing could close the gap between them.

Nor was RADA quite the liberation he'd expected. The Britain of the mid-'50s was still a deferential society and his whole class were expected to stand up and chorus 'Good morning' when their tutor came in to start the day's work – for him a distasteful memory of the nine schools he'd attended.

Nonetheless, he entered fully into the syllabus of speech training, in which he hardly needed instruction, and internal, mostly Shakespeare productions, playing a range of parts of varying prominence: Orlando in *As You Like It*, Proteus in *The Two Gentlemen of Verona*, Lucentio in *The Taming of the Shrew* and Sir Toby Belch in *Twelfth Night*.

What was more, a few weeks into his first term he acquired a girlfriend: 20-year-old Joanna Dunham, who was later to have a successful career in films and on television. Brian found her refreshingly easy to talk to and liked her 'bohemian' fashion ideas such as buying a second-hand fur coat, then dyeing it bright red.

'He always seemed older than the other students in more than just years,' Joanna told me. 'And he *drank*. That was something hardly anyone at RADA did then, though everyone smoked. He would say, just like an older person, "I *must* have a drink."

'I never thought he had any particular acting talent but there was one moment when he did surprise me. We had to do an exercise together for Fernald, a scene from [Anton Chekhov's] *The Seagull*. We chose the scene between Konstantin and his mother where he's adoring to her first, then flies into a terrible rage and tears a bandage off his head.

50

'The words must have had some special meaning for Brian. As he spoke the lines, I could feel he was getting out of control and when he started tearing the bandage off, I felt really frightened. It was almost as if he was having a nervous breakdown there on the stage.'

For a time, Joanna was just a companion with whom to go to films and art galleries, but then Brian spoiled things with the same lunge at heterosexuality he'd previously tried with Sonia Seligson. One night while they were at a party together, he got drunk and started to blurt out some of the darker secrets of his schooldays. 'I felt he seriously wanted to have a relationship with me and that he was trying to tell me something,' Joanna recalled. 'He was very pissed and threatening to drive me home. I behaved very badly I'm afraid. I just ran away.'

After that, there was nothing for it but to work even harder and RADA's next assessment reflected the beneficial result: 'An interesting and rewarding term ... of great variety. There are glimpses of latent power and breadth which augur well. A sensitive intelligence and understanding are expressed with control and a sense of direction and form. His characterisation is subtle and deep. A really promising student.'

At the end of that Easter term, he went home for a week to be with his family for Passover. He returned to London on Easter Monday, intending to spend the rest of the vacation working at Ashcroft and Hawes' bookshop. The prospect of three weeks by himself was not depressing; rather, he felt elated that his success at RADA seemed to have driven away all thoughts of sex.

Two evenings later, he went straight from work to see a play at the Arts Theatre in the West End, then drank a solitary coffee and took the Underground to Swiss Cottage, the nearest stop to his digs.

There he went into the men's toilets out of a genuine need to urinate. On emerging, he saw a young man staring at him in an unmistakable fashion. They exchanged a few words about finding 'somewhere private' but then Brian thought better of it and walked away.

His interlocutor was a plainclothes police officer, part of a two-man trap. Despite having committed no offence, Brian was arrested, taken to Hampstead police station and charged with 'importuning several men' outside the Swiss Cottage toilets.

When his case came before Marylebone Magistrates' Court, the wording on the charge sheet had changed to 'importuning seven men'. Nonetheless, he was told the speediest end to his ordeal would be to plead guilty.

A statement to the solicitor he'd consulted – a local man who neither knew nor cared about him – poured out a confession he'd been unable to make to anyone else: 'I do not think I am an abnormally weak-willed person ... the determination with which I have tried to rebuild my life over the past few months have, I assure you, been no mean effort. I believed that my own willpower was the best thing with which to overcome my homosexuality. And I believe my life may have become con-tented and may even have attained a public success.'

Worst of all was having to give his father's telephone number 'in case I am imprisoned or remanded'. Well-mannered as ever, he apologised for his shaky writing because 'I was unable to procure a typewriter and my hand is nervous.'

In the end, he was merely fined. The only press coverage was a paragraph in the local paper, the *Hampstead & Highgate Express,* to which his name meant nothing, and no word about the episode leaked back to Liverpool. But it had poisoned London for him – even tainted the milieu in which he'd so yearned to be accepted and which had finally seemed to be opening up to him.

He wrote to John Fernald that he'd decided to leave RADA after completing less than half of his course, for reasons he preferred not to go into. 'I would like you to know,' he added '[that it] has proved an invaluable experience and given me a real insight into a great craft. Certainly my appreciation and support of the theatre are unlikely ever to cease.'

A dinner with Harry and Queenie at the Adelphi confirmed the, for them, joyous news. He was ready to return to work in the business where he belonged in the city where he belonged, with no further distractions.

5

MISTER BRIAN AND MR X

Despite the threat of mutually annihilating nuclear war with Communist Russia, the late 1950s in Britain were a time of stability and hope under a paternalistic Tory government that looked to be everlasting. The country still had the standing of a world industrial power, there was virtually full employment and hence a steady rise in living standards after years of post-war self-denial. What had once been luxuries encountered only in American films, like television sets, refrigerators and washing-machines, were easily attainable on the hire-purchase system.

By now, the millions of babies conceived in the war's shadow had grown into a new species called teenagers, generally understood to be aged fourteen to nineteen, all of whom all but a tiny percentage left school to go straight into well-paid work. Such was their spending-power that now they had whole industries dedicated to supplying their every whim and turning over millions a year, most visibly in the sale of pop records.

The Epstein family business, which had decided to concentrate on household appliances and records some time since, therefore boomed equally with both. Nineteen fifty-eight brought its first venture into central Liverpool a shop in Great

Charlotte Street just around the corner from the Adelphi Hotel. The acronym for Isaac Epstein's modest North End Music Stores became a modern storefront logo in wide-spaced capitals: NEMS.

Clive Epstein also had joined the firm's sales staff, although with none of his older brother's false starts and soul-searching. At the Great Charlotte Street NEMS Clive was to run the household-appliance department while Brian ran the record department – and the show.

He had decided the store should have a celebrity opening even more impressive than he'd organised for Clarendon Furnishings with 'Auntie Muriel'. His choice of celebrity showed how much thought he gave to even the smallest detail: the singer Anne Shelton had been a wartime 'forces' sweetheart' but also recently enjoyed a hit single, 'Lay Down Your Arms', so both old and young would be attracted.

Classical music buff though he remained, he kept a dutiful eye on the latest in pop and from time to time even found something to like. He had been all but oblivious of the craze for American rock 'n' roll a few years earlier but in July 1958 its most outrageous figure, Little Richard, scored a late British hit with the old vaudeville number 'Baby Face', rendered in a shriek like a scalded banshee.

Brian was amused by 'Baby Face', Joe Flannery recalled, and played it often at home between his Bach and Sibelius. 'He'd never have believed how Little Richard was going to cross his path one day.'

The Great Charlotte Street venture proved so successful that a year later a second, more extensive NEMS opened in the city centre. This one was in Whitechapel, a winding thoroughfare close to the heart of the city's banking and commercial district as well as the docks. New-built and ultramodern in design, it had three sales floors and a fourth above for offices.

To perform the by now traditional opening ceremony, Brian secured Anthony Newley, a Cockney actor who'd found himself in the pop charts after singing in a film comedy about army life called *Idle on Parade* (a charge once frequently levelled at Private 22739590 Epstein).

His appearance was invaluable publicity for the new NEMS which brought so many rapturous young women into Whitechapel that a police presence was needed and gave Brian a first taste of smuggling a celebrity on devious routes through alleys and back doors to prevent his clothes being torn off his back, Elvis Presley-style. Newley was later to say he'd never received such faultlessly efficient VIP treatment.

At first, the new store's main draw was expected to be Clive's ground-floor department, the array of fridges, washing machines and spin-dryers with names like Hotpoint, Creda and Electrolux that were objects of glamour in themselves. Brian's theoretical domain were its two record departments, one for pop in the basement, the other for classical at the rear of the ground floor beyond the Credas and Hotpoints.

The brothers were supposed to share the space in its expansive windows, much as they'd been made to share sweets as children – and their mother would recall the same kind of arguments over who'd got more.

But Brian's flair for presentation was omnipresent, whether in an eye-arresting display of Vidor portable radios, the latest Ferguson 16-inch television in a living-room setting (some chair-backs resolutely turned to the street) or a promotional push for Sunbeam electric shavers 'on easy terms'. Within, customers browsed the Goblin Teasmades and Morphy Richards toasters beneath his ceiling-wide collage of record album-covers.

With an instinctive feeling for what wasn't yet called hype, he advertised his pop music basement as offering 'the Finest Record Selection in the North', implicitly dismissing other north-western commercial hubs like Manchester, never mind north-eastern ones like Middlesbrough or Newcastle upon Tyne.

He ran it with none of the casualness usual in such places, no jeans or sweaters but always an immaculate business suit, shirt and tie. He was known with old-fashioned formality as 'Mr Brian' – though behind his back he was 'Eppy' – and his young staff in their grey nylon coats were strictly enjoined to call every customer 'Sir' or 'Madam', regardless of age or appearance, just as he did.

His policy was one already fast disappearing from British retailing in the late 1950s and now long extinct: that the customer is always right. If anyone asked for a record not currently in stock, he would order it for them no matter how obscure the label or small the potential profit margin.

Shopkeeping then had no technological aids beyond the adding machine. Brian therefore drew on filing skills acquired in the army to create his own stock-monitoring system. A series of cardboard folders with different-coloured strings denoted which titles were selling well or badly and which needed reordering.

The worst blunder a staff member could commit in his eyes was to let something run out completely. Almost always the result would be one of the blushing tantrums to which he'd been prone since childhood and for which, a few moments later, he'd apologise with such genuine humility it would be impossible not to forgive him.

People of my generation look back at record shops in the late '50s as fondly as our parents did at pre-supermarket grocers' with their odours of bacon and lard and whole cheeses cut with a wire. NEMS in Whitechapel was a classic example, enhanced by Brian's unique mixture of punctiliousness and – the only word for it – benevolence.

Its principal merchandise was the small-format vinyl disc which spun at 45 revolutions per minute. In that era before inflation a forty-five cost six shillings and eight pennies (approximately 34p) year in, year out. Albums, then known as LPs (for long-players) and a tiny fraction of the singles market, were around 30 shillings (£1.50), and four-track EPs (for extended play) at around 10 shillings (50p).

Prospective buyers, often accompanied by one or more friends, would stand in a line of open-sided cubicles and the record would be piped through to them with no limit on length of occupancy or number of repeats.

On Saturdays, the place became so crowded that Brian himself often took a turn behind the counter. It would be while he was so engaged that a customer query would change his life, then the world.

* * *

He and Joe Flannery were still together, though Joe did his best to 'put a wall' between himself and the other Brian, so different from the dapper NEMS executive in business hours, who came perilously into being after midnight. His flat was the sanctuary to which Brian could always return with yet another black eye or bruised face and a bloodied shirt that, despite its costliness, Joe had standing orders to 'put straight in the bin'.

Yet the wall could crumble, as it did one night when Brian was temporarily without a car and asked Joe to drive him back to Liverpool from Southport on the Lancashire coast with a 17-year-old boy he'd picked up there. During the journey, there was an argument between the two of them and the boy pulled out a knife.

Since Brian was plainly incapable of dealing with the situation, Joe put his foot down until the speedometer touched 60 mph and threatened to crash the car if the knife were not instantly sheathed. When they reached Liverpool, he pulled up outside the first police station he saw but the boy jumped out of the car and fled.

Another such encounter had consequences beyond Joe's ability to help. This time it was with an older man who, unluckily, realised who Brian was during daylight hours. Not content with stealing his car and his wallet, the man started blackmailing him and when he refused to pay any more, attempted to transfer the extortion to his parents.

The police therefore had to be called in and Brian was subjected to an interrogation that would have been without the least morsel of sympathy. It being crucial for the blackmailer to incriminate himself in front of witnesses, he was lured to the NEMS store after hours where officers concealed behind washing machines and spin-dryers plainly heard him demand his blood money.

At the unavoidable court hearing, Brian gave evidence in supposed anonymity as 'Mr X' but was easily identified as he entered and left the building. The blackmailer was convicted, received a substantial prison sentence and was led away vowing vengeance on his accuser.

Despite this immeasurable private and public humiliation, Joe Flannery recalled, the idea of a convict with a festering grudge against him seemed to engender a queasy excitement. 'He used to tell me all the time that there was someone out to get him and that his life wouldn't be safe when this person was free again.'

Afterwards he tried to lead his parallel life with a measure of discretion. The easiest way was to visit other European countries – admittedly not many – with a more tolerant attitude towards homosexuality. Amsterdam in particular, reacting against its homophobic Nazi occupiers during the Second World War, offered a freedom that drew him back time and again.

Rather than go on risking life and limb around the docks, he rented a ground-floor flat at 36 Falkner Street in Liverpool's faded but still elegant Georgian quarter. The flat was solely for carnal purposes and he would never spend a whole night there, preferring to go on living in respectable Childwall with his parents and brother.

Across the road from his flat was Liverpool College of Art, where he'd once wanted to study fashion design; backing on to it was Liverpool Institute High School for Boys, which had turned him down aged eleven. Among the mingling students from both that he would scarcely have noticed were a tough-looking one, an angelically pretty one and a younger, shy one – three quarters of his unimaginable destiny.

His affair with Joe Flannery inevitably came to an end, although Joe was still deeply in love with him. 'I realised I couldn't ever have him to myself,' he said. 'The jealousy just hurt too much.'

Aside from those who casually passed through 36 Falkner Street and were instantly forgotten, Brian acquired two friends he was to keep for the rest of his life – literally so as both would be with him on the weekend that ended with his mysterious, lonely death.

Twenty-two-year-old Peter Brown was managing the record department at Lewis's, Liverpool's principal department store, when he met Brian at a mutual friend's birthday party, the only guest wearing a dinner jacket. Discovering that Lewis's had already singled out Brown as potential executive material, Brian poached him to run the record side at NEMS, Great Charlotte Street for a higher salary plus commission.

Born into a modest Catholic family in Bebington, Cheshire, Brown had the same love of refinement as his new employer but with nothing like the same access to it. He was to become almost a facsmile of Brian, copying his clothes, his mannerisms and, most assiduously, his accent.

They took to going on holiday together, usually to Spain for the sunshine, the low prices and hotels and beaches still relatively unpolluted by British package tours, drunkenness and fish and chips. On every visit, Brian insisted on attending at least one bullfight, the inveterate risk-taker fascinated by the slow-motion ritual that could end with the death of the bull or the matador.

In contrast with the suave and getting suaver Brown, Geoffrey Ellis was a slightly mouse-like twenty-eight-year-old with a law degree from Oxford, bound for a senior post with a major insurance company, the Royal. Ellis shared Brian's fondness for expensive restaurants, which usually meant driving into the Cheshire Wirral where homophobic alarm bells didn't ring so deafeningly at the sight of two men spending the evening together. They made frequent use of this gastronomic safe-conduct.

But then Ellis was transferred to Royal Insurance's New York office, departing Liverpool on one of its still plentiful ocean liners. Brian saw him off, envious of his insuring life and wondering if they'd ever meet again.

* * *

While Brian conscientiously kept abreast of the professional music scene as dictated from London, he had no inkling of the amateur one teeming under his nose. It had begun in the mid-'50s with skiffle, the fusion of American blues, country and gospel that turned a generation of self-conscious British boys into aspiring performers and gave the guitar an allure verging on the erotic.

Skiffle produced only one authentic star, Lonnie Donegan, but a few groups made it into the pop charts, notably The Vipers on the small Parlophone label, produced by its managing director, George Martin, whose name Brian would come to know – and bless.

Like every other British city, town and village, Liverpool threw up dozens of skiffle groups with one or two lucky guitar-owners and the others blowing kazoos, scrubbing the glass serrations of kitchen washboards with thimble-capped fingers or plucking at 'basses' made from empty boxes, amputated broom-handles and kitchen string.

When the skiffle craze ended, as it soon did, the scrubbers and plunkers fell away, leaving the guitarists impatient to progress to rock 'n' roll, which they now felt was within their reach. Among them were the art student and two Liverpool Institute

63

schoolboys previously mentioned, known in rough-hewn skiffle style as The Quarrymen.

Despite pop music's massive growth since the 1950s, there had been only two artists' managers whose names were known to the general public, one American with a single client, the other British with many, and neither shedding great lustre on their nascent profession.

Elvis Presley's manager, 'Colonel' Tom Parker, was an ex-carnival showman – as much a walking cliché with his loud Hawaiian shirts and chewed-wet cigars as his protégé was a towering original – who'd regarded Presley as just another fairground scam and shut down his sublime rock 'n' roll as soon as possible to move him into ballads and dim-witted Hollywood movies.

By contrast, Britain's Larry Parnes, a former dress-shop owner, went in for quantity with a 'stable' of male vocalists to whom he gave professional names laden with homoerotic innuendo like Marty Wilde, Vince Eager and – no kidding – Dickie Pride. Such was his avarice in that pre-decimal era of pounds, shillings and pence that he was known as 'Mister Parnes Shillings and Pence'.

Less amusingly, he was a sexual predator operating pretty much openly among naïve and vulnerable young men reliant on him to fulfil their dreams. Part of the deal for several of them was that they live at Parnes's west London flat, there to be groomed in the old-fashioned sense of being coached in showmanship and deportment. Directly opposite was Baden-Powell House, the headquarters of the international scouting movement, and in leisure moments he would ogle the Boy Scouts who constantly came and went, birdwatcher-like, through powerful binoculars.

None of his lodgers being in the least gay nor inclined to become so, they had to acquire the knack of fending him off without jeopardising their management contracts. Vince Eager, the most frequent target, kept the same small antique table handy to use as a shield.

Two of Parnes's discoveries had come from Liverpool: a former Mersey tugboat hand born Ronnie Wycherley, now renamed Billy Fury, and a ship's carpenter born John Askew, now Johnny Gentle. An essential part of his training had been making them speak in a vaguely transatlantic accent, their own native one, which seems to grab the listener by the lapels, being thought too impossibly unglamorous for teenage idols.

Any Parnes discovery appearing live in Liverpool guaranteed a surge in his record-sales at NEMS stores, so when a show at the Empire theatre co-headlined by Billy Fury and Marty Wilde was announced, Brian dutifully went along. It was his first experience of young womanly screams that totally obliterated the music – and of course he hadn't heard anything yet.

Afterwards, he made contact with Larry Parnes, who introduced him to the affable Wilde and the almost catatonically shy Fury. Parnes was sufficiently struck by his astute comments about the show's staging and lighting to consider offering him some kind of PA's job, but there was no other kind of rapport between them.

Parnes could claim to have been the first manager of any consequence to notice Liverpool had its own distinct musical culture – what would later be termed 'the Mersey Sound' – and to put it to use outside its home city, albeit not very far outside.

Ever-thrifty Mister Parnes Shillings and Pence saw the benefit in hiring semi-pro local bands to back his vocalists on their northern tours for a pittance rather than go to the trouble and expense of bringing experienced sidemen all the way from London. And being purely instrumental, their glamour-killing Scouse accents would go unheard.

In early May 1960, he was to send Johnny Gentle on a tour of ballrooms in the Scottish Highlands, accompanied by musicians still unsure whether they were the Silver Beetles or The Beatles – the latest in a series of wrong turnings that would eventually lead them to the right place.

Or, rather, into the right hands.

6

'RIGHT THEN, BRIAN – MANAGE US'

On the cusp of the 1960s, it seemed that British popular music – as comprehensively represented in the audio-booths at NEMS' Whitechapel store and Brian's patent stock-monitoring system – had nowhere left to go.

The jagged rock of the '50s had given way to 'beat' music, a sanded-down version, in its every form intended to reassure the older generation (i.e., anyone over twenty) that it meant no harm whatsoever. Its pre-eminent, almost monopolistic product was Cliff Richard who, only a couple of years earlier, had had the tabloid press asking, 'Is This Boy Too Sexy for Television?' but now was chastity incarnate. He was also showing signs of religious fervour, which in an American teen idol would have been quite normal but in a British one seemed like a betrayal.

Rock, beat or whatever, was still expected to blow over at any moment, so Richard's Australian manager, Peter Gormley – a figure unknown to the general public – was already following Colonel Tom Parker's lead with Elvis Presley by getting him into ballads and film musicals.

While the girls had Cliff, the guys had his backing group (not band) The Shadows, a shiny-suited foursome who performed a little stepdance in unison like a Cuban-heeled gavotte, very occasionally adding a discreet back-up vocal.

The Shadows had a parallel career on their own with lead guitar instrumentals as pioneered by the American Duane Eddy; consequently, there now were as many beat groups (or sometimes 'combos') as there used to be skiffle ones, all devotedly shadowing them. The only people calling themselves 'bands' played traditional jazz in a homogenised form called Trad, which involved dressing up as Mississippi riverboat gamblers, Confederate soldiers or Louis IV courtiers, which appealed to girls as much as boys and frequently got into the pop charts.

Those charts, as ever, were dominated by America, the template for all popular music through the century thus far, from minstrelsy and blues through Dixieland jazz, big band swing, bebop, country, folk, R&B and soul. And now with the '60s, it seemed to be tightening its grip still further.

A Brooklyn teenager named Carole King and her husband, Gerry Goffin, wrote 'Will You Love Me Tomorrow?', the first US number one single by an all-female African-American vocal group (The Shirelles) heralding a flood of classic pop from New York's songwriting 'factory', the Brill Building, by Neil Sedaka, Connie Francis, Bobby Darin, Bobby Vee, The Drifters and The Coasters.

A mousy twenty-year-old named Phil Spector began building new studio effects brick by aural brick into a 'wall' of sound. From Detroit came the first releases of the unprecedentedly black-owned Motown label, assembled as if on the car production line where its founder, Berry Gordy Jr., had once worked. Chubby Checker's 'The Twist' set off the latest of many dance crazes to cross the Atlantic.

Britain's music business, on the other hand, seemed to have come to a standstill sometime during the 1930s. The two dominant record companies, Decca and EMI – the latter an umbrella for several autonomous labels – competed with each other not just in the marketplace but as bureaucracies as labyrinthine and conservative as the British Broadcasting Corporation.

Only the most famous names, which still meant the oldest, had any say in what they recorded. The rest were under the sway of in-house 'artist and repertoire men' (never women) who signed the talent, supervised the sessions and decided on the takes to be released. Extreme formality and class-consciousness prevailed throughout: the engineers were artisans clad in white coats like lab assistants and even jazz drummers were not excused collars and ties as they played.

New artists signed to these two behemoths would usually have to record some American hit, only to see it slaughter their pallid cover-versions in the home charts. Only as second best would an A&R man turn to the small coterie of professional songwriters, all of them London-based and most unable to think 'moon' without rhyming it with 'June'.

A few singers wrote their own material but only the odd song, often under a pseudonym. A notable exception was Billy Fury from the Larry Parnes stable (and Liverpool) who'd composed the whole of his solo album, *The Sound Of Fury*. This might have spurred the A&R fraternity to seek other young talent capable of doing likewise – yet it hadn't.

Such was the lethargic, complacent industry that Brian would soon turn on its head.

* * *

His journey to that moment began at the end of June 1961 when a curly-haired, personable young man named Bill Harry called to see him at NEMS Whitechapel.

Harry had been a student at Liverpool College of Art when he first realised the extent and variety of the city's music scene. By his reckoning it had 350 semi-pro bands playing in styles ranging from hardcore R&B and country to Cliff Richard-style pop at hundreds of venues from plush ballrooms to modest 'jive hives', putting it on a par with 'New Orleans at the turn of the century'.

He now planned to document the phenomenon in a fort-nightly paper named *Mersey Beat*, financed by a £50 loan from a friend supplemented by his college scholarship grant and operating from a single room in Renshawe Street with himself and his girlfriend, Virginia, the only staff. NEMS was high on the list of record shops and musical instrument dealers he hoped would stock it.

Brian showed great interest in the new paper and ordered a dozen copies of its first issue to retail at three old pennies each. He also volunteered to contribute a regular column reviewing the new records that came into NEMS' stock.

Mersey Beat's first issue on 6 July showed it to be more than a factsheet about bands and venues. Half its front page consisted of an article headed 'BEING A SHORT DIVERSION ON THE DU-BIOUS ORIGINS OF BEATLES translated from the John Lennon', a stream of instantly laughworthy nonsense whose author had been at art college with Bill Harry before turning to music full-time.

That first issue sold out immediately and Brian ordered a further two dozen. When they, too, vanished with no sign of a slowing in demand, he ordered twelve dozen of issue number 2.

As well as being publicity for NEMS, his column was a chance, however small, to be the writer he'd styled himself in the angst-ridden will he'd drafted as a teenager. He took obvious trouble with its composition, as he did to give the serial-numbers of the records he reviewed to facilitate customer orders.

He made his debut in *Mersey Beat*'s second issue under his own headline, 'STOP THE WORLD and listen to everything in it'. The lead item was about Anthony Newley, who'd performed the opening ceremony for NEMS Whitechapel, and his hit West End musical, *Stop the World – I Want to Get Off*.

'Tony Newley's new show has somewhat mesmerised the critics despite an overall triumph for a well-deserved success,' he wrote, 'but the record buyers are going to be absolutely certain about the success of its songs "What Kind of Fool Am I?" and "Once in a Lifetime [For Once in My Life]".'

There was a strong bias towards musical theatre, with reviews of other cast albums for *The Music Man* and *West Side Story*, followed by dutiful mentions of Elvis Presley's new film *Wild In The Country* (coming soon to the Gaumont cinema), Chubby Checker's 'Let's Twist Again' and, slipped in at the end by the unreformed classical buff, pianist John Ogdon's recital of works by Busoni and Liszt.

Occasionally he could blow a small trumpet of his own, as when in July he reviewed John Leyton's 'Johnny Remember Me', a sombre ballad about a man mourning a dead wife or girlfriend that was widely predicted to be a flop. Nonetheless, his instinct was to order it in bulk so, unlike other Liverpool dealers, NEMS could cope with the orders when it went to number one.

Three years later when there was already a demand for his autobiography, Brian would claim to have been totally unaware of The Beatles' existence throughout that summer and autumn of 1961. Of all the Fab Four anecdotes told and retold down the years, it is among the most cherished. But according to Bill Harry, an unimpeachable witness, it was total fabrication.

'Brian knew perfectly well who the Beatles were from the moment *Mersey Beat* came out with the article by John on its front page. The day I delivered the second issue with his first record-review column, he invited me into his office and went through the issue page by page, asking questions about everything in it and a good part of it was about them.'

Harry gladly gave him a full briefing: how they'd started at the bottom of the heap in Liverpool but been toughened and tightened beyond recognition by months of playing night-long sets in Hamburg's red-light district to audiences of drunken sailors, sex-workers and gangsters. And how when they'd first come home, their pounding new sound – never mind beyond-ludicrous name – had led to a widespread assumption that they were German.

During their second Hamburg stint, they'd come to the notice of the bandleader Bert Kaempfert who also acted as a talent scout and producer for the German Polydor label. *Mersey Beat*'s lead story in its second issue, on the page facing Brian's record-column, was that Kaempfert had signed them to record on Polydor. 'He can't have missed it,' Bill Harry says.

Harry dutifully covered the other young talent giving voice all over Liverpool, like Rory Storm and the Hurricanes with their featured drummer Ringo Starr, Gerry and the Pacemakers fronted by a boy with a letterbox smile named Gerry Marsden, and a superpowered blues chanteuse who'd recently changed her name from Priscilla White to Cilla Black.

But The Beatles were such a dominant presence in the paper that readers were starting to call it 'Mersey Beatle' and newsprint-wise were constantly in Brian's face. The 14 September issue had a double-page spread about them, pushing his record column (now less about musical theatre and more about current pop) into the top left-hand corner.

Their name headlined sizeable display advertisements for The Cavern club and a dance at Litherland Town Hall and there were further humorous contributions from a now anonymous John – cod small-ads among the genuine ones and a featurette by 'Beatcomber', parodying J. B. Morton's eccentric Beachcomber column in the *Daily Express*. 'I am an unmurdered mother of 19 years,' ran one paragraph. 'Am I pensionable?'

He certainly noticed The Beatles but that wasn't the same as taking notice of them. He'd just turned twenty-seven, in those days considered the threshold to middle age, and looked even older with his carefully maintained 'Mister Brian' gravitas. Feeling himself automatically excluded from the rowdy young culture The Beatles personified, he never once suggested to Bill Harry that he might meet them.

He'd done so, of course, many times without realising it, since for years past they'd been regular visitors in his record department, sometimes buying but more often crowding into an audio-booth and having covetable new releases piped through to them again and again under his tolerant regime so that they could memorise the words or figure out the chords.

In the summer of 1961, as it happened, he was suffering a

resurgence of the boredom and restlessness that had bedevilled his teens. With NEMS Whitechapel running with soldierly efficiency and an able lieutenant in Peter Brown, he hankered after some new challenge, ideally with more scope for his artistic side than dressing windows or designing 'special offer' posters.

To try to clarify his thoughts, as well as attend bullfights, he'd taken a long holiday in Spain with Brown. It was on a Saturday morning just after his return that ...

* * *

In Brian's telling, the most portentous moment in pop music history has a beautiful simplicity. A leather-jacketed young man named Raymond Jones comes into NEMS and asks him for 'the new single by The Beatles'.

He's never heard the name before but, pursuant to his own strict customer-service policy, undertakes to order it for Jones and writes a memo to himself, 'The Beatles – check on Monday.' It's when he checks on Monday that the twentieth century's greatest romance starts to unfold.

Why bother to invent and stubbornly maintain this fiction? Because by 1964 when his autobiography came out, The Beatles were massively famous and he alone basked in the glory of giving them to the world. Anyone else who'd played a part in it therefore had to be edited out of the narrative.

In an odd reversal, the one true element of that Saturday-morning fable was turned into myth. It would later be claimed there'd been no such person as Raymond Jones but that he'd been invented by Alistair Taylor to be a kind of leather-jacketed Everyman. I can vouch for his existence because I've talked to him.

74

The single in question was the first product of The Beatles' contract with the West German bandleader Bert Kaempfert and Polydor Records, which *Mersey Beat* had banner-headlined the previous July in plain sight of Brian on the adjacent page. Intended primarily for Kaempfert's German-speaking public, it was hardly avant-garde, a cover of 'My Bonnie Lies Over the Ocean' souped up with a rock beat.

Nor was it really a Beatles record since its lead vocal was by Tony Sheridan, another British musician working in Hamburg whom Kaempfert also had under contract. And because 'Beatle' sounded like the German word 'peedle', meaning little boy's willy, their name had been temporarily changed to the Beat Brothers. Altogether, it was miraculous that Raymond Jones had ever heard of it.

Polydor product in those days wasn't distributed in the UK but someone in the business like Brian had no difficulty in contacting the label, intending to order a single copy for Raymond Jones and thereby honour NEMS' customer charter.

It turned out that the minimum order was twenty-five copies, which his assistant in the record department, Alistair Taylor, warned was way too many for such a curiosity. But, remembering his successful punt with 'Johnny Remember Me', Brian placed the order and hand-wrote a sign for the main street window: 'Beatles Record Available'.

Within a few days, a cover-version of one of the world's most hackneyed songs in which The Beatles appeared anonymously and inaudibly apart from their backing, sold out two orders, totalling fifty copies. And the salesman in Brian prompted him to check them out in case further singles might be pending.

According to Bill Harry, they'd just returned from a second

stint in Hamburg's red-light district, swapping all-night sessions there for lunchtime ones at The Cavern club in Mathew Street. If Brian cared to meet them and catch one of their shows, Harry said he would arrange it.

It was only then that he discovered The Cavern was just a couple of streets away from NEMS Whitechapel – or, as Beatles fans would one day meticulously measure it, 250 footsteps.

* * *

So on 9 November 1961 he trod them for the very first time accompanied by Alistair Taylor, promoted for the occasion from his assistant to his *personal* assistant.

Mathew Street was indeed close at hand but over the frontier of Liverpool's dockland, a narrow cobbled lane between towering Victorian warehouses, blocked by heavy trucks and strewn with empty crates, cabbage stalks and squashed oranges to the peril of Brian's beautifully polished brogues.

Bill Harry had set up his visit to The Cavern as if he were royalty, arranging with its owner, Ray McFall, for him and Taylor to be admitted without the usual non-member's entrance-fee of one shilling and sixpence (7p) and to be ceremonially greeted at a makeshift entrance, resembling a ship's companionway. Ushered past the waiting queue, they descended a straight flight of eighteen stone steps with the growing heat from below coiling like snakes up their trouser legs.

At the bottom was a cellar consisting of three brick tunnels with low barrelled ceilings, measuring no more than about fifty feet by thirty, that today would be instantly condemned as a multi-deathtrap. It had no emergency exit, no air-conditioning, no extractor fans, smoke alarms or sprinkler system, no main drainage even: the primitive toilets emptied into a cesspit that instantly made its presence known.

The place was packed to capacity and far beyond, mostly by young women in beehive hairdos, balloon skirts and stiletto heels, crowding the rows of kindergarten-sized chairs before the stage in the central tunnel and jiving or twisting around their massed handbags on the floor rather than leave them vulnerable to theft on their empty seats.

The odours of sewage, disinfectant, mouse droppings, mould and tinned oxtail soup (this being lunchtime), mingling with those of the cheeses stored in the warehouse above, impregnated Brian's business suit beyond rescue by any drycleaner and the bright-blue clouds of cigarette smoke filled his lungs and stung his eyes.

The resident deejay, Bob Wooler, announced that they had a special visitor that day, Brian Epstein of NEMS. One can picture his extreme discomfort and how it melted away when The Beatles took to the rickety stage.

On him, it must be said, their first impact was as four young men who were highly attractive in very different ways: angel-faced Paul on bass, solemn George on lead guitar, taciturn Pete Best on drums, but none so devastatingly as John, in the subordinate role of rhythm guitarist yet his leadership plain in every gesture.

Even Brian's limited experience of beat groups told him this one was radically different. Instead of the usual frontman with back-up, they were a cohesive unit, taking turns as lead vocalist but giving equal weight to their shared harmonies. Instead of the usual matching suits, they wore all-over black leather that looked much slept in; instead of the usual elaborate cockade, all of them but Pete had hair brushed forward almost to eye-level; instead of the scowl obligatory for pop beatmakers since the heyday of Elvis, their faces were animated and intelligent.

Most unconventional of all was their repertoire. They had spent months playing in West Germany, where rock 'n' roll had never died, and back in Britain still blasted out the best of Gene Vincent, Carl Perkins, Buddy Holly and Little Richard with the fervour of revivalist preachers.

They were skilled mimics, able to supply note-perfect covers of all the latest pop hits, even those by black female vocal groups like The Shirelles' 'Boys' which they did without bothering to change its girlie lyrics. To keep them going through the long Hamburg nights, they'd learned standard old vaudeville chestnuts and Broadway show tunes. And sometimes, rather diffidently, knowing the Cavern crowd's preference for comfortable golden oldies, they'd slip in an original composition by John and Paul.

They were as much a comedy act as a musical one, talking in cod German or Speedy Gonzales Mexican accents, singing television jingles for Camay soap or Sunblest bread or imitating characters from their favourite radio programme, *The Goon Show*. At intervals John would shamble around the stage in a cruel parody of a disabled person which in those days offended no one.

Professionalism, in the sense that Brian understood it, was non-existent. Throughout their performance, they chain-smoked cigarettes, wolfed snacks, carried on conversations with friends or foes in their audience and accepted or rejected song requests.

Yet while they were on, the business executive on his

kiddie-chair, as a rule such a stickler for perfection, forgot the heat, forgot the smells, forgot even his painful self-consciousness in his fascination with those four black leather-clad figures and longing somehow to be a part of them.

Afterwards, he tried to speak to them in the ratty communal musicians' room behind the stage, but could make contact only with George, who rather uppishly inquired, 'What brings Mr Epstein here?' then turned away before Brian could think of an answer.

Alistair Taylor's reward for accompanying him into this teenage netherworld was to be given lunch at his current favourite city-centre restaurant, The Peacock. Taylor was full of how 'absolutely bloody marvellous ... incredible', The Beatles had been. 'What would you think if I thought of managing them?' Brian asked – a notion so far-fetched that his assistant laughed out loud.

But after that he returned to The Cavern several times, taking along various young NEMS employees to catch their act. The unanimous rave reviews convinced him this wasn't just about his head being turned by four pretty lads, one in particular.

Five weeks after first seeing them he reappeared at the club alone, carrying the executive briefcase that to his employees always meant serious business. He picked his way through the crowd to the band-room, spoke to George again and requested a meeting with The Beatles in his office at the NEMS store at 4.30 that afternoon.

* * *

Such an approach from a prominent local businessman might have been expected to cause them at least a frisson of excitement.

79

But their low-achieving career thus far had made them cynical and suspicious of strangers, even one so obviously affluent who drove a luxurious Ford Zephyr Zodiac.

They consented to the meeting but, on their own initiative took along the Cavern's deejay, Bob Wooler. The portly, dignified Wooler, more like a Roman senator than a disc-spinner, was an important ally whose plugging of 'My Bonnie' had first alerted Raymond Jones and many more of their supporters to it.

Their manner was elaborately casual, so much so that Paul decided to go home for a bath first. The others purposely dawdled on the short walk from Mathew Street to Whitechapel, stopping at both the two pubs that lay en route. It was half-day closing for NEMS and Brian had to unlock the front door and usher them through the ghostly washing machines and tumble-driers where, a few months previously, unsympathetic police officers had waited to ambush his blackmailer.

They were already half an hour behind schedule and the news that Paul was still enjoying a leisurely soak in distant Allerton triggered one of the angry flushes that Brian's staff and family knew so well. He responded stiffly that Paul was going to be very late. 'But very clean', a deadpan George pointed out.

'Brian hated to be kept waiting,' Bob Wooler would tell me. 'That was his first introduction to many hours of being kept waiting by The Beatles.'

In the end, with Paul finally present, he summoned the nerve to volunteer himself as their manager while owning up to being totally without experience of the role. To his surprise, that didn't bother them at all – suggesting he'd been more impressive than he realised. The only question came from Paul, who asked if he'd want to change the kind of music they played and was assured that he wouldn't.

John spoke for the others without troubling to take a vote: 'Right then, Brian – manage us.'

7

'I'LL ALWAYS TAKE CARE OF JOHN'

Harry and Queenie Epstein had been away from home for a week and knew nothing of what had gone on during their absence. When they returned, a flushed and excited Brian sat them down and made them listen to 'My Bonnie'. He told them it was by a group named The Beatles, spelling it out as people needed to do in those days, and that he'd decided to be their manager.

For Harry and Queenie, it was painfully reminiscent of his previous, unsuitable career choices – couturier, artist, actor – before he'd come to his senses and gone into retail. And what was to happen to the record department he'd built up with such care and pride, his father asked? Brian replied airily that it wouldn't suffer; managing The Beatles would take him only 'two half-days a week.'

While his embarrassed parents succeeded in concealing his new venture from most of their friends, it was impossible to do so from their next-door neighbour. As for many years past, this was the prominent solicitor (and scot-free sexual predator) Rex Makin, who'd always enjoyed discountenancing Brian in the guise of straight-talking. When he consulted Makin informally on the kind of contract he might offer The Beatles,

83

Makin derided it as 'just another Epstein idea', even though Epstein ideas in the commercial sphere thus far hadn't been half bad.

Meanwhile, he demonstrated the seriousness of his intentions in ways calculated to impress The Beatles the most. At Frank Hessy's musical instrument store, which supplied most of the Liverpool groups, they owed £200 in instalment payments for guitars and amplifiers, equivalent to around £3,000 today. Brian paid it off in full with a personal cheque.

He also offered regular jobs to their two-strong support team who'd previously been doing the job for love and beer and the chance to meet girls it afforded. Neil Aspinall was a close friend of Pete Best and a boarder at the Bests' family home, studying to become an accountant in between driving the group to and from gigs in his van. Tony Bramwell was a childhood friend of George who'd begun by carrying George's guitar into venues so as to get in free himself, and from that had morphed into a roadie without the title.

The Beatles' instant agreement to Brian's impulsive proposition had made everything seem wonderfully straightforward, but when he looked into their affairs during those last weeks of 1961 he found complications and potential obstacles everywhere. They had been in existence under various names for six years, during which three people could claim to have been their de facto manager, often all at the same time.

Firstly there was Allan Williams, a bibulous Welshman who'd put them on at various low-level clubs he owned around central Liverpool despite thinking them 'a right load of layabouts'. Williams had arranged their first Hamburg residency and driven them there himself minus the necessary work-permits;

if stopped at the West German frontier, he'd said, they should pose as college students on vacation.

However chaotically, Williams had at least pulled them out of their Liverpool rut, yet he had been shabbily treated over the second Hamburg visit, just ended, which they'd negotiated directly with the club-owner concerned.

Because of this, they'd docked Williams's £15 per week commission, impervious to his protests that without him they would never have appeared there in the first place. Still angry and hurt, he had no objection to Brian's taking them over, but cautioned him not to touch them 'with a fuckin' bargepole'.

Secondly there was the Cavern deejay, Bob Wooler, who'd talked them into what little stagecraft they practised (like starting to play before the stage curtains opened, if there *were* curtains) and lent them the rare import singles from his extensive private collection that gave them such an edge on their rivals.

But away from the microphone, he was a shy, reticent man to whom it never occurred to claim a piece of them. On the contrary, he wholeheartedly welcomed Brian's takeover and throughout the cataclysmic years to come would always be available to him as an unacknowledged, unpaid consultant.

Finally, and most formidably, there was Pete Best's mother, Mona, who'd started The Casbah 'coffee club' in the basement of her house in suburban Haymans Green where The Beatles had first appeared when they were still The Quarrymen and to whom they largely owed their entrée to The Cavern.

If they had a manager at present it was Mrs Best, since most of their bookings came via her and they still used her house as a base camp. But she made way for Brian without protest because of what she thought he could do for her son.

85

Like Pete, Paul and George were under twenty-one, so he needed their parents' consent before he could make any sort of deal with them. It was a process in which he sold himself as skilfully as anything from his family's store.

He found an immediate empathy with Paul's widowed father, Jim, a self-taught musician who'd led an amateur jazz band during the 1920s and '30s and had once bought a piano from the original North End Music Stores. Yet even this kindly man showed a degree of anti-Semitism, reminding his son in an age-old trope that 'Jews are good with money.'

George was the only one in the group with a full set of parents, so Brian had not only to pass inspection by his bus-driver father, Harold, but his vivacious mother, Louise, and to an extent his older brothers, Harry and Peter.

Harold and Louise had always been totally supportive of George, buying him an expensive Hofner President guitar even to play simple skiffle and allowing him to turn professional at seventeen for The Beatles' tour of Scotland with Johnny Gentle from the Larry Parnes stable. If he wanted Brian to manage him, it was fine with them.

John was of age – just – so technically entitled to make his own decisions about his future. However, Brian had been warned he was still much under the sway of his aunt, Mimi Smith, who'd raised him single-handedly after his mother, her younger sister Julia, had proved unequal to the task.

What was more, she had always been fiercely opposed to his music, cautioning him with seemingly unassailable logic, 'The guitar's all very well, John, but you'll never make a living from it.' Conscious of the delicate task ahead, Brian set aside a whole afternoon for it.

To his surprise, the seemingly tough street-kid had grown up in the middle-class suburb of Woolton, in a neat semi-detached house named 'Mendips', with stained glass windows, faux-Tudor beams and a living room whose row of bells had not so long ago summoned live-in domestic help.

Mimi, although an admirable woman in many ways, was a social snob and – as she later told me – Brian came as a huge relief after the 'roughs', including his fellow Beatles, John usually went around with.

'There was a knock on the door and standing there was this smart young man ... he had a clean white shirt on and a tie and he said, "Hello, I am Brian Epstein" and my first impression was "You'll do." He was very educated, very polite, knew his p's and q's, came from a good family.' What worried Mimi, she recalled, was what had impressed Jim McCartney and the Harrisons – his obvious wealth and substantial business background. '"It's all right for you," I told him. "If this group business turns out to be a flash in the pan, it won't matter. It's just a hobby to you ... but what happens to *them*?"

'Brian said, "It's all right, Mrs Smith, I promise you. John will never suffer. He's the only important one. The others don't matter but I'll always take care of John."'

* * *

Brian's objective, even before getting The Beatles under contract, was to sign them to a London record company, a glory none of Liverpool's 350 beat groups had yet come near.

For him it was a straight choice between the industry's twin giants, Decca and EMI, which between them supplied the bulk of NEMS' stock. He chose the latter, self-proclaimed 'greatest recording organisation in the world' whose mighty roster extended from Frank Sinatra, Nat 'King' Cole and Judy Garland to Tennessee Ernie Ford, Gene Vincent and Cliff Richard and the Shadows.

His importance as a retailer secured him an immediate appointment with EMI's marketing director, Ron White – though he made out that it was merely to talk about the discounts NEMS received on bulk orders. Once inside White's office, he whipped out a copy of 'My Bonnie', asked him to listen to The Beatles' uncredited backing on it, showed him a photograph of them in their black leather and announced they were an act 'the greatest recording organisation in the world' would be bereft without.

White explained that as marketing director he had no influence over the signing of talent but promised to pass the details to EMI's A&R department. Noticing the single's label, he asked whether The Beatles were already contracted to Polydor. This raised the spectre of their pre-Brian deal with Bert Kaempfert which gave Kaempfert exclusive world rights to their output for ten years and bound them to record four tracks a year.

Indeed, Kaempfert could have sunk any hope of Brian getting them a British record deal. But he was that rarity in the music business, a fair-minded, kindly man who agreed to release them from the contract in exchange for one more studio session when they next returned to Hamburg.

They still all but monopolised every issue of *Mersey Beat* but Brian was now looking to publicise them over a wider area. He therefore wrote to the huge-circulation daily *Liverpool Echo* in which NEMS regularly advertised and which ran a weekly record-review column under the byline 'Disker'.

Its author, Tony Barrow, happened to be a Liverpudlian whose day job was working for the Decca organisation in London as a writer of album-cover copy. Brian's letter somehow found its way to Barrow, who was sufficiently intrigued to invite him to call at his office at Decca's headquarters on Albert Embankment.

This time, as well as 'My Bonnie', Brian took with him a tape-recording of The Beatles live at The Cavern which he said – untruthfully – was to be the basis of a television documentary about them, but its sound quality proved hopelessly bad. Barrow regretted it was too late for him to review 'My Bonnie' in the *Echo* but said that if they ever won a recording contract he'd be happy to do a 'local interest' story about them.

It was then that Brian first reached beyond the stars to assert that one day they'd be 'bigger than Elvis Presley', whose British label, HMV, was a satellite of Decca. It prompted a snigger from Barrow's office-mate for, as everyone in the know knew, nothing could ever be bigger than that.

Having heard nothing further from Ron White at EMI and feeling he'd already dipped a toe into Decca, he next went to see their marketing director, Beecher Stevens, again supposedly to discuss bulk-purchase discounts. With Stevens he took a different tack, putting forward a plan to give The Beatles access to Decca's studios and manufacturing facilities without actually becoming Decca artists. The company would merely manufacture their records, which he'd then release on his own NEMS label.

He was in fact anticipating the indy companies of the not-so-distant future that would give first-rank performers – The Beatles among them – the creative freedom of owning their own label while outsourcing its manufacturing and distribution. But he found he had no need to elaborate on his idea. The seemingly ambivalent Tony Barrow had had second thoughts and told Stevens his act might be of interest, and Stevens had passed the word to the head of A&R, Dick Rowe.

Rowe was a respected figure currently enjoying the kudos of having produced Britain's tenth most successful single that year, Billy Fury's 'Halfway to Paradise'. As such he was too grand to follow up Barrow's tip in person, so on 13 December a young assistant in his department named Mike Smith was dispatched to Liverpool to check out The Beatles on their home ground.

Brian treated Smith to a lavish dinner, then escorted him down into The Cavern and to his front-row kindergarten chair as though to the Royal Box at Covent Garden. Simply bringing a London A&R man here so speedily and seeing how it sent The Beatles' prestige into the stratosphere was almost triumph enough for him.

Their live show converted Smith in an instant and on the strength of his report Dick Rowe agreed to audition them under studio conditions as Decca protocol demanded. This was to take place at flatteringly short notice on New Year's Day, not then a public holiday.

To Brian the news more than compensated for having finally heard back from Ron White at EMI. White said that three of the company's four label-heads had listened to 'My Bonnie' but all been equally unimpressed. The fourth, who'd been on holiday at the time – but whom White didn't think worth trying now – was one George Martin.

* * *

90

It was with the highest hopes at the turn of the year that The Beatles and their still unofficial manager travelled down to London for the Decca audition, though not all together. Brian went ahead a couple of days beforehand to stay with Queenie's sister, his aunt Freda, who lived close to Decca's recording studios in West Hampstead; John, Paul, George and Pete made the journey on New Year's Eve in Neil Aspinall's van.

Neil had never driven to London before and got seriously lost somewhere in the Midlands. There were numerous hold-ups due to snow and freezing fog and the journey ended up taking ten hours. Brian had booked them into a small hotel in Woburn Place, Bloomsbury, and told them to turn in early since the audition was scheduled for 11 a.m., when they'd normally be dead to the world. Instead, they wandered around the riotous West End and saw in the New Year that would be the making of them – or, at least, three of them – watching the ritual mass drunken bathing in the Trafalgar Square fountains.

As they stood there, a stranger sidled up, showed them some funny-looking green strands he called 'pot' and offered to share it with them if they'd let him 'smoke' it in the relative seclusion of Neil's van. The Liverpool lads fled.

Next morning, they somehow made it to Decca's studios at the appointed time, to find Brian already waiting impatiently. Their obvious failure to get enough sleep earned them their first managerial telling-off, accompanied by one of his deep flushes.

It had no effect whatsoever on John, as Pete Best would recall. '[He] basically turned round and said, "Brian, shut up. We're here for the audition, right?"'

But Mike Smith wasn't: their supposed enthusiast and sponsor didn't show for another half-hour and proved to be nursing a major hangover from the previous night's partying. Brian seethed and blushed at this casual treatment but managed to bite back his annoyance.

For The Beatles the session was both uncomfortable and disappointingly impersonal. The studio to which they were shown had only just been reopened after the Christmas break and was still freezing cold. Then the engineer told them their amplifiers were substandard and they'd have to use the ones on site without any time to get used to them.

Normally in what Decca clinically termed 'a commercial test', auditionees did a maximum of four or five numbers before being firmly ushered out of the studio. Calling on the stamina they'd acquired in the Hamburg stews, The Beatles did fifteen for Smith and his boss, Dick Rowe, punctuated only by a brief lunchbreak. And by the end, despite the chill and the unfriendly amps, they'd managed to crank themselves almost to Cavern level. The problem was with those fifteen songs, all of them Brian's choices despite his promise to be musically non-interventionist.

Nowadays they're generally agreed to show The Beatles' magpie talent at its best: their ability to play almost anything in any genre and flavour it with their particular inventiveness and charm. And among the note-perfect covers and pastiches and piss-takes are three Lennon–McCartney compositions, 'Like Dreamers Do', 'Love of the Loved' and 'Hello Little Girl', like appetisers for the feast to come.

But in the simplistic British pop of 1962, versatility was suspect and conformity was all. What was to be made of a beat group whose beat might be rock 'n' roll, country, Latin or slow foxtrot and who veered unpredictably from Chuck Berry's

'Memphis Tennessee' to Harry Warren's 'September in the Rain' and Lieber and Stoller's 'Three Cool Cats' to Harry B. Smith's 'The Sheik of Araby'? Or, for that matter, of beatmakers who ignored the time-honoured formula of frontman and back-up and sang in twos or threes or in unison?

Afterwards, The Beatles felt gloomy about their performance, but Brian reassured them that it had been 'marvellous'. Before their nightmare homeward journey, he took them to a restaurant in Swiss Cottage – a district for him fraught with memories of his entrapment by the police – and tried to cheer things up by letting them order wine.

Three days later, *Mersey Beat* published the results of a poll among its now 5,000 readers to elect Liverpool's most popular group. The Beatles came top, beating Gerry and the Pacemakers, the Remo Four, Rory Storm and the Hurricanes, Kingsize Taylor and the Dominoes and the Big Three. The front page was filled by a photograph of the winners in their black leather, cropped to hide their shabby footwear and with Paul's surname spelt 'McArtrey'. Like all the other contestants, they'd voted for themselves multiple times – an unnecessary measure since Bill Harry had fixed the result in their favour.

But there was no word about the Decca audition, which Brian wanted kept secret until its far more important result was made known. Its only mention was in Disker's *Liverpool Echo* column, filed by Tony Barrow from inside Decca, where all the signs seemed positive. 'I said it was only a matter of weeks before The Beatles came back to record their first single.'

Barrow then learned to his astonishment from Dick Rowe's office that they were to be rejected 'because groups with guitars are on the way out' – a prophecy rivalling the one in 1927 that talking pictures would soon blow over.

Rowe told me the real reason years later, after his reputation as The Man Who Turned Down The Beatles had been rescued by signing the Rolling Stones to Decca (on George Harrison's recommendation).

The Beatles' audition had coincided with that of Brian Poole and the Tremeloes, another 'group with guitars' from Dagenham, in the east London suburbs. 'I told Mike Smith we could only afford one of them and he'd have to choose. He said, "They're both good but one's a local group, the other's from Liverpool." We decided to take the local group. We could work with them more easily and stay closer in touch because they were in Dagenham.'

Brian's response was to go back to Decca's marketing people and remind them of his importance to the company in retailing terms. But they had no influence over the A&R department and in any case were wearying of his 'bigger than Elvis' line. 'You've got a good business, Mr Epstein,' one of them told him condescendingly. 'Why not stick to it?'

'I heard afterwards that he'd guaranteed to buy 3,000 copies of any single we let The Beatles make,' Dick Rowe said. 'But I was never told about that at the time. The way economics were in the music business then, if we'd been sure of selling 3,000 copies, we'd have been forced to record them whatever kind of group they were.'

To Rowe's credit, he tried to soften the blow by suggesting Brian should hire an independent producer to work with them and possibly give them a more commercial edge. He suggested Tony Meehan who'd recently quit as The Shadows' drummer, at the height of their success, to go into producing still aged only nineteen.

A meeting between the two took place in Rowe's office but was not a success. Brian was told that hiring an outside studio would cost £100, which he considered extortionate – although little enough compared with buying up 3,000 copies of a single just to get The Beatles on record. Besides, as an ex-Shadow Meehan had an inflated ego that wouldn't have sat well with Liverpudlians, especially not John.

Brian backed away from the arrangement, writing to Dick Rowe that 'Mr Meehan's' help would no longer be needed as 'since I saw you last the Group has received an offer of a recording Contract from another Company.'

It wasn't a complete fib, since the Group still had recording commitments to the easygoing Bert Kaempfert which might mean further releases on Polydor. But to get them signed to a British label, the whole point of the exercise, he'd have to start again from the bottom.

8

'THEY LOOKED AS IF THEY'D BEEN STEAM-CLEANED'

Putting The Beatles under contract was a lengthy process owing to Brian's wish that its terms be as fair as possible. Their lack of representation other than parental, and evident readiness to sign anything offered to them, only increased his determination that this should be so.

He had got hold of a standard management contract back in December but been horrified by its predatoriness and had it extensively modified by a Liverpool solicitor, David Harris. Its third and final draft, dated 24 January 1962 – and one day to be sold at auction for £275,000 – gave him sole responsibility for finding The Beatles work, managing their schedule and 'all matters concerning clothes, makeup and the presentation and construction of the Artists' act and also on all music to be performed'. His commission was set at 10 per cent rising to 15 per cent if their collective income should ever exceed £120 per week.

The signing of the contract took place at Pete Best's home with his mother, Mona, proudly looking on – circumstances that would later seem horribly ironic. In the general excitement no one noticed that Brian himself deliberately omitted to sign his own name, thereby rendering it legally null and void.

By his lights, he had already failed The Beatles twice, with EMI and Decca, and leaving his signature off the contract was a kind of insurance for them. 'It was because even though I knew I would keep to [it] in every clause, I had not 100 per cent faith in myself to help The Beatles adequately,' he would later admit. 'In other words I wanted to free [them] of their obligations if I felt they would be better off.'

The first gig he arranged for them was on 1 February, via a promoter named Sam Leach at the Thistle Café, West Kirby, a seaside town on the Cheshire Wirral ten miles from Liverpool.

Beating a big drum for them in a small space came naturally. On Brian's insistence Leach billed the event as the 'Grand opening of the Beatle Club', although no such club existed and they were never to revisit the Thistle Café. Their fee was £18, of which his commission was just under £2.

His father's misgivings notwithstanding, he'd been given office space on the top floor of the NEMS Whitechapel building; for, Harry Epstein reasoned, it would ensure he didn't neglect the record department and kept his promise to devote only two half-days a week to The Beatles.

As back-up for his regular office secretary, Beryl Adams, he took on 17-year-old Frieda Kelly, a shorthand-typist at NEMS who'd already seen The Beatles at The Cavern more than a hundred times, to deal exclusively with them and organise their expanding fan club. Frieda initially had a whip-round among the four to cover the running costs until she realised Brian meant to do that, too.

There was little difference between the way he'd always run

the record department and the way he now set out to run The Beatles. This, too, spoke of his passion for efficiency and his flair for presentation and publicity; occasionally there were even reminders of his life long ago in the army.

The customer in his mind always being paramount, it offended him profoundly to see their casual, even contemptuous attitude towards their live audience, not realising that, for the female element particularly, it was a large part of their appeal. Therefore, he instructed them that they must stop smoking and swearing and eating onstage and – even in the reeking bowels of The Cavern – end every performance with a deep bow in unison.

They had never before been amenable to any kind of discipline. But there was no arguing with the weekly £25 each Brian paid them which Tony Bramwell hand-delivered in brown wage-packets every Friday as if they were an addition to the NEMS workforce. At the time, George's father, Harold, earned £10 a week as a bus-driver, so even this most rebellious Beatle on the quiet paused the chain-smoking that one day would kill him, and fell into line with the bow.

Yet they could relapse into their old habits at any moment. Frieda Kelly told me of Brian's blushing annoyance when the Cavern's owner, Ray McFall, telephoned to complain that insufficient Beatles had turned up for that day's lunchtime session. "'There's only *three* of them!" he kept saying. "And Gerry Marsden's singing with them, standing on an orange-box so they needn't bother to let the microphone down to his height.'"

Their out-of-town bookings, however small, were organised like the 'movement orders' Brian used to deal with as an army clerk even though merely a quartet rather than a regiment

99

needed moving. Well in advance, they and their now dedicated driver, Neil Aspinall, would receive a lengthy typed briefing about the venue, the promoter and the start- and finish-times, always stressing the need for punctuality and sobriety.

Pulling up at some tiny village hall far out on the Wirral like Barnston Institute – normally an outpost of the cosy, jam-making Women's Institute – they'd find it pre-plastered with posters designed by Brian, heralding the advent of MERSEY BEAT POLL-WINNERS! and (again, not wholly a fib) POLYDOR RECORDING ARTISTS!

He would usually come to see them in his Zephyr Zodiac, as conspicuous among the teenage throng as a peacock in a sparrow's nest, and ready to challenge any departure from the written agreement or disrespect towards them on the organisers' part.

After their appearance at Aintree Institute, near the Grand National racecourse, the promoter Brian Kelly handed over their £15 fee entirely in small change – not only silver half-crowns and florins but copper pennies and halfpennies. Brian was outraged and demanded that in future they be paid 'in pound notes in a civilized manner'.

He soon realised that his organisational and artistic talents were not enough. Getting work for his boys, as he already referred to them, meant cultivating tough promoters like Kelly who'd been their main employers outside The Cavern. And here the immaculate appearance, posh accent and expansive ways that had always been his greatest assets in business became a positive handicap.

The ultimate objective for all Liverpool groups was the Tower Ballroom across the Mersey at New Brighton, a magnificent space with quilted walls that had once been the ground floor to a 173-metre replica of the Eiffel Tower. Its manager Tommy McArdle, a former middleweight boxing champion and celebrated chucker-out of drunks, was nonetheless thoroughly intimidated by Brian's invitation to 'come over and have lunch' at one or other of his current favourite gourmet restaurants.

He was not alone in feeling himself wanting on the crucial promotional front. Mona Best, who'd effectively handed him The Beatles for the greater good of her son Pete, complained continually about the paucity and quality of their gigs since his takeover. He'd begun to dread phone calls from 'that woman' – though not as much as he soon would.

Meanwhile, he was making regular trips to London to try to find The Beatles a record label, but this time with no inside contacts like Tony Barrow or Dick Rowe. He now had something better than 'My Bonnie' as a calling-card, having managed to buy their Decca audition tape (destined to sell at auction in 2019 for £62,500.)

After the two multi-label giants he'd been dealing with, the remaining choices seemed meagre and small-scale. There was Pye Nixa, which had Lonnie Donegan, the one-time 'king of skiffle' now in steep decline; Oriole, which had Russ Hamilton, a Liverpudlian singer-songwriter who'd pre-dated Billy Fury, now totally forgotten; Philips, which had Marty Wilde, or Top Rank, which had Vince Eager. At the very bottom, and not even to be considered, was Embassy, which produced quickie cover-versions of current hits by unknown performers to be sold exclusively in Woolworths stores.

Few of the A&R men to whom Brian came 'cold' in this way found time to see him or listen to his tape and his 'bigger than

Elvis' line met with the same mocking smiles, particularly when uttered in the same breath as 'Liverpool'.

Exploring every possible avenue, he approached Joe Meek, an electronics genius who produced grandiose singles like 'Johnny Remember Me' – which had done so well for NEMS – in his flat-cum-studio above a leather goods shop in Holloway, north London.

Meek shared Brian's sexual orientation and likewise kept it secret, except from the young session musicians he employed, who had to practise the same tactful fend-offs as the members of Larry Parnes's stable. He listened to The Beatles' tape but had no interest in meeting them as there was 'nothing new about their sound'.

Brian's friend Geoffrey Ellis, home on a visit from New York, was disconcerted by the transformation in someone Ellis remembered as a classical music buff. Their first reunion had to be cut short because Brian had to attend a Beatles performance at a New Brighton pub. 'Thank God I don't have to come with you,' Ellis told him.

Continuing what Harry and Queenie Epstein considered his sudden descent into the underworld, he no longer frequented upscale city-centre bars like the Adelphi's cocktail lounge and The Basnett, but was increasingly to be found with his boys at the Iron Door Club in Temple Street, a more grown-up version of The Cavern that served alcohol.

At the Iron Door late one night, he became aware that a tall, diffident-looking man seemed to be trying to get his attention. It was Joe Flannery, his long-ago nursery companion and in adolescence the only steady gay relationship he'd ever had.

Since their unrancorous parting, Joe had become immersed

in Liverpool's beat scene as manager of Lee Curtis and the All Stars, who regularly alternated with The Beatles at The Cavern. The group's frontman was Joe's youngest brother, Peter, whom his homophobe father used to accuse him of wanting to molest when Peter was barely able to walk.

Brian found Joe as easy to talk to as of old, and poured out the dual frustration of pitching The Beatles to indifferent ears in London and trying to engage with rough-and-ready dance-promoters on Merseyside. 'He said he was cheesed off with it all,' Joe said. 'He was thinking of chucking it in and going back to learning to act at RADA.'

Joe by then was living with a factory supervisor named Kenny Meek (whom he introduced to everyone as his 'cousin'). But Brian's charm and sophistication – and vulnerable moments like this – had lost none of their power to melt him. 'I said I'd negotiate The Beatles' gigs and deal with the contracts involved while he concentrated on getting them a recording deal.'

'Flo Jannery', as John instantly dubbed him, was to do much more than that, turning his house in Gardner Road into the same after-show refuge for them as his little bric-à-brac shop in Walton had once been for the teenaged Brian, cooking them late suppers of cheese or baked beans on toast, usually having them stay overnight in his comfortable lounge, when he noticed 'John always took the couch while Paul made do with two armchairs pushed together.'

There was little profit in it for Joe and no glory: on the contracts he negotiated for The Beatles, when £30 could still buy two shows from them in an evening, he was designated only as 'Management'. Nor did he ever talk about his silent partner role until Bill Harry steered me to him in 1979.

Back then, he recalled, it had been enough for him to be around Brian again or simply hear his voice.

'Whenever he phoned me he didn't say, "Hello, it's Brian", just "Joe ...". I always used to like that.'

* * *

From the beginning, Brian had dreaded the moment when The Beatles would find out about his homosexuality. And that dread was to stay with him to the end of his life. They always knew all about it yet never owned up to their quadruple blind eye.

Indeed, they would have known about it long before knowing him – ever since the *Liverpool Echo*'s story about the dramatic 'queer-bashing' case in which he'd been the victim and given evidence in court under the instantly porous alias of 'Mr X'.

Latterly, as semi-permanent occupants of NEMS' audio-booths they couldn't have missed all the incriminating gossip behind his back: about his being still a bachelor at an age when 'normal' young men were married with children, his suspiciously close male friendships, even his immaculate tailoring and ability to dress a window and design a poster.

With two extended stays on Hamburg's Reeperbahn behind them, The Beatles were no innocents. But even the pioneering gay liberation they witnessed there couldn't curb the homophobia they'd inherited from their elders that was as natural as bad breath.

In these early days, they accepted Brian's sexuality as the price of what he could do for them; later, that acceptance would become a measure of their affection and, ultimately, compassion.

When his new career became public knowledge, there were inevitably whispers about why a well-set-up businessman should be devoting such effort and expense to four scruffy youths. And at times, more than whispers. Before long, his solicitor was having to send a stern letter to a man who'd been heard in a city-centre Kardomah café loudly casting aspersions on his relationship with The Beatles. The letter demanded a written apology and an undertaking that the 'malicious and defamatory allegations' would not be repeated.

Joe Flannery's addition to The Beatles' support team gave rise to still more whispers although there was no rekindling of the sexual spark between Brian and himself, which had always been of the mildest.

Knowing Brian as he did, Joe realised what a strange emotional bind he was in. He loved The Beatles like the children mid-twentieth-century Britain would never allow him. But with his instinct for fatally wrong choices, he was *in love* with John, the one who personified all his most shaming rude-boy fantasies with a ferocious intelligence and whipcrack wit added on.

At first, the gluttonously hetero John was embarrassed to be thus singled out. One night when they were at the Iron Door with the promoter Sam Leach, Brian abandoned discretion so far as to suggest that the two of them 'fly to Copenhagen for the weekend'.

'That was a nice offer,' Leach remarked innocently. 'Shut up,' John hissed back. 'Can't you see he's after me?'

However, as time went on he wasn't averse to 'playing it a bit faggy', as he put it, to gain extra favours for the group or out of pure mischief.

John deferred to Brian about everything relating to The Beatles but otherwise the so-called 'boy born without brakes' could treat him abominably, at one minute sarcastically over-reverential, at the next blisteringly rude to his face about his clothes, his hair, his accent, his sexuality, even his religion. The abuse was turned on so suddenly without provocation that he could only stand there, clutching his executive briefcase to him, colouring deeper and deeper. 'I've sat with him in the car for hours,' Joe Flannery said, 'when he's been crying over some of the things John's said to him.'

People were to wonder that he hadn't fallen for the surpassingly good-looking and charming Paul instead. Frieda Kelly, that closest of onlookers, believed he always felt vaguely guilty about it. Never for a millisecond, for any pragmatic reason under the sun, would Paul have been capable of 'playing it a bit faggy', yet he would always be the Beatle whom Brian tried hardest to impress and whose wishes he jumped fastest to execute.

Pete Best was the only one with John's kind of allure for him, sharpened by Pete being a genuine tough guy rather than a pretend one like John. Decades later, he would claim that Brian had propositioned him outright from behind the wheel of the Zephyr Zodiac during a journey to Blackpool with John and his girlfriend, Cynthia Powell, out of earshot in the back. But the pass had been rejected without awkwardness and, during Pete's remaining tenure as a Beatle, was never repeated.

Only George seemed no part of this convoluted sexual equation despite being widely considered Paul's equal in looks, if not charm. His childhood friend-turned-roadie Tony Bramwell thought that might be changing when he was invited to spend a whole day at the Epsteins' home, apparently tête-à-tête with Brian. Afterwards he was cagey about the visit, almost as if something untoward had happened, and became angry when

Bramwell tried to pump him for details. 'He ... snarled that [they] had just talked and he wouldn't discuss it.'

* * *

There was one final element of The Beatles' image that Brian felt it essential to change – with some regret since it was what had most excited him personally. This was the all-black leather look acquired in Hamburg, which in 1961 still reminded people of Hitler's SS.

He therefore took them to Liverpool's Empire theatre to see a performance by Cliff Richard's backing group The Shadows, step-dancing in unison in matching shiny suits. He told them if they aspired to being anywhere near as successful, this was the only way to go and reminded them that under their contract he could insist on it.

John's mutinous mutters about 'selling out' were silenced when the suits Brian had in mind turned out not to be the kind of flashy tat worn by their Liverpool rivals but in a discreet grey 'brushed tweed', made to measure by the Birkenhead tailor Beno Dorn at £40 apiece, or around £750 in today's money.

The Beatles unveiled their – or, rather, his – new look at The Cavern with some trepidation. Reviews from their female following were mixed. 'It was like being hit with a brick because they'd looked so rough until then,' one said. 'From their skin and shiny hair to their fingernails and clothes, they looked as if they'd been steam-cleaned,' said another.

Harry and Queenie Epstein looked on in dismay, but could do nothing about it, as Brian's obsession with The Beatles far outgrew its supposed 'two half-days a week'. His very appearance changed, in the opposite way theirs had, for he would sometimes discard his tailored suits and Peter England shirts in favour of a black leather jacket and matching polo-neck, then considered rather embarrassing for a twenty-seven-year-old. 'I remember the first time he came to The Cavern dressed like that,' Bob Wooler recalled. 'He had no idea that everyone was laughing at him behind his back.'

The Beatles also introduced him to a discovery they'd made in Hamburg, where they had to perform marathon sets with only minimal breaks. It was a German slimming pill called Preludin whose dulling of the appetite and speeding up of the metabolism allowed them to go without sleep for days at a time.

These 'Prellies' were Brian's first experience of drugs. They were not only highly addictive but increased his already copious drinking since they dried up the saliva and made the lips difficult to moisten. Wooler remembered him 'champing away' between vain attempts to slake his raging thirst.

He was still pitching The Beatles to the last London record labels on his list, always being turned down in the most slighting ways. When he returned home, they'd meet his train at Lime Street station, four expectant faces he dreaded to see fall yet again. He'd break the bad news either in a coffee bar named the Punch and Judy or Joe's Café, a 'greasy spoon' in Duke Street where he had a table permanently reserved for him as if it were the Savoy Grill.

At such low moments it would be John, so often his tormentor for no reason, who was the most understanding and philosophical. There was nothing for it, John would say – they'd just have to settle for the despised 'Woolworths' label, Embassy.

Trying to keep their hopes up, he resorted to an audacious

deception one night as they were all sitting in the pub next door to the Majestic Ballroom 'across the water' in Birkenhead. 'He got me to go out of the room,' Joe Flannery recalled, 'and then come back in and say there was a phone call for him from Elvis Presley's manager, Colonel Tom Parker.'

Skilled actor that he still was, he made it seem utterly plausible that the legendary Colonel should be reaching out from Memphis to a manager of equal consequence on Merseyside.

Which only three years later really did happen.

* * *

Brian would later suggest his fruitless journeys to London on The Beatles' behalf had dragged on for months, but in reality there were only three weeks between Decca's formal turn-down and the moment when his luck changed so unexpectedly.

Early in February it occurred to him that London's supercilious A&R community might take him more seriously if the fifteen tracks on the Decca audition tape he now owned were transferred to an acetate demo disc. A year earlier, before ever equating The Beatles with Hamburg, he'd gone there for a record-retailers' conference that had included a visit to the factory of Deutsche Grammophon, the classical division of the Polydor company. Also on the course had been a man named Bob Boast, general manager of the HMV record store in London's Oxford Street, the retailing 'face' of the EMI organisation.

Boast had mentioned that such a disc-cutting service was available in-store, while one waited, for only £1 apiece. Providentially, among the half-dozen songs Brian picked to be transferred from the fifteen on tape were three original ones by

Lennon–McCartney, even though they'd made no impression on any listener thus far.

It was for him a rather humiliating errand after having previously dealt with senior record company executives; moreover, Bob Boast's disappointing response to the tape was that it wasn't his kind of music. But the engineer who converted it into a disc, Ted Huntley, commented that it 'wasn't at all bad'.

Brian hadn't realised that one floor above the HMV store were the music publishers Ardmore & Beechwood, a company likewise owned by EMI. Huntley's reaction prompted Boast to take the newly cut disc upstairs to its managing director, Syd Coleman, and suggest that Coleman listen to it, which he did along with his deputy Kim Bennett, a former singer turned 'song-plugger' tasked with selling new compositions to recording artists.

A few minutes later, Brian was astonished to be shown into Coleman's office and told that Ardmore & Beechwood wanted to publish one of the Lennon–McCartney songs on the disc, 'Like Dreamers Do'. Despite this huge, unlooked-for accolade, he had to explain that what he really sought was a recording deal for the group to which the songwriters belonged. Coleman was equally astonished that he didn't already have one and arranged for him to meet a colleague and close friend inside EMI, the head of its Parlophone label George Martin.

Parlophone at the time was the smallest and least commercial EMI satellite. Under Martin, it had had a few fleeting pop hits, with Jim Dale, Adam Faith, and the Temperance Seven, but it was known mainly for 'spoken word' records by the Goons comedy team and their two principal members, Spike Milligan and Peter Sellers.

Brian duly made contact with Martin's secretary, Judy Lockhart-Smith – who misheard his first name as 'Bernard' – and an appointment was made for him to come to EMI's high-rise headquarters in Manchester Square on 13 February.

There he met a man as unlike the usual A&R man as he himself was unlike the usual pop manager. For Martin, then aged thirty-six, was tall and elegant with a pure BBC accent as opposed to Brian's northern-flavoured one, and 'the air,' he thought, 'of a stern but fair-minded headmaster'. Uniquely for a producer of pop records, Martin was a trained classical musician, proficient on the piano and oboe and in scoring and conducting: abilities that one day would be put to uses he'd never dreamed.

Brian thought it best not to mention The Beatles' previous turn-down by three other EMI labels and, to his relief, Martin showed no awareness of it. On his side, Martin would remember how 'to start with [Brian] gave me a big hype about this marvellous group who were doing such great things in Liverpool . . . He even expressed surprise that I hadn't heard of them, which in the circumstances was pretty bold.'

Years later, when I talked to Martin on the first of many occasions, he still smiled over The Beatles' eccentric song choices at that time, like Fats Waller's 'Your Feet's Too Big'. But like no one else during Brian's arduous foot-slog, he found things about them to praise: John's song 'Hello Little Girl,' the unusually high timbre of Paul's voice and some of George's lead guitar work.

'There was an unusual quality of sound, a certain roughness,' he would recall. 'Something tangible that made me want to hear more, meet them and see what they could do. I thought, well, there might be something there. At least it's worth following up.'

Martin made no definite commitment but Brian was reassured by his civilised manner together with Judy Lockhart-Smith's sweet, sympathetic smile, and returned to Liverpool to meet his boys at Joe's Café full of optimism.

9

'THE MOST HATED MAN IN LIVERPOOL'

While he awaited George Martin's decision, The Beatles needed Brian to handle a business matter pre-dating his management – and leading to a crisis in which he could be of only marginal help.

They had first gone to Hamburg in 1960 as a five-piece with John's fellow art student and close friend Stuart Sutcliffe on bass guitar and Paul an extra rhythm guitarist, in the Liverpool phrase 'like a spare prick at a wedding'. Stu and John between them had thought of the name 'Beatles', a laboured double pun on beat music and beating all competition, which had been mocked to the skies by rival Liverpool groups yet somehow had stuck.

Stu was an indifferent bass-player but a brilliant painter and during their second Hamburg season had ceded his spot in the line-up to Paul and enrolled at the city's art college under the tutelage of the great Scots-Italian Pop artist Eduardo Paolozzi.

He now was settled in Hamburg and engaged to a talented photographer named Astrid Kirchherr, but on a recent trip home had seen The Beatles at The Cavern for the first time and talked to Brian about a possible future role as their personal designer or art director. Stu was very different from the others, small and delicate and fiercely intellectual with a look of Hollywood's lost icon, James Dean. A captivated Brian wrote to him afterwards, 'I didn't know anyone as lovely as you existed in Liverpool.'

Despite The Beatles' new 'steam-cleaned' image, Brian was happy for them to continue performing in Hamburg's red-light district, at present the biggest deal on their horizon. For the sake of that image, however, he bought up and suppressed some snapshots taken on their previous visits which John had given to *Mersey Beat*'s editor, Bill Harry. 'They weren't very scandalous,' Harry recalls. 'Mostly John out on the street in his underpants or onstage wearing a toilet-seat around his neck.'

Their next Hamburg gig was to have been a return to a club named the Top Ten whose young owner, Peter Eckhorn, The Beatles liked and trusted. They had negotiated their previous wage directly with Eckhorn but when he travelled to Liverpool to re-engage them, he found Brian now in charge and their price per musician raised to a hefty 600 Deutschmarks (about £53.50).

Close behind Eckhorn came a diminutive Hamburger named Horst Fascher, a former middleweight boxing champion who'd been chief bouncer at the Top Ten and kept special watch over The Beatles for love of their unregenerate rock 'n' roll.

Now Fascher wanted them to open a new venue named the Star-Club on 13 April, then appear for seven straight weeks with a guarantee of two further bookings before the end of the year. To cut out Peter Eckhorn, Fascher offered the 600 Deutschmarks each plus a hefty bribe – Brian's first but not last encounter with 'brown bag money'.

Prior to departure, he plastered Liverpool 'jive hives' far and wide with posters announcing that Beatles gigs there were

'PRIOR TO EUROPEAN TOUR', and electrified *Mersey Beat*'s readership with the news that he'd be accompanying them personally by air.

In Hamburg, meanwhile, Stu Sutcliffe had been suffering blinding headaches and fainting fits but had refused to interrupt his painting for long enough to seek medical help. On 10 April he collapsed at the home of his fiancée, Astrid, where he'd been living. An ambulance rushed him to the city's Heidelberg Hospital with a suspected brain haemorrhage but he died on the way, cradled in her arms. He was twenty-one.

The Beatles knew nothing of this when three of them, John, Paul and Pete, flew out of Manchester's Ringway airport on 11 April. George had – appropriately enough – developed suspected German measles and as it was his first-ever flight, Brian had stayed behind to escort him the following day. As the two waited to board, they met Stu's mother, Millie, who told them what had happened and that she was on her way to identify his body. Brian sat with her and did his best to comfort her throughout the flight.

He found Stu's death had deflated a group he'd only ever seen in antic high spirits. John was stricken above all, having hero-worshipped Stu at art college as the kind of 'real' artist he believed – and would always believe – he himself could never be. It was Brian's first glimpse of the vulnerable soul beneath his relentless clowning and ruthless wit.

Initially, the mourning had to be private between the four and Stu's fiancée, Astrid. All Brian could do was help Millie Sutcliffe through the formalities following her son's death, including a post-mortem, and the arrangements for transporting the body back to Liverpool for burial. But in the aftermath he became friendly with the androgynous young woman who'd befriended his boys during their earliest days in Hamburg so much to their lasting benefit.

Astrid was the first photographer to shoot them with their faces becomingly half-shadowed, like art objects rather than leaky-booted scruffs, and had done Stu's hair in the fringed 'French' style that turned into the Beatle Cut. Brian realised the extent of her contribution and promised it would be properly acknowledged, but amid the whirlwinds soon to come, it never would be.

This second time in Hamburg for him included no conscientious revisiting of the Deutsche Grammophon factory. Like The Beatles, he spent most of his few days there asleep, his nights under the hyperactivating influence of Preludin slimming pills. And the city's St Pauli district, for them almost a second home, gave him a heady taste of carnality and criminality without danger.

The Star-Club's owner, Manfred Weissleder, also owned St Pauli's biggest strip-club and was its most feared denizen. A huge, fleshy man with a dusting of golden hair like a James Bond villain, he was rumoured to be closely involved with Hamburg's mafia since his many establishments were immune from the protection rackets otherwise endemic. He in turn gave protection to the musicians on his payroll in the form of little star-shaped lapel badges, the mere sight of which made any would-be aggressor instantly back off, mumbling apologies.

Even fear of Weissleder couldn't curb the violence that could break out during The Beatles' performance – though never silence it. Star-Club customers, mostly sailors from the nearby docks with a leavening of local gangsters and pimps, routinely carried tear-gas pistols, knives and 'brass knuckles' and the

2,000-capacity space regularly billowed with choking yellowish fumes and ran with blood.

They were no match for Horst Fascher – who'd done time for accidentally killing a sailor in a street brawl – and his team of waiters-cum-bouncers known as 'Hoddel's Gang', themselves armed with coshes and adept at wrestlers' drop-kicks. 'The scariest guy I had,' Fascher told me, 'was a doorman with one arm.'

To Brian it would have been mesmerising to witness such mass sadism at close quarters, just as it was to walk down St Pauli's main throughfare, the Reeperbahn, where every variety of sex was openly catered for. But despite the flowing alcohol and abundant 'Prellies', he seems to have resisted its myriad temptations rather than risk his boys 'finding out' about him.

As always, he had no idea of the jokes on that score that John, in particular, was making behind his back. 'One night, I heard there was an English guy drunk in the next-door bar, who I first thought must be a musician,' Fascher recalled. 'But when I go in there, I find Brian Epstein sitting up at the bar, passed out cold with his head on the counter.

'So I go back into the club and tell John to come and help me get him out of there. When John comes into the place, he just picks up a half-empty glass of beer from the counter, pulls back Brian's collar and pours the beer down his neck. I asked him if that was any way to be treating The Beatles' new manager. "It's OK," John said to me. "I already gave him one up the ass."'

Luckily, he didn't have to hold out for long. In a world without mobile phones, he needed to get back to Liverpool to see if there'd been any further developments with George Martin.

* * *

There hadn't. And whenever he tried phoning Martin, the producer was always said to be in a meeting, then failed to call him back. Alistair Taylor would remember him almost weeping with frustration and even considering reprisals, not only against Parlophone but every EMI label by banning their products from NEMS stores.

It wasn't until 9 May, six months to the day after Brian had first seen The Beatles at The Cavern that Martin agreed to meet them immediately after their return from Hamburg.

In those days, the UK's fastest and most dramatic mode of communication was the Post Office telegram. Brian immediately sent one to John, Paul, George and Pete in St Pauli and another to *Mersey Beat*'s Bill Harry, ever so slightly doctoring the facts:

> CONGRATULATIONS BOYS. EMI REQUEST
> RECORDING SESSION. PLEASE REHEARSE NEW
> MATERIAL.

> HAVE SECURED CONTRACT FOR BEATLES TO
> RECORD FOR EMI ON PARLAPHONE [SIC] LABEL IST
> RECORDING DATE SET FOR JUNE 6.

Many years later, it would emerge that Martin hadn't been acting on his own initiative but on the orders of EMI's managing director, Len Wood, after machinations typical of that cumbersome, over-politicised and straitlaced corporation.

The original intention had been merely to sign up Lennon–McCartney's songwriting partnership on the recommendation of Wood's publishing head, Syd Coleman, to whom Brian had played The Beatles' demo disc with such little hope above the

HMV record store. But Martin at the time happened to be in bad odour with EMI's management for seeking a pay increase and – far worse in its eyes – carrying on an extra-marital affair with his secretary, Judy Lockhart-Smith. It was seen as a slap on the wrist to make him work with a group from a faraway, grimy city, with a beyond-ridiculous name and seemingly no earthly chance of success.

But it was never to feel that way. Martin was instantly won over by The Beatles' charm and deference towards him for the albums he'd made with their comedy heroes, Peter Sellers and Spike Milligan. Nor was he at all the 'toff' he sounded, having grown up in poverty in north London and, like many men of his generation, acquired an upper-class accent during wartime military service, in his case with the elite Fleet Air Arm. The very anomalies that seemed to distance him from The Beatles – comedy producer and trained classical musician – would be what made them perfect for each other.

For EMI it was scarcely a major investment. The contract Martin offered Brian and he gratefully accepted was a standard industry one for four years at a royalty of one old penny per record sold, rising after a year by one farthing – a minute coin worth a quarter of an old penny that had disappeared from general circulation the previous year.

Martin later told me how, unbeknown to Brian, his attitude to his new charges was at first wholly self-interested. He'd always envied his fellow EMI label boss, Columbia's Norrie Paramor, whose hit singles with Cliff Richard and the Shadows endlessly duplicated themselves whereas every one of Parlophone's comedy records had to be conceived and constructed from scratch.

The Beatles, he thought, might be his Cliff and the Shadows and, with an A&R man's absolute power, considered making Paul their lead singer in the customary such-and-such and the so-and-so's format. Then the musician in him realised the folly of consigning John and George merely to background 'oohs' and 'aahs'.

Martin at that stage wasn't a great fan of Lennon–McCartney songs and there was an awkward moment when he announced the Beatles' debut single, by the 'professional' Mitch Murray (himself only twenty-two), would be a sunny little ballad entitled 'How Do You Do It?' which had already been turned down by Parlophone's biggest name, Adam Faith. Despite pleas from Brian not to rock the boat, they protested it wasn't their style and would make them a laughing stock back in Liverpool. Martin made them demo it nonetheless, but the result was so determinedly lacklustre that he gave way and settled for John and Paul's 'Love Me Do' instead.

His authority was reasserted later when he took Brian aside and announced that Pete Best's drumming wasn't good enough to be recorded so he'd have to use a session-player in Pete's place.

In the recording business this was perfectly normal. Martin wasn't demanding that Pete be fired and he could quite easily have gone on being a Beatle in their live shows. But in the two years he'd been with them, he'd never really fitted in with his reserved manner and crisp, non-Beatley hair. John, Paul and George seized the opportunity to get rid of him and shift the blame elsewhere.

Shabbily, they made Brian do the dirty deed, citing Martin's thumbs-down to his drumming. Pete replied that he'd been good enough to have played with them for the past two years as well as sharing their many degradations in Hamburg without a word of complaint. But there was no appeal and he left Brian's office, as he later told me, feeling 'cut and dried and hung out on the line'.

Far more of an ordeal for Brian was the wrath of Pete's mother, Mona, to whom this represented the grossest ingratitude for all she had done to support and promote the group as well as injustice to the member whom many people regarded as its star.

It also had serious practical implications since Pete's best friend was Neil Aspinall, The Beatles' now indispensable driver-cum-roadie, who boarded at the Best family home and, in a plot twist worthy of Gilbert and Sullivan, had been having an affair with Mona Best, resulting in her pregnancy.

But Pete, a gentleman throughout, told Neil not to think of quitting at such a pivotal moment while Mrs Best undertook to bring up their newborn son, whom she'd named Roag, without any paternal pressure on his young father. And while subjecting Brian to many blush-making tirades, she seems never to have demanded the compensation Pete could reasonably have claimed.

Not so easily swept under the carpet was the simultaneous pregnancy of John's long-suffering girlfriend, Cynthia Powell, which in those days for most young people could only lead to marriage. Here the consequences for The Beatles looked far more serious, for all precedent dictated that pop stars with wives or too-visible girlfriends risked alienating their entire female fan-base.

John and Cynthia's wedding promised to be a rather melancholy affair since her widowed mother was abroad and his domineering aunt Mimi wanted nothing to do with it. So

Brian, sublimating his real feelings for John, took charge with his usual efficiency: he volunteered himself as best man, obtained the licence for the civil ceremony and offered the couple the use of his hidey-hole in Falkner Street flat for the remainder of Cynthia's confinement.

On 23 August – John and Cynthia's wedding day – *Mersey Beat* reported that Pete Best had left The Beatles by mutual 'amicable' agreement and was to be replaced by Ringo Starr from Rory Storm and the Hurricanes. To compound Pete's woes, the paper added that Ringo would be flying down to London with them on 4 September to record their debut single, 'Love Me Do'.

Brian had played no part in choosing Pete's successor as a manager might normally expect: the others had been so pally with Ringo in Hamburg that he'd seemed like a Beatle in waiting and now they slipped him on like a cosy old corduroy jacket. 'Brian just felt relieved that Ringo wasn't good-looking with that sad puppy-dog face,' Joe Flannery said. 'He didn't want there to be another Beatle he might fall in love with.'

Mersey Beat's story about an 'amicable' change of drummer fooled no one: Pete's many fans realised he'd been dumped and were outraged. Hundreds of letters demanding his reinstatement flooded into the paper and a round-the-clock mourning vigil was kept outside the Best home. When Mona Best opened her front door to take in the morning milk, she saw grief-stricken young women sleeping rough all over her garden.

There were riots outside The Cavern and Ringo's debut with The Beatles was punctuated by shouts of 'Pete Best for ever – Ringo never!' After George received a black eye from a male Pete supporter, Brian refused to show his face there unless the owner, Ray McFall, provided him with a bodyguard. 'He kept telling me, "I'm the most hated man in Liverpool,"' Joe Flannery recalled. 'And he was loving it.'

He tried to soften the blow for Pete with a promise to build another group around him. In practice this only meant re-homing him in an existing one, Lee Curtis and the All-Stars, managed by Joe Flannery and fronted by Joe's youngest brother, Peter.

Joe agreed to the transaction out of love for Brian despite knowing it would inevitably dilute the spotlight on Peter. He further agreed to an elaborate bit of subterfuge, typical of Brian. 'First I had to talk Pete into joining the All-Stars after being a Beatle, then tell him, "I think I can arrange it with Mr Epstein."'

* * *

Whatever the fate of 'Love Me Do', Harry Epstein now took Brian's pop management seriously enough to incorporate it into the family brand. The summer of 1962 saw the creation of a satellite company, NEMS Enterprises, to be run by his brother Clive and himself without any paternal interference. 'Enterprises' was appropriate as it marked his expansion from management, first into promoting, then big-time showmanship.

At the time, Greater Merseyside's most energetic impresario was a tousled twenty-seven-year-old named Sam Leach, whose association with The Beatles pre-dated Brian's and who had once seemed yet another contender to manage them. Leach's principal venue was New Brighton's Tower Ballroom where his multi-group spectacles known as Operation Big Beat pulled in crowds of up to 3,000 and deployed as many bouncers as Horst Fascher at the Hamburg Star-Club.

Leach thought big – but Brian thought bigger. First in partnership with Leach but soon independently he began putting on Tower Ballroom shows headlined by major recording stars with a single in the charts or a national tour in progress. The first was the Cockney rocker Joe Brown whose 'Picture Of You' was currently in the UK Top 10, the second the American Bruce Channel whose 'Hey Baby' had inspired John's harmonica riff on 'Love Me Do'. Each time, The Beatles were second on the bill, to indicate they were only a line of type less important.

'Brian would watch the pop charts all the time to see who was selling the most records and then book them,' Joe Flannery said. 'When they came up to Liverpool, he'd make a big day of it with a record-signing session at the shop and the show in the evening. The Americans used to think it was wonderful. They weren't used to getting that kind of VIP treatment in England, even in London.'

His greatest coup was announced in a full-page advertisement in the 6 September *Mersey Beat*:

NEMS ENTERPRISES PRESENT
MERSEYSIDE'S GREATEST-EVER ROCK
SPECTACULAR HEADED BY AMERICA'S
FABULOUS LITTLE RICHARD AT THE TOWER

This most uproarious of original rock 'n' rollers had waned in popularity in his own country, especially after a spell in the ministry, but his following throughout Europe remained fanatical. He, too, happened to be touring Britain and Brian had been able to book him for a single night at the Tower Ballroom on 12 October headlining eleven local groups headlined by The Beatles.

Putting them on the same stage as one of their greatest musical heroes ended what they'd viewed as Brian's probationary period. On 2 October they signed a second management contract to replace the one that had included Pete Best – and lacked a manager's signature – raising his commission to 25 per cent. A drafting error by Clive Epstein, hastily rectified soon afterwards, allowed each side power to terminate the agreement at six months' notice.

Little Richard duly materialised on Merseyside, the baggy, shiny suit and Struwwelpeter hair shown in the NEMS advert rather disappointingly replaced by sober sharkskin and a short-back-and-sides. With him came the tour's promoter, Don Arden, a thuggish character known in the business as 'the Al Capone of Pop'.

Joe Flannery witnessed a pre-show row between him and a furiously blushing Brian in which the Al Capone of Pop came off decidedly worse. 'I can remember his voice ringing round the Tower Ballroom bar: "I'm going to telephone your office tomorrow, Mr Arden, and after that I don't think you'll be working there anymore."'

Other local promoters of the Little Richard tour had told horror stories of his unreliability, his bizarre whims and fancies, his frequent refusal as an ordained minister to sing anything but hymns and his paradoxical fondness for onstage stripteases, ignoring the audience's pleas for 'Good Golly Miss Molly' or 'Lucille'. But that night in New Brighton, he ululated every one of his Golden Oldies with scarcely a pause.

'Brian seemed to be able to do anything with him,' Joe remembered. 'When he finished his act, something went wrong with the mic for the next act, Pete MacLaine and the Dakotas.

Brian could even get him to walk across, nice as you please, and hand his personal microphone to Pete MacLaine.'

Backstage after the show he remained seraphically amiable, posing for photographs with the awestruck Beatles clutching all their hands at once and coaching Paul in the window-rattling shriek he called his 'little holler'.

Two weeks later, he returned to Liverpool, this time to appear at the Empire theatre with Craig Douglas, Jet Harris and the Jetblacks and The Beatles. Brian had devised the event to give them their first performance at the Empire.

Joe Flannery claimed to know the reason for this seemingly inexhaustible willingness to oblige Brian and make The Beatles look good. 'Richard was gay ... or, to be precise, he was everything ... and he and Brian had spent the night before the Tower Ballroom show in a suite at the Adelphi Hotel.'

Neither party was ever to admit to such an encounter and Richard's autobiography, *The Quasar of Rock*, made no mention of it, but twenty-five years later, during a book-promotion tour of America, I was able to investigate further.

Waiting for a short flight from Philadelphia to Pittsburgh, I noticed a fellow passenger with an unmistakable cupid's-bow mouth and pencil moustache – and, despite his name, not very little. He was travelling without his usual bodyguards, who could number as many as twenty, and aboard the tiny propeller-plane we were seated side-by-side with his left knee jammed against my right one.

He was terrified of flying and, as we left the ground, broke into loud prayers to the Almighty and confessions of past sins, dabbing at his glistening face with tissues from an economy-size box. The first few minutes were extremely bumpy and from our

126

front seats we could see the open doorway to the cockpit and a stirrup hanging from the ceiling, which the pilot's hand would grab just before each bump.

'Oh Lord, oh Lord!' moaned my neighbour. 'That cat's on about page three of "How To Fly."' It was like being given a private Little Richard performance with seatbelts.

I felt that mutual terror had bonded us so when the plane levelled out and his prayers subsided, I said, 'May I ask you something?'

'Sure,' he replied. 'Anything you want.'

'On 2 October 1962, when you appeared with The Beatles at the New Brighton Tower Ballroom, had you spent the previous night with Brian Epstein at the Adelphi Hotel in Liverpool?'

I think I may have been the only person ever to reduce Little Richard to silence. Then he broke into denials almost as passionate as his prayers: 'No! No! No! *No!* I never even had a *sandwich* with Brian.'

Knowing that, in certain circles, 'sandwich' can mean something far from Prêt à Manger, I didn't press the point ... but I still wonder.

10

'HAVE YOU HEARD ABOUT THE BOYS?'

Brian received an advance copy of 'Love Me Do' just before Rosh Hashana, the Jewish New Year, when there was a large family gathering at his parents' house. A drawing-room sneak preview of the single drew a mixed response; his paternal aunt Stella from Southport winced and pleaded for 'something by Andy Williams' while his young cousins jumped up and started doing the Twist.

As always, he could depend on Queenie, who at once wrote off to BBC Radio's *Housewives' Choice* programme, requesting it for a non-existent niece and signing herself 'Alice'.

EMI made little effort to promote what several of George Martin's colleagues took to be another Parlophone comedy record. After its release on 5 October 1962, the single was allotted a few meagre ads in the music trade press, then left to sink without trace.

Brian had once been prepared to buy 3,000 copies of any single Decca let The Beatles make; now, according to Joe Flannery, he ordered 10,000 copies of 'Love Me Do', thinking that more than enough to get it into the Top 20.

But although it instantly went to number one in *Mersey Beat*'s chart, the huge Liverpool sale he expected failed to materialise. Many of The Beatles' female following had made pacts with each other not to buy it, believing that a hit single would take them away for ever. Nor would such a massive bulk purchase have had any impact on the national charts, which were based on returns from a pre-ordained circle of retailers, NEMS not among them.

In years to come, Clive Epstein would firmly deny that he or their straight-as-a-die father were a party to such attempted chart-rigging. Yet Brian had always been allowed total freedom in what he ordered without reference to them since the outcome was usually positive. Flannery recalled him almost showing off the stacks of unopened cardboard boxes of records. 'He even sang a little song he'd made up about them, "Here we go gathering dust in May" to the tune of "Here We Go Gathering Nuts in May."'

With 'Love Me Do' not charting and money still no object, Brian hired a young PR man named Tony Calder, whom he'd met at the Decca offices, to introduce The Beatles to selected newspaper and magazine journalists in London. It was the first inkling that they were quite unlike the usual dull, incoherent British popstars; that they possessed unprecedented charm, articulacy and quickness of wit.

Calder's inspired move was to sell 'Love Me Do' to the nationwide ballroom-chains Mecca and Top Rank, both of which featured pop record interludes with deejays who could play it, so creating that most potent of all publicity, 'word of mouth'.

Further unlooked-for help came from Kim Bennett at EMI's music publishing company, Ardmore & Beechwood, who'd helped steer Brian to George Martin. Bennett managed to get

'Love Me Do' onto the playlist of the British Forces Network, broadcasting to the army, navy and air force bases that still dotted the world. As a result, it made a slow chart-ascent from number 49, eventually squeezing into the Top 20 at number 17.

Apart from still greater hometown glory, the chief gain for The Beatles was that EMI no longer regarded them merely as a stick with which to chastise Martin, and Martin now regarded them – and Brian– with total seriousness. With their second single there had been no question of using a 'professional' songwriter; Martin had accepted John and Paul's vastly more exuberant 'Please Please Me', worked extensively on it with them, then so far forgotten his headmasterly mien as to announce, 'Gentlemen, you have just made your first number one record.'

When it came to publishing 'Please Please Me', Brian wanted nothing more to do with Ardmore & Beechwood, thinking they'd performed poorly with 'Love Me Do' (Kim Bennett's hefty contribution unknown to him). Still a little Elvis-fixated, he was planning to approach Hill & Range, administrators of the precious Presley songbook in the UK. But Martin instead advised going to a 'hungry' small publisher who would work for his songwriting boys that bit harder.

The hungriest Martin knew was Dick James, a former dance-band vocalist turned song-plugger – in fact, the one who'd sent him 'How Do You Do It?' only to have The Beatles reject it (and, on learning whence they hailed, had chuckled, *Liverpool! So what's from Liverpool?*'). James had been in business as a publisher for only a year, working out of a tiny office in Charing Cross Road, and was palpably struggling when Martin sent Brian to see him.

That same morning, Brian had an earlier appointment with another publisher in the same building, but arrived, bang on time as always, to be told his interlocutor hadn't come in yet or bothered to send him any explanation or apology. Fuming, Brian went on to James's office with an hour or so to kill, intending to wait outside. By a coincidence for which he'd give thanks for the rest of his life, James happened to be at his desk early and so could see his flush-faced young visitor at once.

He proved to be a large, bald, jovial man, Jewish like Brian – though it was never to be a particular bond between them – whose voice still had cadences of his years on the bandstand with Henry Hall and Geraldo and his best-remembered hit, the theme-song from a children's television series, *The Adventures of Robin Hood*, produced by Martin:

Robin Hood, Robin Hood, riding though the glen.
Robin Hood, Robin Hood, with his band of men ...

James at that stage was interested only in 'Please Please Me' and its B-side, 'Ask Me Why'. When Brian asked what he could do with them that Elvis's publishers couldn't, his answer was to ring up the producer of television's most-watched pop music show, *Thank Your Lucky Stars*, a friend from his plugging days, and play 'Please Please Me' down the line.

The producer booked The Beatles on the spot. Two decades later, James's *faux-naïf* payoff to the coup still gave him obvious pleasure. 'After I rang off, I turned back to Brian and said, "*Now* can I publish the songs?"'

He was to do much more than that after listening to an early pressing of the album George Martin had just made with The

Beatles in a single nine-hour session that left John, in particular, barely able to speak.

Traditionally, 'LPs' had merely been a way of getting pop fans to buy a hit single for a second time, the remainder usually makeweight 'standards' that were seldom played more than once. But on The Beatles' *Please Please Me*, half the tracks were by Lennon–McCartney and almost all were good enough to have been singles in their own right.

Under the standard miserly publisher's contract, James would have taken 10 per cent of the retail price of sheet music (in those days a lucrative secondary market) plus up to half the royalties from radio and television play and other artists' cover-versions.

Instead he proposed that a company be formed publishing only Lennon–McCartney compositions and rather sweepingly called Northern Songs. Forty-nine per cent would be owned by James and his business partner, Charles Silver, 19 per cent by John, 20 per cent by Paul, 10 percent by Brian through NEMS Enterprises and a token fragment each by George and Ringo.

For those days it was both imaginative and generous even though DJM had the majority shareholding and would take an additional handling fee 'off the top'. '"Why are you doing this for us?" Brian asked me,' James recalled. 'What I said to him was the truth. I was doing it because I had such faith in the songs.'

His addition to the Brian–George Martin alliance would mean that the biggest act in entertainment history – unrepeatably, unbelievably – was in the hands of three fundamentally honest men.

* * *

For now, The Beatles noticed little difference save that, as their booking agent as well as manager, Brian was sending them all over the country rather than just all over Merseyside and Cheshire to extract the maximum value from their marginal hit single.

They were playing continual one-nighters in theatres, cinemas, municipal halls and clubs interspersed with their first appearances on BBC Radio in London, often travelling hundreds of miles in one day, crammed with their equipment into Neil Aspinall's van. Nor was there any let-up with the onset of Britain's heaviest and most prolonged snowfall for almost a century.

Brian's objective now was to get them onto one of the 'package' tours that continually circulated, largely made up of acts who'd done better in the charts than number 17. Poring over their posters, he noted that most had the same promoter, Arthur Howes. Rather than approach Howes through his office and risk a brush-off from an underling, Brian found out his home phone number and rang him there on a Sunday.

Warmed by Epstein respectfulness and charm, the cold call paid off. Howes agreed to try out The Beatles for two shows at the Embassy cinema, Peterborough, as the opening act on a bill headed by the Australian yodeller Frank Ifield.

Their appearance, on 2 December 1962, was a resounding flop. Even with their new suits and deep bows, they seemed too perversely out of the ordinary and both their sets – hard though it be to imagine – were listened to in silence and grudgingly applauded. The *Peterborough Standard* dismissed them as 'loud'.

Arthur Howes was somewhat more discriminating and in early February 1963 gave them another shot as £80 bottom-of-the-bill on a national tour headlined by the schoolgirl chanteuse Helen Shapiro. This gave rise to a brief period of notoriety when they gatecrashed a golf club dance in Carlisle in order to raid the buffet and were requested to leave. The resulting press coverage revealed a far worse offence – backsliding from Brian's 'grey brushed tweed' to black leather jackets.

In late February, Britain's Big Freeze still showed no sign of thawing. A nation largely off work and bored to distraction ensured a bumper audience for ABC television's *Thank Your Lucky Stars* show at teatime on the twenty-third.

Not just its usual pop fan audience but whole families huddled around fires or heaters with toast or crumpets or fishpaste sandwiches and received their first exposure to The Beatles' revolutionary hair and cheery grins and perfectly proper bespoke suits, and to 'Please Please Me's wailing harmonica, guttural guitar and winning three-part harmony (they were only lip-synching but no one noticed). It was two minutes two seconds' worth of publicity beyond price.

Within days, the single reached number one on the charts of Britain's most popular music trade papers, the *New Musical Express* and *Melody Maker* – though only number two on that of *Record Retailer*, the final arbiter.

Brian's secretary, Frieda Kelly, recalled how completely his usual executive poise went out of the window. 'I'd never seen him so excited. It was the first thing he said to anyone who rang up: "Have you heard about the boys?" If anyone came to see him, it was the first thing out of his mouth: "Have you heard about the boys?"'

'The most hated man in Liverpool' had become a superhero for taking its name to undreamed-of heights. Congratulatory messages to The Beatles poured into NEMS, some written on toilet-rolls or cylinders of wallpaper, together with giant cuddly toys, cakes and – from one fan with connections to the banana-importing business – a live tarantula in a box.

At the time, Brian was having meetings with the Russian-born entrepreneur Giorgio Gomelsky, who'd sought his authorisation to make a film about what had then seemed merely an interesting fringe pop act. Now their conversations were continually disrupted by calls from promoters hungry to book The Beatles at any price he cared to name.

'I would be there when promoters rang him up, offering him £50 for one appearance,' Gomelsky remembered. 'Brian would say, "I don't know," and start looking in his diary. So the promoter would offer £60. "I don't know," he'd still say. So then the promoter would offer £70, thinking he was stalling for more money. He wasn't − he just couldn't find the right page in his diary.'

There was also a reunion with the great Larry Parnes, who hardly recognised the unassuming young man who'd commented so astutely on Billy Fury's showmanship backstage at the Liverpool Empire in 1959.

'Mr Parnes Shillings and Pence', hitherto a dealer in solo pop icons, had since adjusted to the group mentality and wanted The Beatles for a series of Sunday concerts the next summer at the end of Great Yarmouth pier. Brian tried hard to do the deal for the sake of the exposure it would afford his boys, but in the end was defeated by Parnes's inveterate penny-pinching.

'I was offering £30 per show and he wanted £75,' Parnes recalled. 'He said that if I'd meet his price I could have an option to do shows with The Beatles for the next five years. He came down from £75 to £35, I went up to £32. He wouldn't budge and neither would I.'

* * *

Yet The Beatles' breakthrough, and all the extra care and protection it would demand, suddenly wasn't enough for Brian. He was already well acquainted with Gerry and the Pacemakers, their greatest rivals at The Cavern and Hamburg's best-behaved Scouse group when his boys were among the worst. He therefore took them to George Martin, who recognised a natural in their ebullient singer/lead guitarist Gerry Marsden, signed them to Parlophone and for their debut single gave them the 'professional' song The Beatles had scorned, 'How Do You Do It?'.

Less straightforward was the case of Billy Kramer, born William Ashton, a 19-year-old trainee locomotive engineer from Bootle who, with his backing group the Coasters, had come third in *Mersey Beat*'s latest popularity poll.

Though spectacularly handsome, he had little of Gerry Marsden's animation and, moreover, was prone to extreme stage-fright. He already had a manager, an elderly boilermaker named Ted Knibbs, who was trying to toughen him up by making him rehearse in crowded rooms while standing on a chair.

In late 1962, Brian bought his contract from Knibbs for £50 cash, paying £25 and promising the balance would soon follow. It never did, but Knibbs made no attempt to collect and charitably attributed his loss to a lapse of memory rather than deliberate sharp practice.

'First we're going to throw out the Christmas tree,' Brian told his new acquisition, meaning the same kind of makeover he'd given the black-leathered Beatles, in this case replacing Kramer's gold lamé stage jackets with further bolts of discreet tweed.

Kramer's backing group, The Coasters, didn't want to turn professional so Brian brought in a more accomplished outfit from Manchester called The Dakotas. At John Lennon's suggestion, he inserted a would-be glamorising J between 'Billy' and 'Kramer.'

His preoccupation with this modestly talented hunk was surprising to some people but to many others not so. Kramer would always maintain their relationship had been solely professional, yet Brian was openly smitten by him, always referring to him as 'My Billy'.

When he took Kramer to George Martin with what he clearly regarded as fresh Parlophone material, Martin was underwhelmed by the new protégé's vocal range but – showing how the balance of power between them had shifted in two months – Brian insisted that 'My Billy' should be signed.

Martin recorded him and The Dakotas doing a Lennon–McCartney song from The Beatles' still-unreleased *Please Please Me* album called 'Do You Want to Know a Secret?' (a sly allusion to Brian's own widely-known 'secret' that had completely passed the producer by).

Simple though the song was – having been written for George's limited vocal range – Kramer proved unequal to its falsetto line 'I'm in love with you-*oo-oo-oo-oo*'. Martin artfully camouflaged the wobble by double-tracking the vocal and playing his own piano fill underneath it.

Meanwhile, the group Brian would never have presumed to call 'his' Beatles were on another Arthur Howes package tour, this one jointly headlined by two imported American chart-toppers, Chris ('Let's Dance') Montez and Tommy ('Sheila') Roe. The £80 booking had been made when The Beatles were still next-to-nobodies, but he wouldn't renege on it even though there were now promoters who would have paid ten times as much.

The tour was like a barometer-reading of things soon to come. On its first night, The Beatles went down so infinitely better than either American that Howes promoted them to the top of the bill. From there, by bewildering contrast, they found themselves headed for Stowe, the boys' boarding school in Buckinghamshire, for another pre- 'Please Please Me' engagement that Brian insisted on honouring.

Back in January, a pupil named David Moores had written and asked him if The Beatles would give a performance there. It didn't hurt that the Mooreses were Liverpool's wealthiest family, owners of the Littlewoods mail order business, philanthropists and patrons of the arts.

On the Roe/Montez tour, The Beatles' set had been twenty minutes but to Stowe, for £100, they gave a whole hour, playing in the school's Roxburgh assembly hall to rows of orderly schoolboys.

* * *

NEMS Enterprises was growing apace. A London office was soon needed to provide an address for The Beatles' ever-expanding fan club, to send out signed photographs and answer fan mail which, on Brian's orders, they still did by hand. The company's diversifying roster also created a need for a full-time press and publicity officer who, Brian insisted, must be absolutely sincere about the product he or she was pushing.

Here the perfect candidate was to hand in Tony Barrow, the *Liverpool Echo*'s Disker columnist who'd tried so hard to persuade Decca to sign The Beatles. Barrow recalled being introduced to them in a pub around the corner from EMI headquarters and John casually giving him the lowdown on his new employer.

'John said, "If you're not Jewish and you're not queer, what are you doing working for Brian?" It wasn't in front of Brian but it was in his earshot.'

The poky upper floors of 13 Monmouth Street, Seven Dials, were rented to house both the fan club and Barrow's press office. In building relationships with journalists he was extraordinarily thorough – the quality Brian admired most. He even discovered my existence as a trainee reporter on an obscure weekly paper in Cambridgeshire and began sending stylish releases addressed to me personally that did wonders for my low status in the office.

One showed The Beatles in their chic 'shortie' raincoats posed on what looked like a Mersey mudflat, with a comment from the *Thank Your Lucky Stars* emcee, Brian Matthew, that they were 'musically and visually the most exciting group to emerge since The Shadows'. Another depicted Brian as a schoolteacher with headshots of all his young protégés seeming to revolve around his own headmasterly mortarboard.

NEMS Enterprises' publicity department was briefly joined by a 19-year-old freelance PR named Andrew Loog Oldham whom Brian put on a monthly retainer of £25 to cover the few areas Tony Barrow didn't.

Already a practised hustler, Oldham had hoped to attach himself to The Beatles, but Brian would allow only Barrow anywhere near his precious boys. Instead, Oldham found himself confined to the outer circle of Gerry and the Pacemakers and Billy J. Kramer and the Dakotas.

Soon afterwards, he happened on a volcanic blues band called the Rolling Stones playing in the back room of a pub in Richmond-upon-Thames, fronted by a rubber-lipped economics student then known as Mike Jagger. In an exact reprise of Brian at The Cavern, he discovered they were without proper management and volunteered himself despite having no previous experience.

Without any resources to back up this hubris, he offered Brian 50 per cent of the Stones in exchange for some minimal funding, office space and a telephone line. But Brian felt that with two new Liverpool acts as well as his boys, he had more than enough to think about, and so he missed the chance to run both great supergroups of the 1960s.

* * *

At the start of that momentous summer of 1963, NEMS Enterprises' enterprises could hardly have looked in better shape.

The Beatles' third single, 'From Me to You', was number one in every UK chart; their art-studenty *Please Please Me* album likewise (and destined to stay in the Top 10 for more than a year). They had just completed the most successful of their package tours, starting out by supporting their great hero, Roy Orbison, and ending as its headliners, which the gentlemanly Orbison had accepted with good grace.

Everything that had seemed so eccentric about them was becoming the pattern for all British pop groups ... their masked foreheads ... their round-collared suits, cribbed from the Parisian couturier Pierre Cardin ... Paul's 'violin' bass like the progeny of a Stradivarius and a giraffe. In April, 'How Do You Do It?' by Gerry and the Pacemakers made number one and in May, 'Do You Want to Know a Secret?' by Billy J. Kramer and the Dakotas reached number two, behind 'From Me to You.'

During John's almost continuous absences from Liverpool on

tour, his wife Cynthia, still occupying Brian's flat in Falkner Street, was now at an advanced stage of pregnancy. It was more prison than refuge for she was still under orders to stay well out of the sight of John's female fans.

The flat was anything but secure: the front door of the house stood permanently open and dubious characters from Brian's secret life were always wandering in looking for him. Sitting room and bedroom were separated by the communal hallway, so Cynthia could never feel completely private.

In the eighth month of her pregnancy, while The Beatles were on tour with Tommy Roe and Chris Montez, she developed severe internal bleeding and was ordered by her doctor to stay in bed for three days or risk a miscarriage.

Torn between concern for her and the necessity of maintaining her low profile, Brian turned to a petite young woman named Dot Rhone who'd formerly gone out with Paul McCartney. Dot had special cause to sympathise with Cynthia's predicament: towards the end of her relationship with Paul, she too had fallen pregnant, but the pair had been saved from a shotgun wedding like John and Cynthia's when Dot miscarried at three months. Below Brian's flat was a small basement one, currently unoccupied, which he made haste to rent. The kindly Dot agreed to stay there so that in any future medical emergency Cynthia needn't be alone.

On 8 April, when John was on the road again, she safely gave birth to a boy at Sefton General Hospital. The baby was named Julian, and Brian, once more far exceeding managerial obligation, became his godfather. There being a temporary gap in The Beatles' frantic schedule, he decided to grant them their first holiday since he took them over.

For John, it would have been an opportunity to take his exhausted wife and newborn son away somewhere for some concentrated bonding; instead, he went to Spain for twelve days alone with Brian.

His decision has gone down in history as an act of appalling selfishness and insensitivity for which he never felt any need to apologise. 'The holiday was planned and I wasn't going to break [it] for a baby,' he would recall. 'I just thought what a bastard I was and went.'

But it was equally an astonishing lapse on Brian's part that could only advertise the infatuation with John he believed he'd kept hidden until then. In effect, the rashness and risk-taking of his private life briefly took over from the caution and correctness of his public one. The headiness of seeing all three of his groups topping the charts, one of them twice over, may well have been a contributory factor.

John would later say they'd had 'a pretty intense relationship' but that he'd been merely an observer of Brian's sexual adventures under the forgiving Spanish sun. 'I watched [him] picking up boys. We used to sit in a café in Torremolinos ... and I'd say "Do you like that one? Do you like this one?" I was rather enjoying the experience, thinking like a writer all the time, "I am experiencing this ..."'

As to whether that 'pretty intense relationship' was ever consummated, Brian seems to have confided only in his close friend Peter Brown. Five decades on, Brown still maintains a loyal silence but for the observation that 'Brian had a tendency to prefer oral sex'.

John would still stick to his 'just looking' story when recounting the trip to the unshockable woman who shared the last decade and a half of his life. 'He said that one night, Brian had come on to him,' Yoko once recalled, 'but he just said, "If you feel like that, go out and find a hustler."'

What seemed like finally owning up, not long before his death, may only have been sour Lennon humour: that he'd tried 'it' twice, 'the first time to see what it was like, the second to make sure I didn't like it.'

Back in Liverpool at the time, there was much gossip about the trip but only within The Beatles' social circle, even *Mersey Beat* tactfully ignoring it.

Then on 18 June, Paul's twenty-first birthday was celebrated by a large-scale knees-up in the garden of his auntie Jin in Huyton, which many members of that circle attended. In true Liverpool style, the alcoholic provision was enormous.

At the height of the jollifications, The Cavern deejay Bob Wooler, who was no teetotaller, made a caustic remark to John about his Spanish 'honeymoon' with Brian. John had already taken a great deal of ribbing about it and, as always uncontrollable under the influence, he laid into the older man with both fists.

Billy J. Kramer was standing nearby with a female companion and as John lurched past he tried to grab her breasts. When Billy J. protested, he would later claim that John also threw a punch at him, shouting, 'You're nothing, Kramer, and we [The Beatles] are the greatest.'

It was a shocking act of violence on someone who'd helped The Beatles immeasurably during their early days and was incapable of defending himself. Brian did his best to smooth things over, apologising profusely and driving Wooler to the nearest casualty department, where he was found to have a black eye and bruised ribs.

The next day, he sent him a telegram as if from John: 'REALLY SORRY BOB. TERRIBLY SORRY TO REALISE WHAT I HAD DONE. WHAT MORE CAN I SAY?' He subsequently offered £200 in compensation, which Wooler accepted though the psychological effects of the assault would be permanent.

But, as Brian realised, this was a moment of extreme peril for himself and everything he held dear. If the story of John's assault on Wooler were to reach the national press, it would be infinitely more damaging to The Beatles than wearing black leather jackets to a golf club dance.

Any dirt-digging journalist who looked behind it was bound to find out about his homosexuality – possibly even about his past court appearances in that context – and drag him into lurid headlines as the corrupter of the young men who were his stock in trade. That would be the end of NEMS Enterprises and probably of him, too.

It was now that The Beatles' new press officer, Tony Barrow, proved his worth. Rather than try to suppress the Wooler-battering story, Barrow persuaded a friendly Fleet Street contact, the *Sunday Mirror*'s Don Short, to write it up as an anguished confession from John, using quotes confected by himself and headed 'BEATLE IN BRAWL – SORRY I SOCKED YOU':

'Why did I have to go and punch my best friend? I was so high [then meaning drunk] I didn't realise what I was doing . . . Bob is the last person in the world I would want to have a fight with. I can only hope he realises that I was too far gone to know what I was doing.'

No other paper bothered to investigate further. In a few days, amazingly, the whole affair had blown over, leaving the way clear for Beatlemania.

11

THE NEMPEROR

Since the 1960s, many performers have been said to induce mania in their audiences. Initially, they were pop singers and groups (Bay City Roller-mania, Osmond-mania, David Cassidy-mania, Jackson Five-mania, Wham!-mania, Bros-mania, Take That-mania, Spice Girl-mania, Guns N' Roses-mania, Coldplay-mania, One Direction-mania, Justin Bieber-mania, Taylor Swift-mania) but they've since come to include actors (Leonardo DiCaprio-mania, Tom Cruise-mania, Benedict Cumberbatch-mania) and even plastic dolls (Barbie-mania).

In all those human examples, after a few airport riots and hotel sieges, the paroxysm soon subsided. Only Beatlemania didn't – and still hasn't.

Similarly, young women had screamed over male sex symbols from Franz Liszt in the early nineteenth century through Rudolf Valentino on the silent screen and Frank Sinatra at the New York Paramount in 1947 to Elvis Presley when he turned the guitar into a phallus in the mid-'50s. But never, before or since, was there screaming like that of Beatles fans.

Actually, what suddenly began in August 1963 was more

like a huge, concerted wail or ululation, toneless, almost de-humanised, that nothing could make stop or draw breath and obliterated every word The Beatles sang and note they played.

Its trigger was their fourth single, 'She Loves You' – John and Paul at this point believing there had to be a 'you' or 'me' if they wanted another hit – which had 500,000 advance orders, stayed in the UK charts for thirty-one consecutive weeks, eighteen of them in the top three, and ultimately become the best-selling British single of the decade.

Unlike its many descendants, Beatlemania was always peaceable and good-humoured, however massively disruptive. Nothing evokes the 1960s' first, innocent phase like the black and white footage of those surging, shrieking crowds held in check by yesterday's unmilitarised bobbies, the only casualty an occasional helmet knocked askew. And should things ever get a bit out of hand, there would be Brian, beautifully tailored and old-worldly courteous, a reassurance to any remaining doubters that there truly was nothing to fear.

The media – then predominantly newspapers – certainly played a part in building The Beatles up, although not to the heights they eventually reached; it was more a case of them building the papers up. Even mass-circulation titles thus far had barely acknowledged pop music other than to deplore or sneer at it. But the summer of 'She Loves You' also brought Fleet Street a hard news overload.

The Profumo Affair, the biggest politics-and-sex scandal of the century, shivered Harold Macmillan's somnolent Tory government to its foundations. A Royal Mail train en route from Glasgow to London carrying a fortune in registered let-ters and packets was ambushed and robbed of £2.61 million, around £48 million in today's money. The first potato famine since the mid-1800s all but obliterated the nation's staple meal of fish and chips.

News editors, casting around for some light relief, leapt on The Beatles, the mayhem of their concerts and the fact that their predicted mayfly lifespan showed no sign of ending. Their Liverpudlian charm and candour proved the perfect respite from the sleazy aristocrats and scheming politicos who'd been revealed like ants with the lifting of a stone. And for every paper that splashed them, whether multimillion-selling tabloid or 'quality' broadsheet, circulation surged.

It wasn't only in being articulate and funny that they defied the norms of British pop stardom. Brian had dreaded the revelation that John was married would fatally alienate his female fans, as had happened to Marty Wilde a few years earlier. But in his case, few of them cared, most thinking it only made him more interesting. Likewise, Paul's dating of the young actress Jane Asher, when it got out, only created British pop's first celebrity couple.

With the rise of the Rolling Stones under Brian's former PR man, Andrew Loog Oldham, his boys ceased to be in any way controversial, their once-outrageous mop-tops now seeming neatly barbered in comparison with the Stones' collar-curling shagginess, their ever-obliging smiles all the brighter against the Stones' scowls and sneers.

They were not just a part of what we now call 'the national conversation' but more and more seemed to monopolise it. Any public figure seeking attention, from an archbishop in a pulpit to a backbencher in Parliament, had only to utter their name to win an instant headline. Psychologists delivered weighty interpretations of the screaming of their fans ('an unconscious preparation for motherhood,' one concluded), musicologists analysed their lyrics and chord patterns when there wasn't yet much to analyse, historians discovered parallels between them and music-makers in Ancient Greece or Rome.

Yet they never stopped thinking – and never would – that this all but nationalised Beatlemania could come to an end at any moment. Hence John and Paul's mass distribution of their songs among other artists, even some (like the Stones) who might challenge them in the charts: both were convinced that one day their faces would no longer fit as performers and they'd have to earn their living solely as composers.

It was in the same belief that George Martin called for a new Beatles album every six months and a new single every three, and Brian kept them on a perpetual round of live concerts country-wide, TV and radio shows and personal appearances that only young Scousers whom Hamburg had turned to leather internally as well as sartorially could have withstood.

While being lauded in newsprint as 'Pop Music's Svengali', 'The Man With the Midas Touch' and 'The Fifth Beatle', Brian had already had his first encounter with the oh-so-subtle British anti-Semitism and homophobia that were always to shadow his success.

Recently, an entire edition of the *Thank Your Lucky Stars* television show had been devoted to Liverpool's up-and-coming musical talent with The Beatles as headliners. By rights, Brian should have been its presenter as well as sole provider; instead, the job went to the BBC deejay Pete Murray.

* * *

Insanely famous The Beatles might be in Britain, but record industry folklore held they would go no further except perhaps to a few easily pleased countries around Europe. Up until now, America, the crucible of popular music in every form, had felt no need of pale facsimiles from across the Atlantic. And the small handful of British acts to have got under its guard and into its charts – such as the Chas McDevitt Skiffle Group or the boy soprano Laurie London – usually did so only once.

It was no help whatsoever that EMI owned a major American record label, Capitol, since this operated independently and shared the domestic-owned labels' indifference to British sounds. When George Martin had sent 'Please Please Me' to Dan Dexter, a junior Capitol executive, Dexter's lofty response had been 'We don't think The Beatles will do anything in this market.' A personal phone call from Brian, pleading their case, had fared no better. The only American home Martin could find for 'Please Please Me' and their first undisputed UK number one, 'From Me To You', was an obscure Chicago label named Vee-Jay, the latter eventually appearing on *Billboard* magazine's chart at number 116.

George Harrison's married older sister, Louise, lived in Benton, Illinois (making George the first Beatle to visit America while the four were still totally unknown there). After the Vee-Jay releases, Louise wrote to Brian offering to be their 'ambassador' in the Chicago area and keep him up to date with the US charts.

He sent her photographs and press-releases which she dutifully hawked around radio stations and newspapers. She also attempted to check in with Vee-Jay but when she drove to the address given on the record-cover found only an empty parking lot.

151

'She Loves You' and the Beatlemania it visited on Britain left Capitol's Dan Dexter still unmoved. Instead it was picked up by Philadelphia's tiny Swan label, on which it went to number one – but not until a year later.

* * *

One day that September, the pun-loving Bob Wooler phoned Brian and inquired, 'Is that the Nemperor?' For another young talent had been added to NEMS Enterprises' roster, making it no longer exclusively a boys' club.

He had originally wanted to sign 16-year-old Beryl Marsden (no relation to Gerry) who sang regularly with a Liverpool group, The Undertakers, earning comparisons with America's 'Little Miss Dynamite', Brenda Lee. He'd gone as far as seeking Beryl's parents' consent, but then she'd decided she preferred to be managed by his old friend Joe Flannery.

So instead he turned to an exuberant redhead, born Priscilla (or Cilla) Maria Veronica White, who moonlighted from her office job to tend The Cavern's cloakroom, wait tables at the Zodiac coffee lounge and get up and sing, mainly jazz, with groups like the Big Three and Kingsize Taylor and the Dominoes. Brian had been aware of her, though not her wineglass-shattering voice, since the first issue of *Mersey Beat* to which she'd contributed fashion tips as 'Swinging Cilla'.

Her first audition for him, doing George and Ira Gershwin's 'Summertime' from *Porgy and Bess*, backed by The Beatles, was a disaster since they played the whole song in a different key from hers. Things went much better when he saw her at Liverpool's musicians' hangout, the Blue Angel club, and she made her debut as a NEMS artist supporting The Beatles at the

Odeon cinema, Southport. Brian took his parents along to see her and Harry Epstein predicted that 'She'll be the next Gracie Fields.' The comparison with the down-to-earth northern lass who'd kept up the nation's spirits during the Second World War would prove spot-on.

She was launched as Cilla Black, a rebaptism for which Brian took credit 'because her voice sounded more black than white'. Actually it had happened by accident when Bill Harry, captioning her photo in *Mersey Beat*'s first issue, could remember only that her surname was a colour and had picked the wrong one.

Brian took her to George Martin, who privately thought her 'a Cavern screamer' but by now could not demur when he insisted that 'my Cilla' be signed to Parlophone.

For her first single Martin allotted her Lennon–McCartney's 'Love of the Loved', from the Decca audition tape, which John had thought perfect for Beryl Marsden. NEMS' most stylish press-release yet characterised her as 'The Gal with the Bright Red Hair and the Jet Black Voice' and pictured her in a denim skirt daringly breaking just on the knee.

'Love of the Loved' reached only number 35 so was Brian's first failure, but that only increased his determination to make 'his' Cilla a star.

After success on record, the customary next step for every British pop act was to appear in a feature film, several usually lumped together in what was no more than series of musical numbers connected by the flimsiest plot.

Brian had received approaches for The Beatles to make just such a self-confessed 'exploitation' movie for United Artists which, like all Hollywood studios then, maintained an office in London. Both its producer, Walter Shenson, and its director,

153

Richard Lester, were American, but of a deep-dyed Anglophilia common in the UK film industry in those days. In addition, Lester had directed *The Running, Jumping & Standing Still Film*, a 'short' by the Goons comedy team, whom all The Beatles had adored since their schooldays.

Lester was assigned a rock-bottom budget of £20,000 to shoot the film early in 1964 and instructed to complete it in five months since UA believed its subject would be 'a spent force by the end of the summer'. Its being in black-and-white with the working title 'Beatlemania!' signalled the low level of its expectations.

To negotiate terms, Brian should have employed a specialist film agent, but by now he felt that no kind of deal-making was beyond him and so arranged to meet producer Shenson and UA's London boss, Bud Ornstein, by himself.

'I knew Bud well, so I went over to his flat before Brian arrived to talk over the contract we'd be prepared to agree to,' Shenson told me. 'I knew nothing about pop music or managers. I said, "What do you think he's going to ask for?" ... Bud and I agreed it would be fair to offer the Beatles 25 per cent of the picture.

'Then Brian came in. He seemed very nice. We put to him the fee we'd thought of – The Beatles would get a salary of £25,000 – and he agreed to that. Then we asked him, "Mr Epstein, what would you consider a fair percentage of the picture?"

'Brian thought for a minute, then he said, "I couldn't accept anything less than seven-and-a-half per cent."'

* * *

In an era before anything resembling a rock 'culture', The Beatles joined the top echelon of British show business chiefly by becoming visible in television comedy and variety programmes like *The Billy Cotton Band Show*, Morecambe and Wise's *Two of a Kind* and, pre-eminently, *Sunday Night at the London Palladium*.

This hour-long spectacular, broadcast live from a hallowed relic of the music-hall era, with archaic 'turns' like acrobats, trick-cyclists and high-kicking Tiller Girls, wound up a bleak Sabbath when most entertainments were closed, so had a regular audience of around 15 million.

The Beatles' bill-topping appearance on 13 October 1963 unprecedentedly brought TV cameras into a Palladium act's dressing-room before curtain-up. It was the night that the term 'Beatlemania' was coined by a *Daily Mirror* duty-bound to record frenzied crowds, although the fan presence outside was, for once, rather muted.

The programme's finale brought its performers together on a revolving platform, each waving goodbye from behind a giant letter from its title, flanked by high-plumed Tiller Girls. The Beatles protested this massive loss of cool, John loudest of all, but Brian said they had to go through with it, so they did.

In fact, he loved the old-fashioned, spangly side of British showbusiness. When NEMS began to need legal representation in London, he naturally chose its leading entertainment lawyer, David Jacobs, whose international clientele included Marlene Dietrich, Zsa Zsa Gabor, Diana Dors and Laurence Olivier.

In 1959, Jacobs had famously won £8,000 in libel damages from the *Daily Mirror* for describing the American pianist Liberace as 'a deadly, winking, sniggering, snuggling,

155

chromium-plated, scent-impregnated, luminous, quivering, giggling, fruit-favoured, mincing, ice-covered heap of mother love' – which had the mega-camp ivory-tickler, as he put it, 'crying all the way to the bank'.

Jacobs was almost as flamboyantly gay as his client, 6ft 3ins tall and so charismatic that he could appear in court wearing thick pancake makeup yet still somehow win over a judge or jury.

His lavish cocktail parties not only introduced Brian to names he revered but demonstrated how many shared his sexual orientation yet managed not to be haunted by it. The most notable was Lionel Bart, who'd made – and was rapidly losing – a fortune from the stage musicals for which he'd written both words and music like *Oliver!* and *Blitz!*. At his own parties, a large bowl of £5 notes was left on his hall table from which guests could help themselves.

Bart in turn introduced Brian to Jacobs' most celebrated American client, Judy Garland, who'd transfigured his boyhood as Dorothy in *The Wizard Of Oz* but now, addicted to drugs and alcohol, her Hollywood career in ruins, was reduced to singing 'Somewhere Over the Rainbow' to largely gay audiences in British cabaret clubs. Like her celluloid presence in the darkness of some long-ago Odeon or Gaumont cinema, her physical one, however depleted, literally stopped his breath.

On 4 November 1963, The Beatles received the showbiz establishment's highest accolade when they took part in the *Royal Variety Performance*, traditionally the West End's most glamorous night of the year. The Queen being heavily pregnant with her fourth child, the future Prince Edward, the event was graced by Queen Elizabeth the Queen Mother, her younger daughter Princess Margaret and son-in-law the Earl of Snowdon.

Five hundred police had to be drafted in to control the crowds outside the Prince of Wales theatre chanting 'We want the Beatles' and the top of the bill, Marlene Dietrich, a legend since the 1930s, was able to pass through completely unnoticed.

In the preceding days, Brian's boys had demanded so much of his attention, he'd forgotten he'd left his dinner jacket in Liverpool and, since he couldn't endure a rental, it had to be couriered down to him at huge expense. He didn't join his parents in the front stalls until minutes before curtain-up, looking like someone about to face a firing-squad.

Backstage, John had been so disgusted by the largely middle-aged, plutocratic audience, he'd threatened not to ask them to clap along with 'Twist and Shout' but to 'rattle their fuckin' jewellery'. Mercifully, when he delivered the line it had no f-word, so came across as a perfect blend of Lennon charm and cheek that had the house purring rather than rattling.

Only one thing soured this fresh Beatles triumph, though at the time it went totally unnoticed. In the black-and-white film footage of the occasion, those presented to the diamond-encrusted Queen Mother include the show's makers as well as its stars – but Brian is nowhere to be seen.

* * *

The next day, he flew to New York with Billy J. Kramer, heedless of the knowing nudges and whispers behind their backs. It was an essential business trip, to try to break Capitol Records' cycle of rejections with The Beatles' soon-to-be released fifth UK single, 'I Want to Hold Your Hand'. He also had to promote Billy J., whose second single, Lennon–McCartney's 'Bad to Me', was to be released on the Liberty label. That was a further win for NEMS Enterprises, but it pained him still to be chasing a similar American recording deal for his boys.

For some time, he'd been receiving transatlantic calls from an excitable New York promoter named Sid Bernstein with the seemingly fanciful idea of putting The Beatles on at Carnegie Hall, the city's foremost classical music venue. But, even if that were serious, it hardly warranted the expense – not to mention awful risk – of taking them there.

The only friend he had in New York was Geoffrey Ellis, now a senior figure in the Manhattan office of Britain's Royal Insurance company. Knowing his tastes, Ellis recommended he stay at the super-luxurious Regency hotel on Park Avenue. It seemed an ill omen for the visit when the Regency lost a pair of gold cufflinks he accidentally left in a shirt. They'd been a gift from his brother Clive, for being best man at Clive's recent wedding.

On Ellis's last trip home a year earlier, Queenie Epstein had still hoped her achingly unmarried son might get over 'this group thing'. Now Ellis was amazed by the completeness of Brian's metamorphosis into pop manager as evidenced by Billy J. Kramer. One evening as the three of them strolled through Times Square, Kramer admired a garish jacket in a store window but was firmly dissuaded from buying it by Brian 'because it's not your image, Billy'.

As a first contact in New York's music world, Lennon–McCartney's new song-publisher Dick James had referred him to James's American lawyer, Walter Hofer. 'He was full of questions,' Hofer told me. 'How did American television work, how did the radio stations work? I gave a cocktail party for him that was a disaster. No one had heard of Brian Epstein, so no one came but a few people from Liberty Records because Billy Kramer was signed with them.'

Brian's crucially important meeting was with Ed Sullivan, whose primetime variety show on CBS television had 'broken' every major American pop act since Elvis Presley in 1956. Normally, the unknown British manager of an unknown British group would have stood little chance of a booking, but it happened that the previous month, Sullivan and his wife had been caught up in the chaos at London Heathrow airport when the Beatles returned from a Swedish tour to be greeted by 20,000 screaming fans and regular VIPs like Prime Minister Sir Alec Douglas-Home and the newly anointed Miss World had been totally overlooked.

When Sullivan first offered them a spot as a novelty support act, Brian showed an acumen his negotiating for their first film had so painfully lacked. He insisted they should be top of the bill, in exchange offering two live appearances and a third taped one for only $10,000, a worthwhile sacrifice for the coast-to-coast exposure they would enjoy.

During his stay in New York, he decided it would be a waste of time to try selling 'I Want to Hold Your Hand' to Capitol Records' chronic refusenik, Dan Dexter. But once back in London, he cold-called the company's CEO Alan Livingston, with whom he'd had no previous dealings.

As Livingston would recount, he came on as a total innocent with lines like 'I understand television is very popular in your country', and 'I believe this *Ed Sullivan Show* has a very loyal following.'

Seemingly in the realm of hopeless make-believe, he asked if Capitol would release 'I Want to Hold Your Hand' and underwrite a promotional visit for The Beatles if they were guaranteed a series of headline appearances on the Sullivan show. Were that impossibility ever to come to pass, Livingston replied, it certainly would.

Brian waited three days, to suggest a period of negotiation, then went back to Livingston with the 'news' of his triumph with Sullivan. When Livingston phoned the show's producer, Bob Precht – who was also Sullivan's son-in-law – to check on its authenticity, he asked when exactly the deal had been done. A week earlier, during Brian's visit to New York, was the reply. Livingston would always tell the story against himself, admiring the way that supposedly naïve young Englishman had 'played' him.

* * *

The onset of Beatlemania in Britain had shown The Beatles to be capable of selling much more than vast quantities of records. For months Brian had been pursued by entrepreneurs of every kind, not so much seeking as begging his permission to manufacture goods in their image.

In those days, merchandising barely existed in Britain and the small amount that did was mainly confined to toy companies producing facsimiles of puppets from children's television shows. No precedent existed, therefore, to warn Brian what further fortunes might be in the offing. He saw The Beatles' merchandising purely as public relations, to maintain the record-buyers' goodwill and keep their 80,000-strong fan club happy.

The first themed Beatles goods simply catered for the desire, as strong for girls as for boys, to impersonate their idols. A factory in Bethnal Green, east London, was producing thousands of Beatle wigs per week, retailing at £1.50 each in today's value. A Midlands clothing firm turned out collarless Beatle jackets in the corduroy they'd made fashionable to fit either sex. Girls, too, wore the elastic-sided, Cuban-heeled 'Beatle boots', obtainable by mail order for £3.80.

At that stage, everything reflected the square-dealing shop-keeper Brian used to be. The Beatle jacket was comfortable, durable and well-lined; the official Beatles sweater ('designed for Beatles people by a leading British manufacturer', as its advert said) was 100 per cent botany wool and hardly extortionate at £1.75.

But the theming didn't – couldn't – stop there. Soon there were plastic Beatle guitars, miniature Beatle drumkits, Beatle badges, jigsaw puzzles, handkerchieves, record-racks, rubber airbeds, aprons, bedspreads, shoulder bags, pencils, buttons and trays. There was a brand of confectionery named Ringo Roll and chewing gum warranted to contain *seven* Beatle photos per packet.

A sizeable portion of the avalanche was unauthorised for though NEMS Enterprises held copyright on the name 'Beatles', anything labelled 'Beetles' or just decorated with insects or guitars flew just as frantically off the shelves. Even to spot the culprits, let alone take legal action against them, would have meant country-wide monitoring NEMS couldn't possibly undertake. So, after a few minor prosecutions, the pirates carried on looting, unchecked.

By the end of 1963, the merchandising had got into a tangle that Brian had neither the time nor the patience to sort out. He therefore detailed his London lawyer, David Jacobs, not only to deal with copyright infringements but to award new manufacturing licences at his own discretion. Jacobs, preoccupied with his celebrity clientele, passed the job on to his law firm's chief clerk, Edward Marke.

It was an uncomfortable fit as the firm was also currently dealing with claims for damages by the relatives of passengers killed in a fire aboard a Greek cruise liner, the *Lakonia*. The waiting-room used by these bereaved plaintiffs became full of Beatles picture-books, playing-cards and crayon sets awaiting Jacobs's approval or rejection. He therefore had to find someone else to take on this tiresome business of coining thousands.

His choice was a man named Nicky Byrne whom he'd happened to meet at one of the parties he adorned almost every night of the week. The forty-something Byrne was small and dapper, a former Horse Guard, sometime amateur racing-driver but full-time member of the Chelsea Set, the circle of upper-class bohemians, rebellious heiresses and charming cads that flourished along and around the King's Road.

He was not totally unfitted for the role Jacobs offered, having had experience of both popular music and retailing. In the 1950s he'd run the Condor Club in Soho where 'Britain's First Rock 'n' roller', Tommy Steele, often performed. His wife Kiki, from whom he'd recently parted, was a well-known fashion designer with her own successful Chelsea boutique.

Byrne took some persuading to join the Epstein team. 'Brian had a very bad reputation in the business world at that time. Nobody knew who was licensed to make Beatles goods and who wasn't. I got in touch with my ex-wife, Kiki, to see what she thought about it and mentioned this firm in Soho that was meant to be turning out Beatles gear. Kiki said, "Hold on a minute." She'd had a letter from a firm in the Midlands asking her to design exactly the same thing for them.'

162

Brian circa 1966.

NEMS' first city centre branch in Great Charlotte St, Liverpool, managed by the Epstein brothers. 'Clive ran the appliance department, Brian ran the record department – and the show.'

Bill Harry, founder/editor of *Mersey Beat* with his girlfriend, later wife, Virginia. Contrary to myth, it was Harry who first made Brian aware of the Beatles.

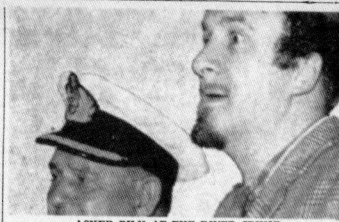

RECORD RELEASES

BY BRIAN EPSTEIN OF NEMS

POPS GALORE!

Now that the disc manufacturers have returned from Europe's sunny breaches they have certainly decided to make up for lost time and the dearth of new releases. Last week EMI and Decca produced the most exciting lists of new records that Decca's in importance was the new Presley "I Feel So Bad" backed by "Wild in the Country". After only being on sale for three days it's sure figure warrants No. 1 spot in NEMS Top Twenty (although John Leyton's "Johnny Remember Me" is a very close second). Merseybeaters will be pleased to know that Billy Fury's "Jealousy" has also immediately found a place in our charts. Eden Kane's "Get Lost" looks like another winner for this artist. Decca also issued Del Shannon's bright follow-up to his "Runaway" success entitled "Hats off to Larry", Duane Eddy bids for the charts once again with "Drivin' Home", Roy Orbison's new disc "Cryin'" and a lovely tear jerker called "Hurt" from Timi Yuro. These four discs are now in the U.S. charts. Another invader which would appear to have a future was issued August 25th by the Mar-Keys "Last Night". For issue on September 8th, Decca line up a Hank Snow recording called "Beggar to a King" and in response to a public request Harry Belafonte's "Hole in the Bucket".

From EMI comes the Shadows "Kon Tiki", a new Connie Francis "Together", The Highwaymen to take away Lonnie Donegan's lead with "Michael", Barry Mann's "Who put the Bomp (in the Bomp Bomp

Bomp)" and the John Barry Seven's "Starfire".

For jazz fans EMI provides Acker Bilk's "Stars and Stripes Forever" (SCD 2155) and Chris Barber with Ottilie Paterson singing "Mamma He Treats Your Daughter Mean". Also not to be left out is a superb single from Peggy Lee "Manana" and "The Folks Who Live On The Hill". Incidentally Cleo Laine's fans will be delighted to hear her Fontana disc "You'll Answer to Me" has also entered our charts. And a well deserved entry it is.

ON MICROGROOVE

The next few days will bring the release of many new LPs and EPs from all the companies. Already received from Philips is a new Doris Day album "I Have Dreamed". The Ray Conniff Singers (as popular as ever) "Somebody Loves Me" and Johnny Mathis "Portrait of Johnny". EMI have enormous lists including the issue of Sinatra's "Swingin' Session", The Shadows' first LP (33SX 1374) and Ray Charles "Dedicated to You." Decca line up an

album from Duane Eddy "Girls Girls Girls", Ricky is 21 (Nelson) and an interesting re-issue on Camden (22/-) by Bunny Berigan and Orchestra.

ACKER BILK AT THE RIVER CRUISE

AROUND AND ABOUT

BY BEATCOMBER

Reviving the old tradition of Judro Bathing is slowly but slowly dancing in Liddypool once more. Had you remembering these owld custard of Boldy Street blowing? The Peer Hat is very popular for nun eating and boots for nude brighter is handys when sailing. We are not happy with her Queen Victorious Gallery is goodly when the rain, and Sit Georgle House is black (and white from the little pilgrims flying from Hejiay College). Talk Hull is very histerical with old things wot are fakes and King Anne never slept there I tell you. Shout Airborne is handy for planes if you like (no longer government patrolled) and the L.C.C.C. (Liddypool Cha Cha Cha) are doing a great thing. The Mersy Beat is selling another three copies to some go home foreigners who went home.

A little guide to entertain may be of some helpless, so here it is:

THE CASBIN — Strickly no members only.

THE SHEATES—The Bohernia of Liddypool.

THE JACKARANDY — Membrains only.

LA LOCANTRY — Next to La Grafty.

LA MATUMBA—For a cheap heal.

THE PHEOLIX—Also Bohumbert.

EL CAMUNAL—Bald Stream.

THE DODD SPOT—Watch out for details.

These are but to name a few of the few with so little for so many, we'll fight 'em in the streets, so to Speke. We've been engaged for 43 years and he still smokes. I am an un-murdered mother of 19 years.

CLAS ADV

HEAR BOB WO Beatles at Al

FABRON wishes Marsden and the wonderf presented to bung booking indebted.

ALPHA SOUND in sound rep

HEAR BOB BE stute.

WANTED! Tale formed.

CARL VINCENT promoters, at the many fan their good w Kennedy who as an hour of

MERSEYSIDE Instrumentalis are invited t 22, 96 Hanove Hours: 10 a.m Saturday.

GROUPS that have already interested in Box No. 9. Letters answe fidence. Guita work as team. Sax players. In apply.

ALAN ROSS w Wooler and B hospitality an and Gerry and some wonderf Bill Harry and wish for the Christmas.

YOU CAN join G by writing to tree, 13.

THE CAVERN

LUNCHTIMES

Tomorrow. Friday 15th—THE BEATLES

Next Monday 18th.
Wednesday 20th.
Friday 22nd. } **Gerry and the Pacemakers.**

Tuesday 19th.
Thursday 21st } **The Beatles.**

EVENINGS

Tomorrow. Friday—
Collegians, Remo 4.

Saturday—
White Eagles Jazzband, Gerry and the Pacemakers.

Sunday—
Doug Richford's London Jazzmen, The Bluegenes.

Next Tuesday 19th—
The Bluegenes, Remo 4, Gerry and the Pacemakers.

Wednesday 20th—
The Beatles, Ian and the Zodiacs, Karl Terry and Cruisers.

Thursday 21st—
DANKWORTH ALL STARS Featuring Alan Ganley (drums), Art Ellefson (tenor), Eddie Harvey (trombone, piano) Ken Wheeler (trumpet, piano), Spike Heatley (Bass).

Friday 22nd—
Red River Jazzmen, Johnny Sandon and Searchers.

Saturday 23rd—
Gerry and the Pacemakers. The Saints Jazzband

LITHI TOW

EVERY T

THE MA

BEAT

JOHN, PAUL,

ALW

IVELY
LITHERLAND

Brian's record-review column in *Mersey Beat*, by now justifiably known as 'Mersey Beatle'.

NEMS ENTERPRISES

PRESENT
MERSEYSIDE'S
GREATEST–EVER
ROCK SPECTACULAR
HEADED BY
AMERICA'S FABULOUS

LITTLE
RICHARD
AT THE TOWER

BALLROOM, NEW BRIGHTON
7-30 TO 1-0 A.M. FRIDAY OCTOBER 12TH

WITH THE BEATLES

★ LATE LICENSED BARS
★ LATE TRANSPORT HAS BEEN ARRANGED FOR ALL PARTS
★ A BOB WOOLER PRODUCTION

You cannot miss this fantastic presentation—buy tickets now at 10/6 from Nems, Rushworths, Lewis's, Strothers and all major record shops on Merseyside and St. Helens, Widnes, Runcorn Chester, Southport (Morrisons)) etc.

THE BIG THREE
PETE MacLAINE AND THE DAKOTAS
BILLY KRAMER WITH THE COASTERS
LEE CURTIS WITH THE ALL-STARS
RORY STORM AND THE HURRICANES
THE MERSEY BEATS
THE UNDERTAKERS
GUS TRAVIS AND THE MIDNIGHTERS
THE PEPPERMINT TWISTERS
THE FOUR JAYS

Brian's poster for the Little Richard spectacular at New Brighton Tower Ballroom. Rumours of a sexual encounter between the two still linger.

George Martin, the inspirational producer whom Brian largely left alone to supervise his boys' 'creative quantum leaps'.

With the Beatles' press officer Tony Barrow, who averted a media scandal after Brian's reckless Spanish 'honeymoon' with John.

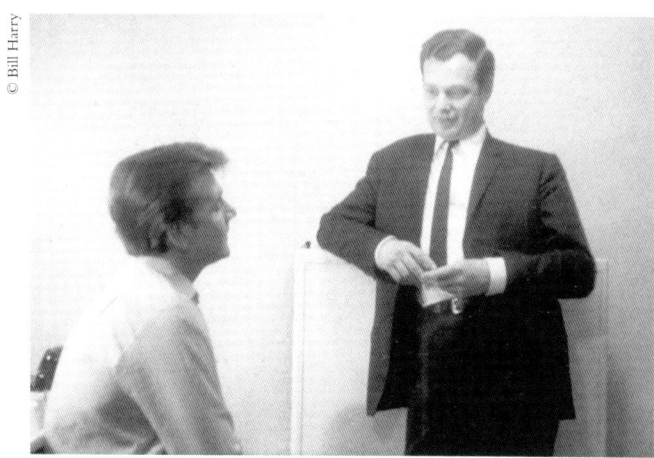

Brian gives Billy J. Kramer a backstage briefing on what his image should be.

With 'my Cilla', the Beatles' only rival for his attention.

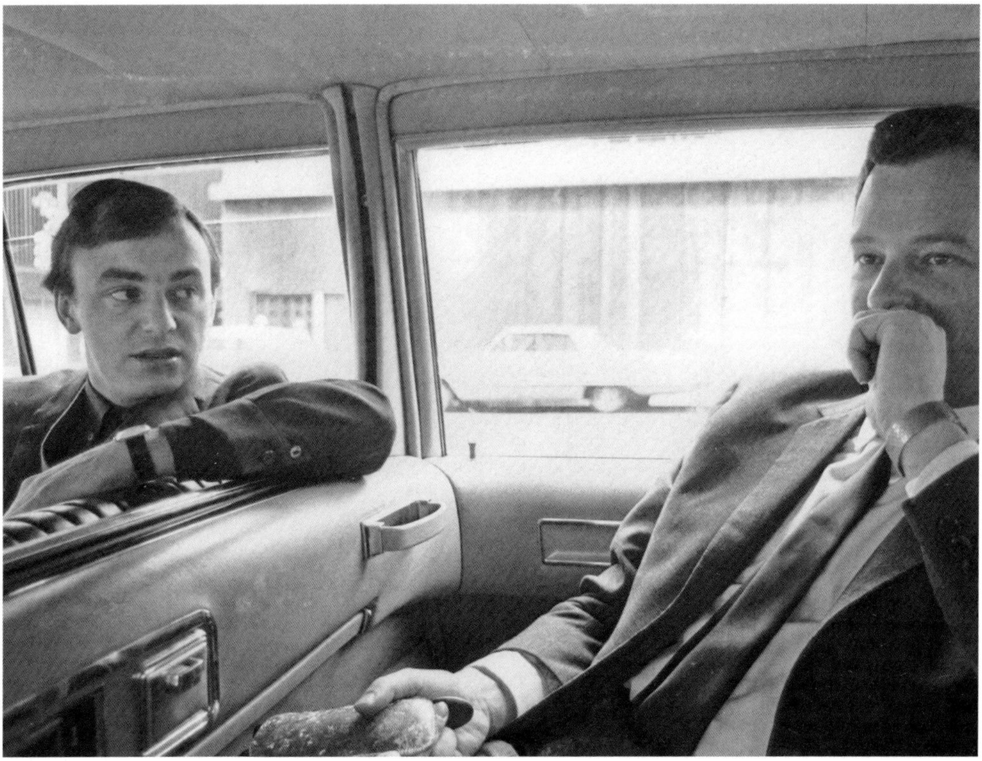

© Shutterstock

Gerry Marsden waits to hear the next step.

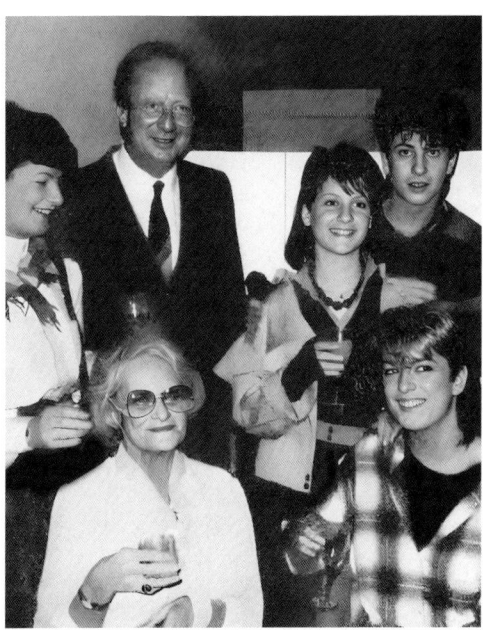

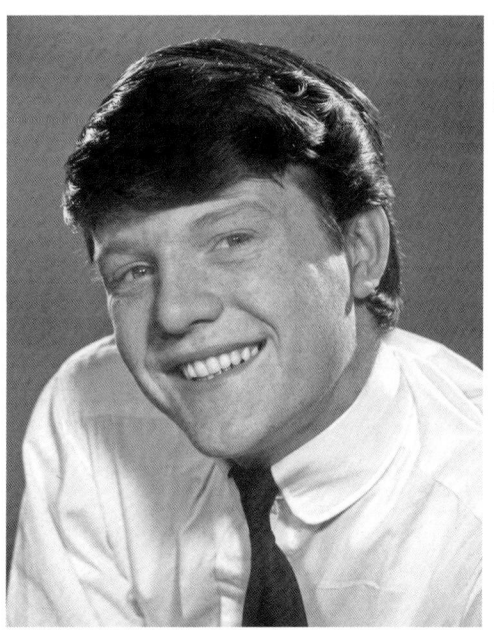

Clive Epstein with his mother and family. After Brian's death, the NEMS crown would weigh heavily on him.

© Shutterstock

Thomas Quigley, renamed Tommy Quickly, a dynamic performer yet Brian's first chart-failure.

© Shutterstock

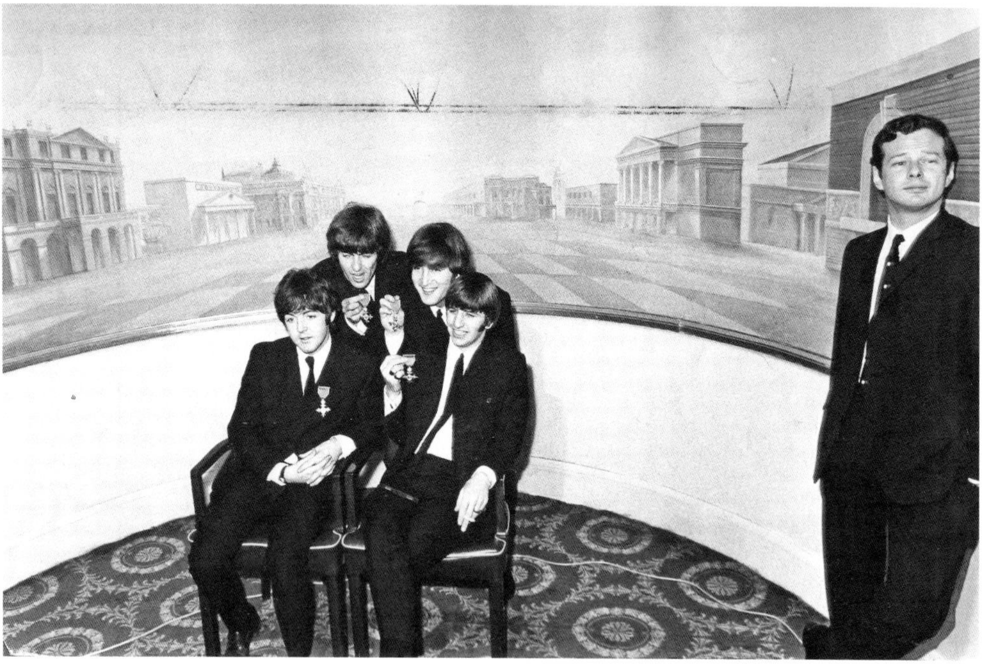

The Beatles show off their MBE medals after the ceremony at Buckingham Palace. Brian, disgracefully, received nothing.

© David Magnus/Rex/Shutterstock

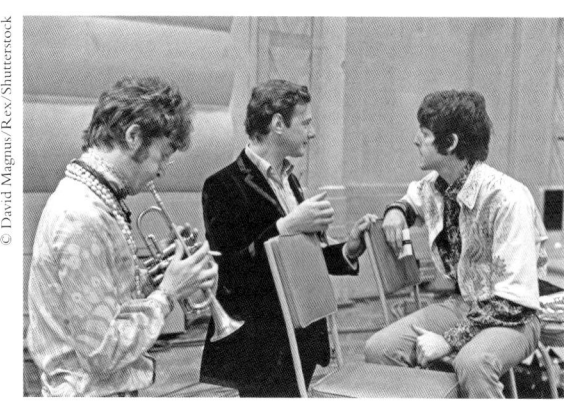

Brian during the *Sgt. Pepper* sessions, when he was starting to look younger than his boys.

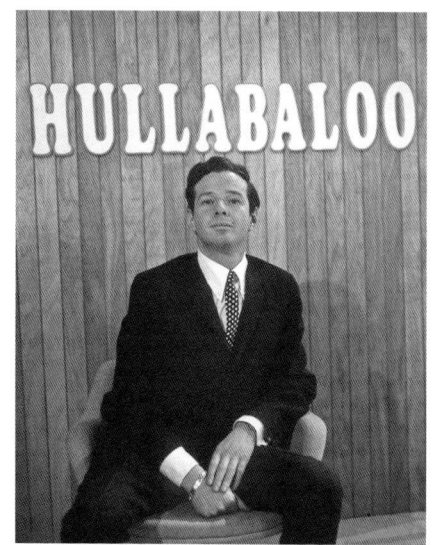

Brian's debut as guest presenter of American pop show *Hullabaloo*. One of several attempts to prove he had a life away from the Beatles.

Brian, Cilla and Billy J. with the NEMS second division, all vying to be his 'Flavour of the Month'.

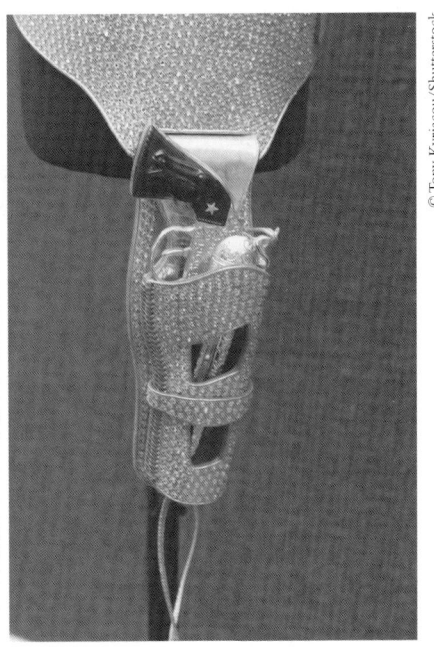

Fancy holster presented to Brian by Elvis Presley and Colonel Tom Parker. Brian had the replica six-shooter made to fit it.

Singer Alma Cogan, 'The Girl With The Giggle In Her Voice' whom Brian dated, never dreaming she was simultaneously having an affair with John.

Brian with his mother. Queenie never stopped hoping he'd 'marry and settle down'.

Police guard 24 Chapel Street after Brian's death.

The audience at the Saville Theatre hears the shocking news.

English Heritage blue plaque marking the site of NEMS offices next to the London Palladium. Mysteriously, Brian's home in Chapel St, Belgravia has always been denied one.

Daily Mirror front page after Brian's death.

Rather than work through NEMS Enterprises, Byrne set up a company named Stramsact to assign Beatles merchandise licences in the UK and Europe. A subsidiary named Seltaeb – 'Beatles' spelt backwards – would handle American rights, if any, ahead of The Beatles' visit in February 1964 to appear on *The Ed Sullivan Show*.

He also recruited five co-directors, all considerably younger than himself – in fact rather young to be company directors of any kind. Only one of them, 26-year-old John Fenton, possessed a smidgen of experience, having already done some licensing deals for David Jacobs; two others, Mark Warman and Simon Miller-Munday, twenty and twenty-two respectively, were simply friends who'd been nice to Byrne during his break-up with Kiki.

The most picturesque member of the group was 23-year-old Lord Peregrine Eliot, heir to the Earl of St Germans and a 6,000-acre estate in Cornwall, who'd shared a London flat with Miller-Munday. Though rich in land and heredity, he needed funds to recarpet his vast ancestral home, Port Eliot. For £1,000 cash, His Lordship received 20 per cent of the company.

The sixth director, Malcolm Evans, a junior floor-manager with Rediffusion Television, was the most random recruit, having met the others at a Nicky Byrne party of which the high spot was the pushing of a grand piano through the Chelsea streets. 'Nicky had somehow persuaded the entire Count Basie Orchestra to play at his party,' Evans said. 'I remember that they were accompanied on the bagpipes by a Scottish pipe major in full dress uniform from the army barracks across the road.'

The contract between Stramsact-Seltaeb and NEMS

Enterprises was left to David Jacobs to draw up, approve and even sign on Brian's behalf. 'I was at my solicitor's office just round the corner,' Nicky Byrne said. 'He told me, "Write in what percentage you think you should take." So I put down the first figure that came into my head – 90 per cent.

'To my amazement, Jacobs didn't question it. He said, "Well, 10 per cent is better than nothing."'

* * *

An unexcited Capitol Records had scheduled the US release of 'I Want to Hold Your Hand' for mid-January 1964, three weeks before The Beatles' appearances on the Ed Sullivan shows which, Alan Livingston hoped, might push it into the lower reaches of the Top 100 (no one conceiving it could possibly have any success beforehand). But Brian refused to wait that long to introduce his boys to America.

The country's three television networks, ABC, NBC and CBS, maintained London bureaus and on Brian's direct instructions Tony Barrow pitched all of them the idea of a news story on the wildness of Beatlemania in Britain and throughout Europe.

All three took the bait and were steered by Barrow to the same Beatles gig in Bournemouth, a South Coast seaside resort whose elderly population made it more synonymous with walking-frames than holding hands.

ABC never aired their story, NBC allotted theirs three minutes during the *Huntley–Brinkley Report* on 18 November, but CBS (which also owned *The Ed Sullivan Show*) put together a more substantial item, satirical in tone – those wacky Brits! – yet still invaluable, which was scheduled for both its

164

morning magazine programme and evening news bulletin on 22 November 1963.

However, it was destined to be shown only that morning. By evening, every other story had been swept away by the horrifying events in Dallas, Texas.

12

'No, not my boys!'

Cilla Black's addition to NEMS's roster alongside Gerry and the Pacemakers and Billy J. Kramer and the Dakotas had created more work than even its energetic press and publicity officer Tony Barrow could handle, so in late 1963, Brian hired a second one solely to look after The Beatles, albeit under his close supervision.

Brian Sommerville was a former lieutenant-commander in the Royal Navy who'd gone on to work for a film publicist, then in the promotions department of the *Daily Express*. Despite this media background, he seemed an odd choice to inherit The Beatles, having no interest in pop music and sporting a comb-over that sat oddly among his new charges' sacred mops.

In fact he owned his appointment to a brief affair with Brian that none suspected at the time and Sommerville didn't reveal until I interviewed him two decades later, even then going into no further detail.

From the beginning, he put The Beatles' backs up by treating them like dilatory naval ratings (so earning the nickname 'Baldilocks' from John). But their regard for Brian was such that they agreed not to make waves over it.

Sommerville was 'blooded' by a six-week British tour, then a NEMS-promoted Christmas show at the Finsbury Park Astoria cinema in north London, joining The Beatles' tiny backup team of their roadie Neil Aspinall and a hulking ex-Cavern club bouncer named Mal Evans – in reality too gentle to bounce anything but a ball – who'd recently become Aspinall's deputy.

Along with this resounding impresarial debut in the metropolis, Brian had again felt the stealthy touch of anti-Semitism or homophobia or both. The Beatles' pre-Christmas engagements included BBC-TV's *Juke Box Jury* in which ordinarily panels of mixed celebrities passed judgement on newly released singles but now was completely given over to them.

Because of their tight schedule it was to be pre-recorded at the Liverpool Empire before an audience largely composed of their fans – and would attract a viewership of around 23 million. Brian had been expecting to join his boys on the panel, back in the role of record-reviewer he used to enjoy so much, but the invitation never came.

On the familiar circuit of the British tour, Sommerville recalled he could seem detached to the point of indifference. 'He'd float into The Beatles' dressing-room, usually with a piece of paper for them to sign. But if there was any trouble, you could count on Brian to be miles away. He had the wonderful knack of being able to disappear during a crisis.'

Sommerville soon learned not to overstep his own role as a kind of backstage butler showing local journalists into the sacred presence, then shooing them out after their allotted few minutes. 'The worst rows Brian and I had were after I'd made some comment and the press quoted me instead of him. "You had no *right* to do that," he'd say.'

The blunt ex-sailor was frequently baffled by Brian's relationship with his boys: how on some nights he visibly plucked up courage before entering their dressing-room and on others would watch their show from the rear stalls, anonymous in his dark blue Aquascutum overcoat and polka-dotted silk scarf, with tears glittering in his eyes.

And for all his achievements on their behalf, one of John's stinging put-downs could still reduce him to silence, blushing his deepest scarlet. George Martin told of such a moment at Abbey Road studios while they were working on a track that stubbornly refused to come right.

'Brian appeared in the control-room with one of his boyfriends and did something I'd never seen him do before. When John had finished a vocal, Brian switched on the intercom and said, "I don't think that sounded quite right, John." John looked up and in his most cutting voice said, "You stick to your percentages, Brian. We'll take care of the music."'

* * *

Before flying to America The Beatles were to give their first shows in Paris with an eighteen-day season at L'Olympia, its nearest equivalent to the London Palladium, sharing top billing with the French chanteuse Sylvie Vartan and Latino-American Trini Lopez and playing two, sometimes three sets per day.

For Brian, nothing would suffice but that his boys should occupy a suite at the five-star Hotel George V where they proceeded to run up a fortune in room-service. However, in an early example of product placement, Brian Sommerville negotiated a deal with the then British European Airways: two weeks of unlimited free London–Paris flights for The Beatles

169

and their party in exchange for carrying shoulder-bags inscribed The BEAtles. In Brian's eyes that more than compensated for Sommerville's failure to charm them.

On their opening night at L'Olympia, violence broke out between rival photographers while they were in mid-performance that overflowed onto the stage. Sommerville was felled by a rabbit-punch and as Brian tried to interpose himself, protesting, 'No, not *my* boys!', a thuggish paparazzo used the old bouncer's trick of standing on his toes while shoving him backwards.

To round off the evening, back at the George V news came from London that the Dave Clark Five's 'Glad All Over' had replaced 'I Want to Hold Your Hand' at number one, prompting a glut of headlines that The Beatles must be sad all over.

Two days later, as they resigned themselves to only half-conquering Paris, a telegram from New York announced that the song now on the wane in Britain was at the top of *Cash Box* magazine's chart.

They celebrated by jumping on their beds and biffing each other with pillows – the closest they ever came to trashing a hotel room – then having dinner with Brian and George Martin, who happened to be in town. The restaurant was Au Mouton de Panurge in Rue de Choiseul whose menu referenced the lavatorial humour of the fifteenth-century writer François Rabelais by serving soup in chamber pots. During the evening, Brian was so carried away as to call for an empty one to wear on his head at a rakish angle.

Yet he didn't realise – and never would – that he'd been directly responsible for this stupendous moment, when he instructed Tony Barrow to pitch his boys to the American TV news networks seemingly with so little profit at the time.

On 22 November, CBS had pulled its five-minute item about Beatlemania in Bournemouth when the news of President John F. Kennedy's assassination had banished all other stories from the airwaves.

Now, after endless airtime devoted to the assassination and its aftermath, CBS's news bosses – among them Walter Cronkite, 'the most trusted voice in America' – recognised the nation's desperate need of some light relief. The three-week-old Bournemouth clip was therefore resurrected and aired on 10 December. Millions of teenagers across the land were thus made blissfully aware of The Beatles but unable to buy their new single.

The resulting frustration was personified by 15-year-old Marsha Albert of Silver Springs, Maryland, who, to paraphrase Chuck Berry, wrote a little letter and mailed it to her local deejay, in this case Carroll James on Radio WWDC. James's interest was piqued but with 'I Want to Hold Your Hand' not scheduled for release in the US until mid-January, he could only get hold of a copy by having it brought from London by a friend who worked as a flight attendant for Britain's international airline, BOAC.

James invited Marsha Albert to introduce it on his daily radio show, then began playing it non-stop. Neighbouring stations, then others further and further afield, began following his lead with taped copies of his precious vinyl disc.

Capitol Records' immediate reaction to this unauthorised mass release was to send out lawyers' 'cease and desist' notices to the guilty deejays. But then Alan Livingston saw the absurdity in so doing. 'We spend fortunes paying these guys to play our product,' he said in a veiled reference to the payola then rife throughout the US record industry. 'Now are we going to pay money to people to *stop* them?'

If Livingston had been slow on the uptake before, he was greased lightning on rollerskates now. He brought forward the single's release-date from mid-January to 26 December, when the nation's entire college and high school population would be on their Christmas break, so at liberty to absorb 'I Want to Hold Your Hand' through their very pores.

And rather than the cautious first pressing of 20,000 Livingston had initially ordered, three record plants began working around the clock to manufacture a million.

* * *

On 7 February, Pan American Airways' Clipper flight 101 left London Heathrow airport for New York, seen off by 3,000 screaming fans who soon would seem a comparatively intimate gathering.

In First Class were Brian and The Beatles and in Economy a contingent of supportive journalists with tickets supplied by NEMS Enterprises; not that any of them needed bribing to write glowingly about the trip however it should turn out.

Most of the remaining seats had been booked by British businessmen with hot new ideas for Beatles-themed merchandise, hoping Brian might be more receptive at an altitude of 30,000 feet. During the flight, he would receive a succession of handwritten pitches, to all of which he replied politely in the negative.

For his boys, pillow-fighting euphoria had turned to deep misgivings about their ability to 'crack' America when so many British artists before them had failed. The normally unflappable

Paul kept his seatbelt fastened throughout the flight as if expecting to be turned around and sent home again. 'They've got everything over there,' George fretted to the *Liverpool Echo*'s elderly correspondent, also named George Harrison. 'What do they want *us* for?' Even John's relentless clowning and gurning seemed to have a touch of desperation.

As flight 101 touched down on a snow-flecked runway at newly sanctified John F. Kennedy airport and a 20,000-strong crowd came into view, its screams already audible through the Plexiglas windows, they thought Kennedy's successor at the White House, President Lyndon Johnson, must also be about to land.

The black-and-white images of The Beatles descending the aircraft stairs in their shortie raincoats, frozen by astonishment as much as the Arctic temperature, are the most famous of their over-photographed career. Most managers at this point would have thrust themselves into shot, but all one can see of Brian is a blurred face and knotted cravat several steps behind.

Straight off the plane, they had to face a giant press conference whose avowed aim was to tear these upstart limeys apart. It soon descended into chaos with Brian now totally invisible and Brian Sommerville tetchily dealing with the volley of questions, mostly about the Beatle hairstyle he himself so conspicuously lacked. But thanks to The Beatles' unquenched wit and good humour, even after a nine-hour flight and a going-over by US Customs, their scheduled massacre turned into a triumph.

It wasn't until they were safely in their suite on the twelfth floor of the Plaza hotel, tuning into the transistor radios like miniature Pepsi-Cola dispensers they'd received as welcome gifts, that Brian fully grasped the magnitude of American Beatlemania.

'I Want to Hold Your Hand' was playing on every pop station, often continuously; so were all three of the Capitol rejects picked up by the Veejay and Swan labels; so were tracks from The Beatles' two British albums. By the beginning of April, they would occupy the top five places in *Billboard* magazine's definitive chart, a feat never equalled before – or since.

American record companies in those days provided all manner of 'services' to the management of their most valued assets, customarily in the form of alcohol, drugs or sex, but Brian's only request to Capitol was for help in finding an English secretary to run his temporary office at the Plaza.

Capitol's classical music division recommended Yorkshire-born Wendy Hanson, a US resident since the late '50s who'd previously been personal assistant to the conductor Leopold Stokowski and the librettist Gian Carlo Menotti and once worked for the late President Kennedy.

Summoned for an interview with Brian in The Beatles' suite, she found the place 'a maelstrom of people on the make and multi-transistorised noise and there, absolutely cut off from it all, this baby-faced young man drenched in Guerlain cologne. "Hello, my dear," he said. "Would you like a cup of tea?"'

To Brian, Wendy's classical music connections and stately presence far outweighed her ignorance about The Beatles and pop in general and he hired her on the spot.

One of her first duties was to type a Beatles contract which she then took straight to them for their signatures instead of passing it back to Brian as she was supposed to. Rather than flushing with pique, he was impressed by her authoritativeness and asked her to continue working for him until the tour wound up in Miami.

* * *

While seeming the epitome of British sangfroid to Wendy Hanson, as to everyone around him, Brian was beset by anxieties on many fronts.

Back in Britain, George had had a flirtation with Estelle Bennett of The Ronettes while the black vocal trio were there on tour; now she had reappeared among the New York friends given free access to The Beatles' hotel suite. In the America of 1964, Brian knew that any hint of an interracial romance could have a disastrous effect on their record sales, and Estelle found herself frozen out of their circle so subtly that George was never aware of it.

John had brought his wife Cynthia on the trip, despite Brian's fear that his American fans might be less tolerant of his marriage than his British ones. Cynthia therefore was under strict orders to be as unobtrusive as possible, which often meant appearing in public with a coat over her head like a murder suspect in custody.

Brian himself was horribly vulnerable in a land where hatred of 'faggots' was almost universal, where the libel laws were far looser than Britain's and magazines like *Confidential* and *Whisper* could safely taunt a fellow David Jacobs client with headlines like 'WHY IS LIBERACE'S THEME TUNE "MAD ABOUT THE BOY"?' On future New York trips he would be less reticent, but for now couldn't even smile at a good-looking elevator-operator in case it was taken the wrong – or, rather, right – way.

Above all there was his anxiety over The Beatles' performance for Ed Sullivan so soon after their arrival: not only their all-important live spot but also one to be recorded earlier the same day, plus virtually unlimited photocalls and interviews.

It led him to an early faux pas with Sullivan when he informed America's starmaker *in excelsis* for the past two decades, 'I would like to know the exact wording of your introduction' and Sullivan growled back, 'I would like you to get lost.'

Sullivan was notorious for taking against even the biggest pop stars on his show and deliberately mispronouncing their names, as when he'd called John, Paul and George's hero Buddy Holly 'Buddy Hollered'. What that growl might do to 'The Beatles' hardly bore thinking about.

Then, thirty-six hours before transmission, George – who'd always been prone to sudden, dramatic illness – came down with a strep throat and a high fever. When his older sister Louise arrived from her home in Illinois to be at the show, she found the hotel doctor ordering his immediate hospitalisation and Brian's carefully maintained cool out of the twelfth-storey window.

'He was saying, "Oh no, this cannot happen. We can't allow the press to hear of this,"' she would recall. '"Can he be cured by Sunday night?"' The doctor was persuaded to allow Lou to nurse him at the Plaza in hopes that he could, and Brian Sommerville put out a statement that he was suffering only from 'mild influenza'.

The 73 million people, or 40 per cent of America's viewing audience, who tuned to *The Ed Sullivan Show* got all four Beatles, albeit one still with a temperature of 104. Their introduction by Sullivan was everything Brian could have wished, down to the near-perfect pronunciation of their name.

That night, the mass clustering round blueish television screens took America's crime-rate to its lowest ever. In all of New York's five boroughs, not so much as a car hubcap was reported stolen.

The flood of congratulatory messages included one from Elvis Presley and Colonel Tom Parker, by now only the world's second-best known pop manager. Brian's mind must surely have gone back to that night in a Birkenhead pub when he'd invented a phone message from the Colonel to boost The Beatles' flagging spirits and to all those pitying smiles at his claim that one day they'd be 'bigger than Elvis'.

But his voice was back to cool as he dictated a reply in telegram-ese to Wendy Hanson: 'Many thanks for the cable. Boys and I most appreciative of the gesture.'

* * *

Nicky Byrne and his Seltaeb merchandising team had arrived in New York some weeks earlier to begin setting up deals according to the 90–10 per cent contract in their favour. They'd checked into the elegant Drake Hotel on Park Avenue, rented offices on Fifth Avenue and within hours had been besieged by manufacturers clamouring to get in on the greatest marketing opportunity in the juvenile sector since Walt Disney had created Mickey Mouse.

The procedure was that Seltaeb, having been persuaded of the suitable nature of the merchandise, issued a licence in exchange for an advance on the royalties expected from it. An early licensee, the Reliant Shirt Corporation, paid £25,000 upfront to produce Beatles T-shirts in three factories it had bought for the purpose. Three days after the T-shirts went on sale, a million had been sold.

With magnificent hauteur, Byrne refused to deal with anyone below the rank of company president, several of whom each day would obediently form a line outside his office. The fact that one of his co-directors was an English earl caused much confusion in a land where Earl is a common first name, Lord Peregrine Eliot often finding himself the target of urgent sales pitches beginning, 'Say, listen Earl . . .'

Byrne did business on a munificent scale with tables permanently reserved for him at Manhattan's most fashionable restaurants, two chauffeur-driven limos on standby around the clock and a private helicopter. The five young Brits who were his co-directors lived in similar affluence. Lord Peregrine would have fond memories of dropping by the Seltaeb office each week and helping himself to $1,000 from the petty cash.

Yet they were undeniably getting results. By the time *The Ed Sullivan Show* aired, a corporation named REMCO Industries had produced 100,000 'official' Beatle dolls and were about to produce 100,000 more, while a rival firm's official Beatle wigs were flopping off its production line at the rate of 35,000 per day. One major deal was reportedly in the works between Seltaeb and a major cola company and another with Woolworth and J. C. Penney stores for official 'Beatle counters' coast to coast.

On top of that, Byrne told me, he'd made a crucial contribution to The Beatles' visit. Capitol Records' publicity budget had been so inadequate that he'd enlisted the help of a T-shirt manufacturer and two radio stations, WINS and WMCA, for the same announcement to be broadcast every fifteen minutes: a free T-shirt for every fan who went out to JFK airport and screamed. He further claimed to have bought off a photographer who'd acquired some compromising pictures from Brian's secret gay life and was threatening to make them public.

When Brian finally paused his other preoccupations to meet with Byrne, it was only to realise for the first time what a disastrous deal David Jacobs had made with Seltaeb.

'I'd just banked $97,000, so I handed him a cheque for $9,700,' Byrne recalled. 'He was delighted at first. "Now," he said, "how much of this do I owe you?" "Nothing, Brian," I said. "That's your 10 per cent." He was amazed and furious at the same time. He said, "You must come and work for *me*, Nicky ... I'll make you president of the company ... I'll give you a thousand a year."'

It was hardly an inducement to a man with two chauffeured limos, a helicopter and an expectation of untold millions. 'I said, "A thousand a year? Oh, come on, Brian." Then all of a sudden I realised he was crazy.'

On 11 February the Beatles were to appear at the Coliseum boxing arena in Washington DC. Heavy snow having made flights to Washington erratic – stirring gloomy thoughts of their hero Buddy Holly's death in similar circumstances, also in February – Brian somehow or other whistled up a train with a private carriage attached to it.

At the Coliseum they played to their crazed audience in the round, protected only by four security men whose ill-fitting Beatle wigs could hardly have been official issue. Their number two roadie, 'Big Mal' Evans, had to rotate Ringo's drum-riser manually to give every shrieking block of seats a full-frontal view of him.

Afterwards they and Brian were taken to Washington's large and hugely important British Embassy to make an appearance at a charity ball given by the ambassador, Sir David Ormsby-Gore, and attended by many senior figures from the diplomatic community.

It began in a civilised manner with drinks in the ambassador's residence but at the ball The Beatles became separated from Brian and were jostled by braying young patricians from the embassy staff, the type known in Britain as 'Hooray Henrys', who treated them like servants even when requesting autographs. John walked out immediately, looking murderous and, as the others did so later, a young woman crept up on Ringo with a pair of nail scissors and cut off a lock of his hair.

The next evening they were at New York's Carnegie Hall which the promoter, Sid Bernstein, had presciently booked months earlier for what he'd described only as 'a phenomenon' to conceal the deviation from its usual programme of classical recitals.

The Beatles' two thirty-four-minute sets flattened social boundaries in their way even more rigid than Britain's. Next to Brian's friend Geoffrey Ellis in the VIP seats onstage sat the wife of the state governor, Nelson Rockefeller, and their two teenage daughters.

John hated all of it with a passion that, conceivably, was Brian's earliest warning that he mightn't want to stay a Beatle for ever. 'It wasn't a rock show,' he would recall, 'it was just a sort of circus where we were in cages. We were being pawed and talked at and met and touched, backstage and onstage. We were just like animals.'

'After the second show,' Sid Bernstein remembered, 'I walked with Brian over to Madison Square Garden and we looked in at its 17,000 seats. I knew the Garden wanted The Beatles and could have the tickets printed in twenty-four hours. I offered Brian $25,000 and a donation to the British Cancer [Research] Fund. I knew he was tempted but he gave me that little smile he had.

'"No, Sid," he said. "Let's save it for next time."' But he was never to see The Beatles play there, nor would they until they were individual ex-Beatles.

The tale of how British diplomats abroad had treated a national treasure was quick to cross the Atlantic. In the House of Commons on 21 February, a Conservative MP named Joan Quennell challenged the Foreign Secretary, R. A. Butler, about 'an accident [sic] when young British entertainers known as The Beatles visiting the United States professionally were manhandled by Foreign Office officials at an official function at the embassy to which they had been invited as guests.'

'I am assured by the ambassador that the suggestion that they were manhandled by anyone is quite untrue,' Butler replied. 'The ambassador has in fact received a letter from a representative of The Beatles, thanking him for a delightful evening.'

No prizes for guessing who that 'representative' had been.

13

'HE WAS ALWAYS LOCKED IN A CELL'

In March 1964, a month after The Beatles' American triumph, Brian moved NEMS Enterprises' whole operation to London. He was by now doing more business there than in Liverpool and the hours he was forced to spend shuttling between them were cutting down the time he could devote to his artists.

Not that the 400-mile round trip was any trouble whenever one set of artists were concerned. His old friend and confidant Joe Flannery recalled meeting him one day while he was in Liverpool and agreeing they'd meet for coffee the next morning.

'While we were having our coffee in his office, the television was on – and there was Brian, meeting The Beatles off a flight at Heathrow airport the previous afternoon. Just to be with them for a few minutes he'd driven all the way down there and back in the space of twenty-four hours.'

He'd decided to make a complete break with Liverpool, closing NEMS' latter premises in Moorfields and taking only twenty-five key members of his team, like his 'second pair of hands', Tony Bramwell, Alistair Taylor and The Beatles' two roadies, Neil Aspinall and Mal Evans. In addition, he persuaded Wendy Hanson, his oasis of calm in the Plaza hotel madhouse, to return to London after years of living in New York and become his personal assistant.

Liverpool, understandably, felt exploited and abandoned, though the glamour he'd brought to it would prove everlasting. That was little solace to Allan Williams, Bob Wooler, Mona and Pete Best and many more who'd helped The Beatles' early career, then helped Brian further it with little or no reward, but now found themselves left behind with nothing to live on but nostalgia.

The move south was carried out with an efficiency reminiscent of Brian's brief spell in the Royal Army Service Corps. 'We shut down in Moorfields on the Friday,' Tony Bramwell recalled, 'then opened up in London on the Monday.'

NEMS Enterprises' new headquarters were the fifth floor of Sutherland House, a modern block in Argyll Street chosen by Brian for its position next door to the London Palladium, and, as he often reflected, 'close to the greatest entertainers on earth'.

The company's telegraphic address – unnecessary till now – was 'Nemperor: London', another unpaid debt to Bob Wooler, who'd coined that nickname for him.

He wrote proudly to all his artists of the enhanced service they would now enjoy, not only with ten telephone lines but an ultra-modern 'Ansafone' system and a staff member always on duty out of office hours (so that 'NEMS Enterprises is open to you every hour of every day and night') handwriting his private phone number at the end of every letter.

Since most of his artists would be new to London, each also received a leather-bound book with the addresses and phone numbers of the best restaurants and clubs and contact-details for his growing number of famous friends.

He was equally meticulous in his instructions to his staff: they must treat all visitors with the utmost respect, keep the offices clean and tidy, never talk to the press about their work and, above all, ensure he was always kept informed of The Beatles' exact whereabouts, together or singly.

The one thing that didn't cross his mind, according to Tony Bramwell, was the hefty increase in the cost of living for young Liverpudlians relocating to London, yet such was their loyalty to and affection for him that they all put up with it.

That same month, he and his artists were profiled by *Panorama*, BBC-TV's heavyweight current affairs programme, a distinction given to only one other pop manager, Larry Parnes, five years earlier. But while the all-male teenage members of Parnes's stable (perhaps fortunately for him) had remained mute throughout, Brian's signings like Gerry Marsden and still-in-development Cilla Black clearly had minds of their own, yet were in complete accord about his being 'grrreat', which in glottal Liverpudlian seemed to have double resonance. The Beatles weren't included, their endorsement taken for granted.

Brian himself was interviewed at length by the reporter, Michael Charlton, still as shy and unassuming as was possible in the back of his new chauffeur-driven Bentley limousine.

* * *

As a permanent London base, he favoured the city's two most exclusive neighbourhoods, Knightsbridge and Belgravia, but for him, as he well knew, it wouldn't be just a question of studying an estate agent's brochure and requesting a viewing.

Anti-Semitism flourished nowhere more vigorously than among those elegant white squares, many of whose ritzier

185

apartment blocks made clear without stating explicitly they did not welcome Jews.

Brian found a way in through Isow's Jewish restaurant, a Soho institution owned by the celebrated 'Flash Jack' Isow where he often went with Lionel Bart. It happened that Flash Jack's son, Norman, had just bought a flat without any problem in Whaddon House, a brand-new block in William Mews, Knightsbridge. He could therefore tip Brian off that a fifth-floor penthouse there was currently for rent.

The place came unfurnished so Brian could indulge his love of interior decoration to the full with chunky black leather furniture, G-Plan fitments and a creamy fitted carpet. The outsize living room had a wall of sliding glass doors to a spacious terrace and was dominated by Robert Freeman's photograph of four half-shadowed faces that had jacketed the *With The Beatles* album. There was a scattering of antiques, although Brian had never been a serious collector; as he often said, 'I don't care about their period or history, I just care about their shape.'

Amid the new egalitarianism of the Swinging Sixties, his hiring of a valet seemed like a throwback to the world of P. G. Wodehouse's Bertie Wooster and Jeeves, but Lonnie Trimble was hardly the Jeeves type.

Trimble was a 6ft 4ins African American, born in Atlanta, Georgia, and a veteran of the US Marine Corps. Domestically speaking, he came with impressive references, having worked in Hollywood for the screen goddess Ava Gardner and for the actor Peter O'Toole, soon to find international stardom playing Lawrence of Arabia.

He too was gay – for a black person, a far greater risk than for Brian – but he lived monogamously with another man, which simplified their relationship much to the relief of both parties.

Trimble found Brian a pleasant change from O'Toole, a heavy drinker and hellraiser who'd subjected him to constant racist abuse disguised as banter. For O'Toole's wife, the actress Siân Phillips, and two daughters he'd come to represent stability and calm and for Brian, as time went on, it would be the same.

For a weekly wage of £12, the same as a Beatle deputy-roadie, he arrived at 7.45 a.m. to don a white jacket and black tie and serve Brian's invariable breakfast of grapefruit and tea at 8.30 sharp. He cleaned the flat, valeted Brian's clothes (which he privately thought less 'swinging' than his own, though he liked the Aquascutum topcoats) and food-shopped at Harrods, only a few minutes' walk away. '[Brian] had money everywhere,' Trimble would remember, 'so much money that he could never use it all. He mentioned once that he could lay his hands on £1 million in cash.'

If required – as when Harry and Queenie were visiting – Trimble would cook dinner, usually more grapefruit followed by grilled Dover sole and what his years in England had taught him to call 'a pudding' rather than dessert.

Otherwise, few visitors came to the flat; even The Beatles were seldom seen there. And Brian's insistence on absolute privacy at home could border on the obsessive. One day a NEMS employee who'd brought some papers over from Argyll Street answered a ringing telephone and told the caller Mr Epstein was unavailable because he was in the shower. Brian was furious that such personal information about him had been given out.

His address book at this time acquired an unusual entry

among the growing number of his celebrity friends and professional contacts. Halfway down the J section, along with the Rolling Stone Brian Jones and his lawyer David Jacobs was 'Guardsman B. D. Joyce 1st Battalion Coldstream Guards Chelsea Barracks London S.W.1'.

The Coldstream Guards are the British army's oldest regiment, familiar to tourists in their scarlet tunics and tall bearskins, drilling as one man on the sovereign's birthday and guarding hallowed monuments like the Tower of London. In 1963, Brian Joyce was an 18-year-old private, assigned to such ceremonial duties.

Despite the grandeur and prestige of life as 'a Coldstreamer', the pay was wretched, for Joyce's rank only £4 per week. Many who were gay (something still as taboo as during Brian's service career) supplemented it by going with men, usually in one or other of the royal parks. Others who weren't, like Joyce, would still allow themselves to be picked up and bought drinks all evening before making their excuses and melting away. 'It was a recognised thing,' he recalls.

One evening, he was with two comrades in a West End pub when he attracted the attention of two older men who were there together, seemingly in search of action. One was Brian, the other his would-be clone Peter Brown, still running the NEMS record departments in Liverpool but down in London on a visit. Sequestered in the ranks of the Guards as Joyce had been, he didn't recognise The Beatles' manager.

'He asked me if I liked music and we started talking,' Joyce says. 'Then he said he and Peter were going out to dinner and asked if I'd like to join them. I told him I was with two friends and he said, "They're welcome to come along too."'

After dinner, before the young guardsmen could do their usual disappearing act, Brian invited them back to his new penthouse. But the 'funny business' they expected did not follow. 'We all just sat and talked. There weren't any drugs but I noticed Brian drank a heck of a lot.'

As Joyce was leaving, Brian invited him to a party there a few days later when he found himself mingling with pop royalty like Mick Jagger and Lulu. It was to be the start of an unguarded friendship on both their sides that would stretch over the next four years.

Though Joyce knew Brian had sexual dealings with others from his regiment, he made it clear it wasn't his thing and he had a steady girlfriend who was a nurse. And in all that time he was subjected to only one tentative overture. 'Brian wanted me to go on a Beatles tour with him but I said, "How can I? I'm in the army."

'"Then I'll buy you out," he said. "How much would it cost?" I said, "No one's going to buy me out."'

As time went on, Joyce says, Brian opened up about the loveless encounters, usually in public parks after dark, that constituted his sex life. 'I said, "You want to change your locations, Brian." He was older than me and incredibly famous but here was me telling him to grow up.'

* * *

Settling his boys in London was nothing like as straightforward as settling himself now that the slightest trace of any of them could trigger a full-scale riot.

He had first installed all four, plus John's wife Cynthia and small son Julian, in a three-bedroom flat in Green Street,

Mayfair. It took the fans only a couple of weeks to discover their presence there and for siege conditions to set in.

Brian then moved the Lennons to Emperor's Gate in South Kensington, where the besieging would continue with hardly a break, while Paul – always the most independent – became a secret lodger with the family of his girlfriend Jane Asher in Wimpole Street, Marylebone.

George and Ringo likewise seemed suddenly to disappear from the Beatle-hunting map. For a furnished flat had fallen vacant at Whaddon House two floors below Brian's penthouse, which he hastened to secure on their behalf.

Both had always lived at home, with adoring mums who did everything for them, so were incapable of caring for themselves. Brian stepped into the breach, dealing with their rent and utility bills, finding them plumbers and electricians as required, arranging the collection of their laundry and dry-cleaning, stocking their fridge from Harrods Food Hall and keeping them in booze and cigarettes.

If there was some competition for the two spaces in the block's underground car park between Brian's Bentley, George's E-Type Jaguar and Ringo's Facel Vega (though he had yet to pass his driving test), it was far outweighed by the two Beatles' freedom to come and go unnoticed. So well did the arrangement work that Brian even invited them upstairs to the parties he would sometimes give after Lonnie Trimble had gone home, deluding himself that they saw nothing significant in the total absence of females.

This idyll of anonymity came to an end one night while they were at a party in nearby Lownes Square and a cat burglar came over the rooftops and entered their flat through an unlocked window, stealing a small amount of cash and some souvenirs of their American trip. The burglary got into the papers, making their address public and so turning quiet William Mews into yet another sea of screaming faces.

Soon it got so bad that the property company which owned the mews wrote to Brian requesting that The Beatles should move elsewhere because of the damage their fans were doing. He wrote back with his usual punctiliousness that he would 'consider the position' and 'endeavour to find an alternative', meanwhile suggesting the installation of barriers and 'Trespassers Will Be Prosecuted' signs. But he knew such measures couldn't hope to stem the invasion and, besides, would ruin the charm of the mews for its other residents, not least himself.

Since the same was bound to happen anywhere else in Central London, his two in-house Beatles and John needed to move out of the city, far enough to avoid the worst of the fan onslaught but within limo-commuting distance of Abbey Road studios and their favourite clubs of the moment.

House-hunting for themselves being beyond them, Brian delegated the job to his – and his father's – accountants, Bryce, Hanmer and Isherwood, a Liverpool firm whose London office specialised in showbusiness clients.

The Bryce, Hanmer partner most involved in the search was an expatriate Czech of melancholy mien named Walter Strach who already had the thankless job of trying to control The Beatles' personal expenses – and would eventually find two out of the three semi-hidey-holes required in the Surrey stock-broker belt.

When I interviewed Strach two decades later, he clearly was not a sentimental man yet was at pains to stress how different

Brian had been from the usual hard-faced, hard-headed, hard-hearted, hard-nosed impresario.

'He always worried that he might be taking advantage of The Beatles. He came to me once and said he wanted to give them 10 per cent of his company, NEMS Enterprises, so that they would get back some of the 25 per cent commission they paid him He didn't have to do that but he wanted to. He was a decent, honest human being.'

* * *

Cilla Black had taken wing just as Brian prophesied, albeit after some delay and not with a Lennon–McCartney song nor in her former bluesy milieu. Her second single, 'Anyone Who Had a Heart' was a tempestuous ballad by Burt Bacharach and Hal David striking back on behalf of the Brill Building.

There was also a classy soul version by Bacharach and David's protégée, Dionne Warwick, but Cilla's raw Scouse treatment ('knowing-gi-love you . . .') overwhelmed it, spending three weeks at the top of the British charts, selling almost a million and becoming Britain's fourth most successful single of 1964.

Brian's only solo female artist, then and always, reawoke the would-be couturier who'd so dismayed his parents when he was in his teens. He designed several dresses for Cilla as well as closely monitoring her hair and makeup and trying to smooth down her accent until he realised it was an essential part of her appeal.

As with The Beatles, nothing was too good for 'my Cilla'. When her twenty-first birthday coincided with a week-long residence at the London Palladium, he hosted a dinner for her at the exclusive Le Caprice restaurant – one of those rare moments when he could feel on top of the world.

'Eppy insisted I should try the wild strawberries and cream,' Cilla would recall. 'Unsophisticated as I was, I thought there was too much alcohol sprinkled on the strawberries. "Oh well," Eppy said, "I'll help you out," and he polished off the lot.'

The frontmen of his two founding NEMS groups after The Beatles didn't receive quite the same level of pampering, especially after both began to kick against the image he'd decreed for them.

Billy J. Kramer turned down three Lennon–McCartney songs in a row – causing Brian to rage that Kramer had 'insulted the greatest songwriters in the world' – but then had a US Top 10 hit with his own choice, 'Little Children' by the American team of Mort Shuman and Leslie McFarland.

Likewise, Gerry Marsden insisted on following a hat-trick of happy-go-lucky number ones with a Broadway show tune, 'You'll Never Walk Alone' from *Carousel*, despite Brian's objection that it wasn't sufficiently to formula. It topped the UK singles charts for four weeks and would become the word-perfect anthem from football fans at Liverpool matches.

For a Beatle, on the other hand, Brian's care and attention could be claustrophobic. The four had returned from America to make their first feature film, its title changed from *Beatlemania!* to *A Hard Day's Night*, a line from John's poem 'Sad Michael' but always attributed to Ringo. During the first day's shooting, George met the fashion model Pattie Boyd, who had a one-word speaking part.

Brian stage-managed their first date, deciding it should be at the antediluvian Garrick Club where women weren't allowed to use the main staircase, choosing the menu and wines and joining

193

them for the whole evening. 'George and I just sat there, hardly daring even to touch hands,' Pattie recalls.

The eldest of three sisters, she had always looked after her siblings, so being looked after by Brian together with George was a heady experience.

'I'd never had such fun before. It was like being a child, which I'd never felt like even when I was a child. If George and I were travelling anywhere, we'd be picked up and taken to the airport, where our flights had been booked for us; at the other end, we'd be met by a limo and taken to a hotel where our suite would be waiting. We never knew the details. We just knew Brian would have everything under control.'

He was continuing to sign up new acts almost by the week, like The Fourmost, who combined music with comedy, the soulful Merseybeats, The Chants, his one and only Afro-Caribbean group, and, from outside Liverpool's magic circle, the all-instrumental Sounds Incorporated from Dartford, Kent, who would enjoy sax-heavy hits on their own as well as accompanying Cilla's live performances.

The Epstein magic didn't work for everyone. His first real failure was Liverpool's Big Three, a hard rock trio such as Cream would later become, who, ahead of the Rolling Stones, went onstage without bothering to change from their street clothes. Now they were put into little Beatly suits and made to record a twee pop number entitled 'I'm With You' complete with some reluctant yeah yeah yeahs, which sank without trace. Their hard-man drummer, Johnny Hutchinson – of whom even John Lennon was afraid – had been so enraged that he'd threatened to 'fill Brian in'.

According to George Martin, who produced some of Brian's

discoveries delightedly and others resignedly, he began to see himself as a modern-day Sergei Diaghilev, whose Ballets Russes company in the early 1900s nurtured superstar dancers like Vaslav Nijinsky and Alicia Markova and choreographers like George Balanchine. But now he was definitely on to the non-Nijinskys.

The first was 17-year-old Thomas Quigley from Norris Green, Liverpool, renamed Tommy Quickly, allotted a Lennon–McCartney song, 'Tip of My Tongue' and launched as NEMS' first solo male vocalist. Brian spent a vast amount on him, including a $30,000 launch in America, but it wasn't enough: after six failed singles and three tours with The Beatles, Quigley would retire from the business in 1965 with drug and alcohol problems and suffer a breakdown soon afterwards.

Then came Michael Haslam from Bolton, Lancashire, recommended to Brian by the *Daily Mirror*'s 'agony uncle' Godfrey Wynn and somewhat reminiscent of bland pre-Beatles balladeers like Mark Wynter and Craig Douglas. For a while Brian lavished his whole attention on Haslam, inviting him to stay at Whaddon House – though with no hint of the casting-couch – and granting him the singular privilege of his own front-door key.

But the two singles he released would seem like a precis of his career: 'Gotta Get a Hold of Myself' and 'There Goes the Forgotten Man'. After a dispute with Brian over his expenses claim for buying a pair of socks, he returned to his former £15 per week job at a Bolton tannery, to be greeted by workmates with a banner reading, 'WELCOME BACK MICHAEL TOP OF THE FLOPS'.

Brian's last business link with Liverpool was *Mersey Beat*, the music paper that had led him circuitously to The Beatles just two years earlier. Seeing it as a natural adjunct to NEMS, he acquired a half-share that was effectively a controlling interest, keeping its founder-editor (and his long-time unpaid adviser) Bill Harry in post with a promise of continuing autonomy.

Merseybeat as a sound now being on the wane, he decided it should go national and compete with long-established trade papers like *Melody Maker* and the *New Musical Express*. It moved into new premises, changed to a weekly from fortnightly and to colour from smudgy black-and-white. But as so often with press proprietors, the urge to meddle in editorial matters became too much for him.

Bypassing Harry, Brian installed an advertising manager of greater seniority than him and began to manipulate the content to plug unsuccessful signings like Tommy Quickly and Michael Haslam.

Harry resigned, later to migrate to London himself and become a PR for the likes of Pink Floyd, Jethro Tull, David Bowie and Led Zeppelin, as well as the ultimate authority on the band he'd helped Brian to launch.

Soon afterwards, the paper's running costs became too much even for Brian and he sold out to the publishing giant IPC, which merged it with its existing pop title, *Disc*. On this one, the Nemperor had to acknowledge himself soundly Mersey-beaten.

* * *

'My appreciation and support of the theatre is unlikely ever to cease,' Brian had written a decade earlier and he remained true to his word. Despite the pressure of his music business, he

196

managed to see almost every new play that opened in the West End and always preferred the company of theatre people, to whom questions of sexuality and race were of no consequence.

In tacit proof, he was invited to become a governor of the Central School of Speech and Drama, located at Swiss Cottage, just across the road from where he'd been an innocent victim of police entrapment while himself a drama student.

Aesthetically speaking, he found a kindred spirit in Brian Matthew, who emceed pop shows like *Easy Beat* and *Thank Your Lucky Stars* in an anomalous cut-glass accent and, like him, was a frustrated actor. The two hatched a plan to build a new theatre to be named the Pilgrim near Farnborough, Kent, helped by fundraising concerts by NEMS acts and Matthew's *Lucky Stars* contacts like Dusty Springfield and Kenny Ball's Jazzmen.

Brian's friend Lionel Bart likewise straddled the worlds of pop and theatre, together with that of sexual outlawry. When Bart's latest musical, *Maggie May* – inspired by a mythical Liverpool sex-worker – opened at the Adelphi Theatre, Brian wrote the introduction to its collected lyrics, his first prose work since his *Mersey Beat* record column.

In it he observed that *Maggie May* was 'an inevitable result of the sudden and massive breakthrough in Liverpool culture' while modestly refraining from mentioning who had started it. Bart he described as 'a reticent extrovert' and 'a shy exhibitionist', seemingly unconscious of how perfectly the description fitted him too.

Early in that summer of 1964, he was among the celebrity invitees at the first night of William Douglas-Home's *The Reluctant Peer* and to a dinner with the cast afterwards where he found himself seated next to the play's boyishly good-looking juvenile lead, 23-year-old Peter Bourne.

Initially their conversation was about music, for Bourne's younger brother was Mike Berry, a Buddy Holly soundalike with whom the pre-Brian Beatles had sometimes appeared lower on the bill at The Cavern.

Bourne was still undecided about his sexuality although in later life, his first name changed to Bette, he would become a celebrated drag queen and proponent of radical queer culture.

Nevertheless, that evening he set out to woo Brian, finding it not in the least difficult. Their one-night stand turned into a brief affair that, unusually for Brian, was totally lacking in tension, anxiety or melodrama. Unusually, too, he didn't mind being seen in public with Bourne, taking him to actor-friendly restaurants like The White Elephant, introducing him to Cilla Black and Peter Noone, aka Herman of Herman's Hermits (although never to The Beatles) and waiting for him at the Duchess Theatre's stage door each night in his Bentley.

Bourne received that rare privilege, a key to Brian's flat, but would later say 'the sexual thing' between them was 'practically nil'. As always with him, intimacy could only go so far and it would instantly evaporate if ever Bourne tried to talk about anything serious, such as Brian's 'being Jewish and being gay and trying to make the thing work . . . I could never get really close to him. He was always locked in a cell.'

Only once was there any awkwardness, when Bourne's brother, Mike Berry, whose pop career was in decline, angled for Brian to take over his management. Still bruised by the Tommy Quickly and Michael Haslam episodes, Brian told Bourne curtly, 'I don't think I can do anything for Mike.'

He clearly envied Bourne's growing success in the theatre and once opened up so far as to admit how much he still regretted not pursuing his ambition to be an actor. 'Well, *be* an actor,' Bourne urged him. 'Look, you've got all that money, you can make a choice. Change your name and start again.'

He believed it to be a fatal handicap that he'd failed at the Royal Academy of Dramatic Art. That meant nothing, Bourne said: Laurence Olivier, the greatest British actor of the century, had been thrown out of the Central School, where Brian was now a governor. But at almost thirty he said he was 'well over the hill' – and, besides, what would his parents say?

The relationship came to an end after two months, without rancour on either side. Brian simply asked for his latchkey back and Bourne exited gracefully stage right.

Queenie Epstein still hoped that down in London he might finally meet and fall for the 'nice Jewish girl' Liverpool had unaccountably failed to provide. And in the singer Alma Cogan he seemed to have done so.

Known as 'The Girl with the Giggle in Her Voice', Alma had dominated the pre-rock 'n' roll British charts with novelty songs like 'The Railroad Runs Through the Middle of the House' and 'You Must Never Do a Tango with an Eskimo' and hosted her own television shows in the extravagant gowns she designed for herself.

Although the new sounds of the '60s had effectively killed off her kind of music, she remained a hugely popular figure in upper-echelon showbiz. She and her widowed mother, Fay, threw a lavish party almost every week in the Kensington flat they shared, at which old-school celebs like Noël Coward, Cary Grant and Sammy Davis Junior rubbed egos with newer ones like Tommy Steele, Lionel Bart and Mick Jagger. For special friends they kept open house virtually around the clock.

Alma had met Brian with The Beatles after their debut at the London Palladium and instantly put them on that 'open-all-hours' list. John paid 'Sara Sequin', as he called her, numerous visits though always leaving his wife, Cynthia, waiting in the car outside.

Late one night, while Paul sat at the grand piano in the living-room, tinkering with a melody which had just popped into his head, Fay shouted from the kitchen, 'Scrambled eggs, anyone?' He used 'Scrambled Eggs' as a temporary title before deciding on 'Yesterday'.

After a while, Brian took to visiting Alma and Fay on his own, usually for tea. 'He'd always bring something for Alma,' her younger sister, the actress Sandra Caron recalls. 'But not in fancy paper and ribbon ... something like a new kind of pen he'd seen in Burlington Arcade.'

When Alma talked to Brian, there was never a suspicion of a giggle in her voice, 'She was one of the wisest, most under-standing people I ever knew,' Sandra says. 'He obviously found some kind of deep solace with her.'

It didn't quite amount to dating since neither could go any-where as they might be recognised and gossip be set in motion, which left only a small Chinese restaurant in Kensington High Street. To complicate matters, Alma was having a secret affair with John, conducted in various West End hotels where they'd register as 'Mr and Mrs Winston'. And Lionel Bart, despite his undisguised sexual preference, was so fixated on her that he'd bought a house in Chelsea that had once belonged to Judy Garland in the hope she'd agree to live with him there.

Alma's mother, Fay, longed to see her married to Brian and wanted to go to Liverpool, meet Queenie and arrange a *shidduch* – the formal matchmaking of a young couple that precedes their wedding. But her daughter told her firmly not even to think about it.

'She didn't have the same kind of feeling for Brian that he had for her,' Sandra recalls. 'It had nothing to do with him being gay. She just said he wasn't "The One".'

* * *

On 6 July, the royal premiere of *A Hard Day's Night* brought London's Leicester Square to a standstill like nothing since the Victory in Europe celebrations in 1945.

The duty royal, Princess Margaret, was married to a bisexual husband, so can be presumed to have had a more tolerant attitude to such matters than older members of her family. The invisible forces that had edited Brian from the *Royal Variety Performance* receiving-line were no longer active and he was in plain sight, immaculately dinner-jacketed, to share his boys' triumph.

Four days later, the film received a second premiere, in Liverpool. The Beatles were all in a state of nerves about this first appearance since Brian had spirited them away, conscious that in their home city heckling was akin to a bloodsport.

Instead, they received a heroes' welcome, appearing on the exterior balcony of the Town Hall with the Lord Mayor and Lady Mayoress, who managed to keep smiling when John greeted the adoring throng with Nazi salutes in every direction.

Brian would assuredly have put a stop to this wanton jeopardising of The Beatles' image, and blatant affront to his religion, had he been there. But at the time he was preoccupied with safeguarding another Beatle's good name.

Someone less than adoring in the throng was circulating leaflets with a paternity claim against Paul that the huge media contingent present hadn't yet noticed. Brian and his brother Clive managed to find the leafleteer and negotiate a settlement of the claim before it could go any further.

14

MR BRIAN EPSTEIN AT HOME

Brian spent most of the second half of 1964 taking his boys around pre-conquered Europe, then to instantly conquerable Hong Kong and Australasia and finally to America to meet the demand their brief visit in February had left unsatisfied. For who knew if there'd ever be such a global hunger for them again?

On the eve of their departure back to the States, he gave a party whose classily understated invitations said only '*Mr Brian Epstein at Home*'. It was another top-of-the-world moment: he'd just heard that *A Hard Day's Night* had opened at 500 cinemas across the US, and in its first week taken $1.3 million – between $10 and $15 million in today's money.

The party itself was anything but understated. London's top interior designer Ken Partridge took five days to raise the floor level of Brian's penthouse terrace, cover it with a three-peaked marquee and fill it with thousands of pounds' worth of flowers. In addition to Beatles and their families, the guests included Lionel Bart, Rolling Stones Mick Jagger and Keith Richards, Alma Cogan, Cilla Black, The Fourmost, Dusty Springfield, Tommy Steele, David Jacobs, George Martin and

Brian Matthew, with a Coldstream Guardsman or two in there somewhere.

Harry and Queenie Epstein, the first to arrive, were pleased to see a kosher section among the sumptuous buffet. But Queenie recoiled in horror from Partridge's showpiece floral decoration, red and white carnations in the shape of a palm tree, citing an ancient superstition that red and white flowers together are a portent of death. The on-site florist, Pam Foster, had to rush to nearby Harrods to buy red ink and, like a scene from *Alice in Wonderland*, hurriedly set about painting the white carnations red.

Judy Garland hadn't been on the guest list but, meeting her at Lionel Bart's the previous evening, Brian had invited her along minus an invitation card. When she arrived at Whaddon House, the front-desk porter failed to recognise Hollywood's most tragically famous face and at first refused to allow her upstairs.

Later, across the room, Brian spotted his grandmother deep in conversation with Garland, as he himself longed to be about *The Wizard of Oz*, *Meet Me in St Louis* or *A Star Is Born*. When the star moved on, he asked his grandma what the two of them had been talking about. 'How to make chocolate cake,' she replied.

The Beatles' first dedicated press and publicity officer, Brian Sommerville, had resigned after losing his cool so often and damagingly on their first American tour. His replacement was Derek Taylor, a former *Daily Express* reporter and a devout Beatlemaniac despite having passed the usual cut-off point of thirty. Conscious of George's seeming permanent eclipse by John and Paul, Brian had allowed Taylor to 'ghost' a column for him in the *Express*, after which the two had developed a close rapport.

He was almost a Liverpudlian, from Hoylake in Cheshire, and strikingly handsome with his un-Beatled wavy hair and pencil moustache, which initially led to a spell as Brian's personal assistant. 'I suppose it was because he fancied me that I got the job,' he admitted, 'even though in all the time I knew him he never so much as laid a hand on my knee.'

Like Brian Sommerville, Taylor had to deal with Brian's competitiveness where The Beatles were concerned and the malice it could provoke, even towards someone whose job was to be close to them. 'I'd been told he could be cruel but I only realised it when I had to organise a Beatles press conference. Brian didn't want it to work. If I made a mess of it, even though they'd be part of that mess, he'd be happy because I'd gained no control over them. 'He said, "Go ahead, but this is doomed. I look forward to speaking to you about it afterwards." 'I'd started working for him in April and here he was in May, already treating me with *massive* cruelty.'

* * *

When The Beatles arrived in San Francisco on 19 August for the start of their tour, Brian received a phone call from Colonel Tom Parker offering him help or advice 'as a friend'. He politely declined both, for his boys now demonstrably were '*far* bigger than Elvis'. Presley even in his palpitant mid-'50s pomp had never toured the country on this scale, visiting twenty-five cities in thirty-two days, travelling a total of 22,441 miles – an average 700 per day – and playing to beyond-berserk audiences of between 12,000 and 35,000.

Presley had never commanded the $50,000 minimum per show that the Beatles received for just twelve songs representing thirty mostly inaudible minutes onstage. The numbers were a continual source of wonderment to Norman Weiss of the General Artists Corporation which had booked the itinerary and normally dealt in fractions of them, but Brian remained at his most insouciant. 'Norman,' he joked, 'you've *got* to stop all this money coming in.'

If the income was colossal, so were the expenses, thanks to his cossetting of its headliners. In the spirit of the New York Plaza, The Beatles' hotels were always the best with no ceiling on room-service and he spent $37,000 on the hire of a Lockheed Electra private jet – as it proved, not a very good one – for their longer hauls. The tour's projected $1 million value shrank almost visibly by the day.

In years to come, rock tours would become infamous for the rampant egotism and bloody-mindedness of their stars. But so thorough had been Brian's indoctrination that at every public moment these ultimate stars were never other than perfectly behaved.

Amazingly stoical, too, about the discomfort, monotony and occasional deadly danger they had to endure in the eye of the hurricane: the arrival in city after city on the same paranoid full alert; the journey to venue after venue hiding in delivery trucks or ambulances; the moments of sheer terror inside a limo with its roof caving in under the weight of screaming bodies and escape prevented by the screaming bodies pressed against its doors; the frequent rough handling from the police supposedly clearing them a path.

Health and safety for travelling pop groups was still a largely unknown concept. In Jacksonville, Florida, the Electra landed in the wake of a hurricane and they played the outdoor Gator

Bowl arena on a twelve-foot-high stage, buffeted by winds still so strong that Ringo's drums had to be nailed to the floor.

The implicit sense was that they were doing it for Brian, in return for all he'd done for them. The same applied to the meet-and-greets of local dignitaries, mayors and police chiefs whom they privately bemoaned or mocked yet, for his sake, still donned charming smiles and offered hands to be shaken as professionally as the Queen at a Buckingham Palace garden party.

The tour was accompanied by a large media contingent who repaid their special access by self-censoring anything discreditable they saw or overheard. On the road, this chiefly concerned what was referred to obliquely as 'the girl scene' – i.e., the supplying of four sexually active, if not hyperactive Beatles with female company during their few leisure hours.

Brian's advance costings always made provision for the most highly recommended sex-workers at each stopover since they were the only ones who could be guaranteed not to kiss and tell or kiss and blackmail. And, like the White House press corps in the era of sexual omnivore President John F. Kennedy, the travelling Beatles press corps didn't breathe, let alone write, a word about it.

Among the crowds who thronged their dressing-rooms, always wanting some or other piece of them, none was more persistent than Charles O. Finley, the businessman owner of the Kansas City Athletics baseball team who cornered Brian almost the moment he stepped off his plane in San Francisco.

Kansas City was not on The Beatles' itinerary as it stood but Finley offered $100,000, twice their normal fee, for an extra show at his team's stadium. Brian replied that in the tour's remaining weeks there wasn't a vacant slot. But Finley had promised The Beatles to Kansas City and refused to take no for an answer. He kept reappearing in their dressing-rooms at other venues, each time raising his offer by $5,000. When they reached Seattle, it stood at $150,000 or $5,000 per minute.

By that time it seemed providential, for although buoyed up by cash advances larger than any in entertainment history, the tour seemed set to do little more than cover its colossal overheads. In addition, the US Internal Revenue Service had grown uneasy about all the dollars that supposedly were to be taken out of the country. Under a long-standing Anglo-American tax treaty, the tour's earnings were theoretically liable only for British income tax; nonetheless, the IRS obtained a New York court order freezing $1 million of its proceeds while 'clarification' was sought.

Brian therefore went to The Beatles and asked if they were willing to sacrifice one of their precious rest days to avoid disappointing Kansas City. Without looking up from a game of cards, they said they'd leave it up to him. So, with an extra $5,000 for five minutes more onstage, the city they'd sung about since they were skifflers didn't miss out.

Brian was not with the tour for its whole five weeks, but left its day-to-day management and thousand-and-one new daily problems to Derek Taylor and the two roadies, showing up only in cities of particular importance like Los Angeles, where The Beatles played the Hollywood Bowl, or New Orleans, to fulfil a long-time ambition by dining at its fabled Antoine's restaurant. He always made a point of paying his own travel expenses out of his 25 per cent commission rather than charging them as an extra.

The day after the Hollywood Bowl, he finally came face-to-face with his would-be 'friend', Colonel Tom Parker, over lunch at the Beverly Hills Hotel, hoping that friendship would extend to letting The Beatles meet Elvis.

It must have been the oddest of summit meetings: the old fairground trickster and the fastidious young Englishman. Yet the two got on surprisingly well. If not yet ready to put his Boy in the way of Brian's boys, Parker presented him with a gold-inlaid Wild West gunbelt and holster signed 'From Elvis and the Col', for which he later had a replica six-shooter specially made (and which one day would sell at auction for $48,000.)

* * *

The tour's craziness was not always from adulation. Its southern leg introduced Brian to that dark flipside of Beatlemania, the death threat, after The Beatles ignored his plea to avoid political statements and informed the media (with his implicit support) that they'd appear at no venues where the audiences were segregated.

In Montreal, a French–Canadian separatist group with Nazi undertones announced its intention to assassinate Ringo in the mistaken belief that he was Jewish based on the shape of his nose. The only actual Jew in the tour-party had little time to feel the second-hand slur while hurriedly organising extra security for Ringo, who played that night with an armed guard seated beside him and a large cymbal angled to deflect possible gunfire.

It was during the tour's early stages that The Beatles first met Bob Dylan, then in transit from folk music to rock though not yet at the point where folk fans, who in their sandalled way could be as rabid as Beatlemaniacs, took to shrieking 'Judas!' at the mere sight of his electric guitar.

209

Dylan turned up incognito with two companions at a lavish party Brian was hosting in a suite at New York's Delmonico hotel after the first of three Beatles shows in Forest Hills, Queens. Asked what he'd like to drink, he replied in customary faux-hobo mode: 'cheap wine'. Brian had to apologise that the only wine available was vintage champagne.

The historic introduction to the band took place in one of the suite's vacant bedrooms with far more reverence on The Beatles' part than on Dylan's. To break the ice, he had one of his companions produce a supply of marijuana, wrongly supposing them to be habitual users; in 'I Want to Hold Your Hand', he'd misheard the line 'I can't hide, I can't hide' as 'I get high, I get high'.

That shared joint had its promised effect of breaking down inhibitions in different ways. John, George and Ringo succumbed to helpless giggles while Paul thought he'd discovered the secret of life and made the roadie Mal Evans write it out at his dictation.

For Brian it temporarily lightened one of the two great hang-ups of his life. The present-day Paul recalled him reclining on a bed, still looking immaculate, pointing at himself hilariously and repeating 'Jew . . . Jew . . .'

* * *

Souvenirs of The Beatles' passing were traded like medieval holy relics. In Denver, Colorado, two local businessmen bought up the hotel bedlinen they'd used, placed it in a high-security vault, then had it cut into three-inch squares and mounted on parchment for sale at $10 per square together with a sworn affidavit that a portion of a Beatle's anatomy had rested on it.

Elsewhere, attempts were made to steal residues of their

bathwater and shaving-cream, or counterfeit them, and super-markets in New York reported selling out of 'canned Beatle breath'.

In the face of all this, the clamour for official Beatle souvenirs should have made the mighty Disney organisation look like a struggling market stall by comparison – yet it didn't happen.

While the tour was still traversing America, NEMS Enterprises' risible 10 per cent of the proceeds from the Seltaeb company's merchandising operation was increased to 46 per cent, much to the chagrin of its swaggering British CEO, Nicky Byrne, who'd always held Brian in the greatest contempt.

But by now there was strife between Byrne and his five young Brit partners, especially their in-house earl Lord Peregrine Eliot. After 'six months of good lunacy', as he described it, Lord Peregrine suspected that neither Brian nor 'Uncle Sam' had been paid what they were owed and that under the US–UK tax-treaty, Port Eliot, his ancestral home in Cornwall, might be forfeit.

So while Byrne was away in London, Lord Peregrine and another partner, Malcolm Evans (not The Beatles' roadie), launched a self-absolving lawsuit, claiming he had failed to pass on merchandising royalties where due while spending $150,000 'for his own comfort and benefit' on hotels, round-the-clock chauffeured limousines, a helicopter and charge accounts for his girlfriends at Fifth Avenue couturiers.

That led Brian to accuse Seltaeb of mis-accounting, cancel its exclusive remit to grant merchandise licences to US companies and instruct David Jacobs to deal with the companies directly from London. Byrne retaliated with a lawsuit for breach of contract and claiming $5 million in damages.

Byrne's action, involving thirty-nine separate claims, entered the pretrial stages of a legal epic destined to overshadow the rest of Brian's life and seemingly fulfil the ill-omen in the red and white carnations that had so disturbed his mother.

Meanwhile the existence of two types of licence to retail Beatle-ware, one issued by Seltaeb in New York, the other by NEMS in London, caused chaos throughout the US. Rather than risk purchasing the wrong licence and being sued, department-store chains like Woolworth and J. C. Penney cancelled orders together worth $78 million.

The debacle was by no means all Brian's fault but he felt huge guilt nonetheless, paying all the legal costs out of his own pocket and otherwise trying his utmost to forget it.

* * *

A welcome distraction that October was the publication of his autobiography in Britain, the US and Canada. It had been ghosted by The Beatles' new press officer, Derek Taylor, on the basis of a single weekend of tape-recording at the grande-luxe Imperial Hotel in Torquay. Taylor's role was mainly as an interviewer and most of the words were Brian's own.

'What am I going to call this book of mine?' he'd been rash enough to ask on a visit to The Beatles' dressing-room, prompting the nastiest of all John's put-downs: 'Queer Jew'. In the end it was *A Cellarful of Noise*, an allusion to his great discovery at The Cavern club, soon amended by knowing Liverpudlians to 'A Cellar Full of Boys'.

He promoted it on American television with an appearance as 'mystery guest' on CBS's *What's My Line?* show, whose celebrity panel guessed his line of work ('Theatrical Agent/

Manager The Beatles') within minutes. He made his entrance by signing himself in on a blackboard as 'Mr X', the alias he'd last employed when giving evidence in a shaming court case in Liverpool, long before acquiring that redemptive designation.

In Britain his most successful television appearance was on *Tonight*, the BBC's quirky early-evening current affairs programme whose presenter, Cliff Michelmore, searching but kindly, made him open up as no interviewer ever had before.

'Don't you ever feel you're in a position of exploiting [your artists]?' Michelmore asked. 'Because a lot of people complain about managers – that they're parasitic.'

'I do feel this,' Brian answered, 'and I'm always very careful – *desperately* careful – not ever to exploit them and that this is very important and I was conscious of this when I entered the business.'

'Are you still conscious of it now? Do you consciously feel "I must not exploit this person"?'

An emphatic '*Yes*'.

'But doesn't that make life very uncomfortable for you?'

'No, not at *all*.'

A Cellar Full of Noise makes little mention of anyone else involved in the discovery of The Beatles. Bill Harry gets a couple of lines for incalculable help and advice but there's no trace of Bob Wooler, Joe Flannery, Allan Williams or Mona Best; one feels The Cavern itself was lucky to make the cut.

Yet it has flashes of honesty and self-awareness far beyond the level of a celebrity memoir in 1964. The only omission is his homosexuality, of which the slightest hint could have led to his arrest.

The antithesis of self-aggrandising, he portrays himself as a hopeless dunce at his eight different schools and an abject failure at soldiering and acting when he'd been none of those things, and downplayed his success in his family's business before happening on that cellar full of such profitable noise.

In an era when Jews are still meant to keep their heads down, he is forthright about his faith and the anti-Semitism he experienced at school which he says 'even now lurks around the corner in some guise or other', though he claims it no longer bothers him.

His individual portraits of his boys are notably lacking in gush. John is 'a very exceptional man [but] can be very acid, very cruel [and] sometimes has been abominably rude to me'. Paul 'can be temperamental and moody and difficult to deal with'. George 'is the business Beatle', meaning the most preoccupied with money (for his inattention at business meetings will eventually be his ruin) but also 'has his moods'. Only Ringo receives unqualified praise as 'a very nice, very uncomplicated young man'.

He reveals that a few months earlier he'd seriously considered selling a 50 per cent share in all his artists and NEMS for £150,000 (£2.67m in today's money) in a deal whereby he still would have guided their careers but would have been 'relieved of much worry and strain', presumably arising from the merchandising fiasco.

But he wrote that when he'd put it to The Beatles, they'd been horrified by the prospect, even the unsentimental Paul threatening to give up the business altogether if it should happen. 'And this was the point. The Beatles are not a deal. They are unique human beings and I believe that if the whole thing peters out, I will always be with them.'

He admits to having made money and to 'living well and spending largely' but says he'd done that even before meeting the world's biggest cash cow and that now his income from pop will allow him to expand into legitimate theatre 'in which few make a fortune'. He instances the new playhouse in Kent that he's setting up with Brian Matthew and reveals what has so long been a secret ambition 'to direct or play in a straight drama without the slightest interest in profit'.

The book ends on a top note of passion he has seldom touched in real life. 'Best of all, far more than money can buy, I love to lean on my elbows at the back of the stalls and watch the curtain rise on John, Paul, George and Ringo, Gerry, Billy, Tommy, Michael or the wonderful songbird daughter of a Liverpool docker and christened Priscilla Maria Veronica White who will stun the world as Cilla Black.'

Its final words have an optimism, heartbreaking in hindsight:

'Tomorrow? I think the sun will shine tomorrow.'

15

'OUR MBE MEANS MR BRIAN EPSTEIN'

The British General Election of October 1964 had finally seen off the Conservatives after a season of scandals and infighting they wouldn't match for another sixty years. And it so happened that the new Labour Prime Minister, Harold Wilson, although Yorkshire-born, represented the constituency of Huyton on Merseyside.

Wilson could thus claim an affinity with Britain's foremost national treasure after the Queen – and lost no time about it. While still Leader of the Opposition, he'd volunteered to present The Beatles with their awards from the Variety Club of Great Britain charity as 'Show Business Personalities of the Year' and been photographed in among them like a portly, pipe-puffing roadie.

Always a staunch Labour supporter despite his privileged background, Brian had sent Wilson an eve-of-election message joking, 'Hope your group is as much a success . . .' But if he felt he now had a friend in high places, he was soon to be disillusioned.

In the wake of The Beatles' triumphal trans-American tour, he'd been receiving constant approaches from New York entrepreneurs seeking to buy out NEMS or buy into it. One that stood out for sheer effrontery was from an accountant-turned-artists' manager named Allen Klein, ostensibly hoping to book his client, the soul singer Sam Cooke, on the next such tour whenever it might be.

Klein was a podgy man with archaically greasy hair, a marked resemblance to Lou Costello, the dim one in the Abbott and Costello vaudeville act, but brown button-like eyes that were anything but dim. After an inconclusive meeting with Brian about Sam Cooke, he suddenly blurted out, 'How much do you want for The Beatles?' Brian presumed it was a joke, so merely smiled tolerantly.

But far from it: in New York, Klein had boasted that he'd 'have The Beatles', even setting himself the deadline of Christmas 1965. Now realising that might be over-ambitious, he set about acquiring rather less rarefied names from the British Invasion: the Dave Clark Five, who'd once overtaken The Beatles in the charts, Herman's Hermits, the new northern kids on the block, and eventually their greatest chart-rival, the Rolling Stones.

These months following Brian's thirtieth birthday, when he should have been watching his back, saw him make a concerted effort to prove – to John especially – that there was more to him than just negotiating contracts and calculating percentages.

A Cellarful of Noise led to his recording debut at Abbey Road studios in an early example of an audiobook. With his lightly cultured voice and acting skills, production by George Martin, that proven master of the 'spoken word' record, and supremely alluring content, it should have been an instant hit, especially in America where there was now a Brian Epstein Fan Club.

Yet while he could grant any of his artists an instant release for their product, his own remained embarrassingly stuck in the Parlophone pipeline.

Equally unlucky was his first venture into record-producing, seemingly undaunted by the ever-more dazzling example of Martin with his boys. He had always felt guilty for not signing up Rory Storm, Liverpool's greatest live performer, and for poaching Ringo from Storm's group, the Hurricanes, in 1962 to complete The Beatles' perfect foursome. Now to make some amends he offered to produce Rory for a guaranteed single release on Parlophone.

Out of deference to Martin, the session wasn't at Abbey Road but at IBC in Portland Place, the studios by then chiefly associated with the Rolling Stones. Brian's 'production' was limited to choosing the song to be recorded and supplying Ringo – The Hurricanes' one time drummer – to swell the percussion and the backing vocals.

Unfortunately, little of Rory's wild exuberance made it onto the chosen track, a cover of 'America' from the musical *West Side Story*. The single was a resounding flop and Rory faded from the business, to die aged only thirty-four together with his mother, Vi, at the home they'd named after his band 'Hurricaneville'. It appeared that, depressed by the failure of his career, he'd taken an accidental overdose of sleeping pills and after finding his body, Vi had taken a deliberate one.

Elsewhere, Brian took every opportunity to show himself to be detachable from The Beatles, whether accepting a Carl Alan dance-music award on their behalf from Princess Margaret, opening charity bazaars like the minor personalities he used to book to cut ribbons at his family's new stores in Liverpool, or becoming vice-president of the Finchley (north London) Jewish Youth Club.

And gradually visibility begat celebrity: his name began to appear on lists of Britain's best-dressed men and even London's 'most eligible bachelors'; he appeared twice on *Juke Box Jury*, that former no-go area for him, and was among the first guests on commercial television's new Eamonn Andrews talk show, where he deliberately let drop that his real ambition was still to be an actor.

Derek Taylor would have been invaluable to this solo publicity push but, despite having distinguished himself on last summer's trans-America tour, Taylor had resigned as The Beatles' press officer after experiencing the petty parsimony of which Brian could be capable. He'd been made to pay for a ticket to take his wife, Joan, to the London premiere of *A Hard Day's Night* and after using a company limo to get home, had found the cost deducted from his salary.

Brian had retaliated by making Taylor work out his full three months' notice while seconding NEMS' 'other ranks' press officer, Tony Barrow, to be his personal publicist.

In November 1964, after tireless lobbying by Barrow, he was invited to be a 'castaway' on BBC Radio's *Desert Island Discs*, in which notable figures from all walks of life chose music to console them on an imaginary desert island. It was a highly prestigious slot, rarely bestowed on anyone in the pop business and in Brian's case seemed to indicate that a long-time invisible prejudice against him had been relaxed.

As a mark of his new independent persona, his eight record choices included only one Beatles track, 'She's A Woman', and for obviously diplomatic reasons a George Martin orchestral arrangement of 'All My Loving'. The rest were pieces by Bach, Sibelius and Max Bruch, the Spanish flamenco singer Carmen Amaya and the American jazz combo Quartette Très Bien.

The single luxury he chose to lighten his imagined solitude was 'painting materials' and the one book – revealing spiritual depths few listeners can have expected – was *Elected Silence* by the Trappist monk, theologian and mystic Thomas Merton.

His not-so-secret hankering to be a performer rather than an impresario was abundantly gratified early in 1965 when an American TV pop show called *Hullabaloo* decided to include a black-and-white segment devoted to up-and-coming pop talent in London. Thanks to his identification with the greatest talent ever to have come up there, Brian was tried out as the segment's host.

He ended up single-handedly presenting a straight run of thirteen, his Huntsman lounge suits exchanged for an assortment of geometrically patterned knitwear and often seated unsteadily on a giant cube which made him look even more absurdly young for such an achiever.

He was allowed an overt bias in favour of his own artists like Gerry and the Pacemakers, Billy J. Kramer and the Dakotas or the recently signed Cliff Bennett and the Rebel Rousers. One week, Richard Lester, the director of *A Hard Day's Night*, came on to deliver an advance plug for the next Beatles film, *Help!*, with Brian nodding thoughtfully as if it was all news to him too.

He also introduced many non-NEMS acts like The Searchers, Freddie and the Dreamers, Marianne Faithfull, Herman's Hermits and Wayne Fontana and the Mindbenders. His introductions and links were ad-libbed and could be a little flat but neither the live audience nor the programme-makers in New York seemed to care.

His most revealing encounter was with Andrew Loog Oldham, who'd briefly worked for him as a publicist before going on to discover the Rolling Stones, become their record producer as well as manager and mould Mick Jagger into a Mod Antichrist.

Did he plan to manage more groups, Brian asked. 'No, I never handle the administration side of management,' Oldham said. 'It doesn't suit my temperament . . . Making records is what I really want to do.'

'I don't think it suits mine either actually,' Brian murmured.

* * *

That was no one's impression in February 1965 when Ringo married Maureen Cox, an 18-year-old Liverpool hairstylist he'd first met at The Cavern.

Brian organised the whole event in his customary parental way, volunteering to be best man as he had for John and Cynthia Lennon, booking the couple the earliest possible morning slot at Caxton Hall, the 'celebrity' register-office, to avoid the press, holding the reception in his flat at Whaddon House – even arranging a secluded honeymoon for them at the Sussex seaside home of his lawyer, David Jacobs.

A week later the London Stock Exchange witnessed the novel spectacle of pop music hits being traded like crude oil, coffee or soybeans when Northern Songs, the vehicle set up to handle Lennon–McCartney's prodigious output, was floated as a public company.

Under Harold Wilson's Labour government, the top rate of

UK income tax was 83 per cent with a 15 per cent surtax for the highest earners, who by now included The Beatles. The flotation was designed to capitalise on John and Paul's success more speedily than their record companies' snail-like royalty payments and use one of the last loopholes in Labour's punitive tax regime before it closed for ever.

The company was divided into five million shares of which their music publisher Dick James and his accountant, Charles Silver, held 750,000 each, John and Paul the same quantity each, NEMS Enterprises 375,000 and George and Ringo a token 40,000 each. The remaining 1.25 million were offered to investors.

As well as a story extending far outside Fleet Street's financial pages, the flotation was a huge hit. The company was valued at £2.7 million, whereupon both John and Paul sold 20 per cent of their shares earning each of them £94,240 just in time to dodge Labour's new Capital Gains Tax. With Dick James and NEMS also benefiting, it seemed the most golden of paydays.

Actually it exemplified the short-termism that governed The Beatles' career in these years – the same compulsion to milk them to the maximum while the going was good that tied them to releasing a new album every six months and a new single every three. Brian assuredly could have bought up enough of the public shares to take over James's controlling interest and so prevent Lennon–McCartney's sublime talent being passed like a parcel from one philistine corporation to another in the decades ahead.

But Brian had no more inkling than anyone else – their writers least of all – that into the next century those northern songs would still be playing millions of times a day in every country in the world.

He had now two old and trusted friends working at NEMS, supposedly to take some of the pressure off him. Peter Brown, that long-time 'mini-Brian', became titular personnel manager, though on a personal level a great deal more. And the meticulous Geoffrey Ellis was persuaded to exchange a steady insurance-company job in New York for the managing director's role Brian found too irksome.

Yet he still divided himself into more commitments than there were hours in the day. With a member of The Beatles' inner circle named Terry Doran he'd started a company called Brydor Cars, supplying high-performance motors to them and their superstar friends; with Bud Ornstein, the United Artists executive who'd green-lit *A Hard Day's Night* but now a free agent, he set up a film company named Pickfair.

He held a slew of directorships, to which he continually added – the new Northern Songs public company, John and Paul's Lenmac song-publishing company, George's Harrisongs publishing company, Gerry and the Pacemakers' film company, the Fourmost's publishing company – and was part of a consortium seeking the franchise for a regional commercial TV station, Southern Television.

Meanwhile, he continued to sign up new acts almost as a reflex: an American folk group, the New Christy Minstrels; a British one, The Silkie; a trio named Paddy, Klaus and Gibson containing The Beatles' old Hamburg crony Klaus Voormann; a Devonshire sextet, The Rustiks, who'd won a talent contest he travelled 230 miles to Plymouth to judge.

The Rustiks became the second NEMS act to be produced

by Brian himself. But as Rory Storm had already discovered, that was no instant passport to the charts and they broke up, disheartened, within a year. Others who'd momentarily attracted his attention, then lost it, still waited hopefully on weekly retainers far from munificent. Gibson Kemp from Paddy, Klaus and Gibson was forced to supplement his £15 by literally moonlighting as a nocturnal office cleaner.

* * *

These manifold business commitments didn't prevent him from disappearing to Spain with Peter Brown at the height of its summer bullfighting season to follow the top corridas from Madrid to Seville, Valencia and Cordoba, though never travelling light; during one such bovine odyssey, their rented villa was burgled and *fifteen* suits, all Brian's, were stolen.

The pair belonged to a select group of foreign bullfighting aficionados including the drama critic Kenneth Tynan, whom Brian had often met in London. Another was the great filmmaker Orson Welles, now no longer able to raise finance for his projects in Hollywood and reduced to begging for it piecemeal around Europe.

Brian's fascination with what Ernest Hemingway called 'the only art in which the artist is in danger of death' had only deepened with the years. In the matador's profession he saw an analogy with his own, for they tended to be young men from humble backgrounds dependent on powerful older managers, with thousands of clamorously adoring fans. And he shared their addiction to danger, if not from a charging bull but a charge of so-called 'gross indecency'.

The greatest matador of the day was 29-year-old Manuel

Benítez Pírez, formally titled El Cordobés but also known as 'El Beatle' because of his moptop coiffure. Brian was hugely smitten with him and wanted to put him into a film with the real things, but was put off by his manager, known as El Pipo (The Kid), who gave new meaning to the term bullshit.

Later, on holiday with George and Pattie Harrison in Provence, Brian tried to induct them into his passion by taking them to a bullfight in Arles. It was hardly on El Cordobés level: while one of the matadors was eyeing up a young woman in the crowd, the bull gored him from behind and George fainted.

Brian was never luckier in his associates than during that spring of '65 as the Beatles filmed *Help!* under Richard Lester's efficient direction – partly in the Bahamas as a further tax-avoidance measure – and George Martin uncomplainingly contrived to record the companion album in the spaces between it.

Above all there was Wendy Hanson, his personal assistant, both formidably efficient and an elegant female companion whenever he needed one for appearances' sake. She would accompany him to theatrical first nights and at regular intervals to Monte Carlo where she'd routinely see him lose thousands in the Casino.

Her role was to provide anything a Beatle wanted, to which he could never say no, from a set of high-priced Asprey's luggage for Ringo to a birthday cake at Maxim's in Paris for Paul's girlfriend, Jane Asher, to a temporary shutdown of Harrods so that all four could shop there in peace. Underlying it all was a task for which her former career among temperamental operatic prima donnas and conductors had only half-prepared her – that of organising Brian.

'We were in Nassau while the boys were filming *Help!*, and

226

it had all got a bit dull so he decided we'd go to New York for the weekend. Pan Am couldn't seat us together on the flight, which made him furious. There and then he wrote a letter to Pan Am saying, "The Beatles will never use this airline again." When we got to New York there were, I promise you, twenty Pan Am officials bowing and scraping there on the tarmac.

'The next morning, we were supposed to leave for London. Pan Am sent their own limo to fetch us. I was in the hotel lobby with all my bags – but there was no Brian. I waited and waited – still no Brian. Eventually I went up to his room. There he was, still in bed with not one of his thirteen suitcases packed.

'All the way to the airport the limo-driver was in contact with Pan Am. "We're just crossing the river," I could hear him saying, "we're five miles from Kennedy . . ." They got us onto the flight with seconds to spare, in fact they literally threw our bags into the plane after us.

'Then as we were taxiing along the runway, Brian looked at his watch. "Hm," he said. "Half a minute late in taking off. Typical."'

In New York he placed increasing reliance on his lawyer there, Nat Weiss, likewise Jewish and gay, whom Larry Parnes had recommended to him a year previously. Ahead of his arrival, Weiss would book his favourite suite, 35B at the Waldorf Tower, stock the bar with copious amounts of his favourite liquors and prepare a cassette tape of new American pop tracks to his exact specification for him to listen to and assess on his limo ride in from JFK airport.

In the early days of what became an intimate though platonic friendship, Weiss knew him as the languid young Brit who loved New York's shameless materialism, who bought yet more suits up and down Fifth Avenue, who had a weakness for American French toast and chef's salads and whose heavy consumption of alcohol still produced only euphoria.

'When he was high [i.e., drunk] he'd pile the furniture up, he'd put chairs on top of tables then more chairs on top of those to see the effect. Moving the furniture was a big thing with Brian.

'But however high he got, he'd never talk to strangers about The Beatles. I've seen him at parties when people tried to broach the subject, Brian would suddenly change – it was as if an icy shutter had come down. Anything he ever told me about them was in the strictest confidence, over lunch or dinner.

'For him their relationship was something mystical; he himself used that word. He believed there was a chemistry between the five of them that no one else could comprehend. They weren't a business to Brian, they were a vocation, a mission in life. They were like a religion to him.'

Yet even Weiss, this unswervingly loyal and increasingly essential ally, claimed never really to have understood him.

On the one hand, there was the Brian whose integrity seemed of an earlier generation, whose handshake was as good as a contract and who treated the unknown teenage masses of Middle America with the same scrupulous fairness as he used to the customers in his family's store. 'He always insisted that concert promoters shouldn't take advantage of the fans, that tickets should be kept as cheap as possible.'

There was also the jealous, possessive Brian who would rather The Beatles' press officer bungled one of their press conferences than get too close to them; the munificent Brian whose entertaining was a byword for generosity and style, yet who'd part company with a valuable employee like Derek Taylor over the price of a film-premiere ticket.

There was the super-diplomatic and discreet Brian and the reckless, thoughtless Brian who constantly took matador-like risks in the bullring of Manhattan, persuading Weiss to take him around forbidden gay hangouts – where at any moment the cops could have swooped and his and The Beatles' career would have been over. There was the fastidious, sensitive Brian fatally drawn, in Weiss's non-judgemental words, to 'a very crass, macho kind of person, the hard-hat construction worker type.

'He wasn't just a Jekyll and Hyde character. He was Jekyll and Hyde and about twenty other people besides.'

* * *

In London, his 'houseman' Lonnie Trimble became accustomed to arriving for work in the mornings just as some or other casual pick-up of the night before was leaving. Shouldn't he be a little more careful about his personal security, Trimble ventured. 'Oh, they wouldn't harm me,' he replied. 'I'm Brian Epstein.'

One day, he wasn't fully dressed as usual, impatient for his tea and grapefruit, but sitting up in bed and looking utterly miserable. He quizzed Trimble about his own long-term relationship with a young man named Patrick and asked why, despite its perilous interraciality, it seemed to work so well. 'Because we love each other,' Trimble told him.

Soon afterwards, when least expecting it, he seemed to find something comparable. On a trip to New York, he met a young male model and aspiring actor named John Gillespie, nicknamed 'Diz' after the jazz trumpeter Dizzy Gillespie and bearing a slight resemblance to the singer-songwriter Gene Pitney.

Gillespie was married at the time but within a few months he had divorced, relocated to London and moved in with Brian at Whaddon House. The press ad that reported NEMS' signing of the New Christy Minstrels also introduced him as the first actor on its books. Such was Brian's infatuation that he'd bypassed Peter Brown and Geoffrey Ellis, put Gillespie on a higher-than-normal £50 per week retainer and ordered him an expensive new wardrobe despite having never seen him perform in the theatrical sense.

At first their affair went well, with Brian finally able to 'play house', as Lonnie Trimble put it, and Gillespie charm personi-fied. He met The Beatles and was given a copy of John Lennon's *In His Own Write* by the author, signed with another dig at Brian: 'To Diz. You're A Great Turn.'

However, after a few weeks, Peter Brown recalls, the two began to have alcohol- and drug-fuelled rows and even physical fights that drenched Brian's creamy shag-carpet with hurled drinks, cracked his mirrors and scattered his carefully placed *objets d'art*. 'They fought about drugs and the trollops that Diz brought in,' Trimble recalled. 'He was bisexual but he didn't really like playing the homosexual bit.'

Trimble tried to intercede for Brian as much as he dared. 'I said, "You don't have to love him but at least you ought to sleep with him once a week and give him a kiss when he comes home in the evening and then we'll all be happy."'

When Brian's parents came down from Liverpool on a visit, Trimble made dinner for them all – the usual grapefruit, Dover soles and pudding – but before the soles could be served a quarrel broke out between Brian and Gillespie, who stormed out of the flat with Brian in pursuit. Harry and Queenie sat there for a while but when there was no sign of him they decided to leave.

As Trimble showed Queenie out, she pleaded 'Lonnie ... look after my son.'

Things grew progressively nastier, he recalled, as Gillespie took to stealing things from the flat and demanding larger and larger cash sums from Brian. When at length Brian refused to hand over any more, Gillespie allegedly grabbed a kitchen knife, held it to his throat, emptied his wallet and disappeared, seemingly for good.

* * *

In June 1965, the Queen's Birthday Honours, made on the recommendation of her Prime Minister, Harold Wilson, created each of The Beatles an MBE (Member of the Most Excellent Order of the British Empire) for 'services to music'. It was the first time pop musicians had been so elevated and was a blatant attempt by Wilson to trendify his government (and more particularly himself), that publicity-grubbing premiers would copy for ever after.

Brian, the enabler of those 'services', received nothing. He was mortified by his exclusion, convinced it was due to his Jewishness or homosexuality or both. Nonetheless, he reacted with grace, ordering flowers to be sent to his boys' respective parents on the morning the awards were announced.

Brian's own services to music continued, unacknowledged but unstinted. In July, London's West End was brought to a standstill by the premiere of *Help!*, attended by Princess Margaret and Lord Snowdon, while the soundtrack album topped charts around the world.

That same month he agreed to put together and emcee a concert for the forthcoming Commonwealth Arts Festival, titled 'An Evening of Popular British Music with Brian Epstein' and featuring his latest signing, the Moody Blues, alongside Cliff Bennett and the Rebel Rousers, The Kinks, Manfred Mann and Georgie Fame and the Blue Flames.

The Beatles' 1965 American tour was to begin on 15 August at Shea Stadium in suburban New York before an audience of more than 55,000, the largest for a live musical performance ever known. On the eve of this colossal event Diz Gillespie turned up again in Manhattan.

Unable to trust himself to put a final full stop to their affair, Brian deputed Nat Weiss to negotiate a financial settlement. Gillespie's price for vanishing permanently was $10,000 and a car but Weiss, employing a tough-guy mien, beat him down to $3,000. According to Ray Coleman's biography, *Epstein*, he also had to agree to be locked in a room at the Warwick Hotel where The Beatles had been staying, watched over by a private security guard until the tour had left town.

The Beatles at Shea Stadium film shows Brian standing alone beside the high stage, still besuited despite the tropical heat, watching his boys in their faux military tunics face the ravening terraces as insouciantly as always. He nods his head slightly out of time with the music few spectators can hear – and its makers not at all.

He will mainly have been mentally counting down their thirty-minute setlist to their getaway by Wells Fargo armoured truck, then helicopter. But likely competing for headspace would have been that detainee at the Warwick, the horror and allure of him.

On 26 October the Beatles assembled at Brian's flat before going to Buckingham Palace to receive their MBEs from the Queen. He hadn't even been invited to attend the ceremony but was making sure they looked their best for it and were well set up by Lonnie Trimble with coffee, pastries and fruit. Whatever his feelings, he was all smiles and congratulations and his boys loyally rallied round by telling the *Daily Mirror*, 'Our MBE means Mr Brian Epstein.'

In the end, he couldn't bear to miss the investiture completely, so rode to the palace in The Beatles' limo and waited for them with the driver while they received their decorations two at a time from Her Majesty then displayed them at length for the world's media, without ever revealing his presence.

Afterwards, as the limo nosed its way out through the cheering crowds, his profile was just visible in its front passenger seat.

16

'I DIDN'T KNOW THEY LET QUEERS IN HERE NOW'

At the end of 1964, Brian had paid £40,000 for a Grade II listed Georgian house in Chapel Street, Belgravia – a decided step-up from Knightsbridge – but because it needed extensive work by his favoured interior designer, Ken Peacock, he couldn't move there from Whaddon House until December 1965.

Peacock's refurbishments included a magnificent, curved staircase he had specially made, but it didn't last long. 'There was some trouble one evening with two [male] guests Brian took back. They had a fight on the stairs like they do in a Western and somebody fell through it . . . it was like a pile of sticks on the ground.'

Twenty-four Chapel Street was, as real-estate brochures say, 'arranged over four floors'. The basement was a self-contained flat for the domestic staff it was expected to employ; on the ground floor were the kitchen and a reception area; on the first, a sitting room and Brian's study; on the second, his bedroom, dressing-room and bathroom, the latter with a blown-up colour photograph of El Cordobés covering an entire wall.

The two top-floor bedrooms had been knocked into one

to create what Brian called his 'playroom' for whatever games might occur and to display memorabilia like the bejewelled holster presented to him by 'Elvis and the Col' and the picture he'd had taken of himself, pointing its replica gun at the camera and drawing a bead like a well-tailored Wyatt Earp.

His domestic staff had further expanded with a chauffeur-bodyguard, a burly ex-soldier named Bryan Barrett, to drive the selection of cars that were constantly changing as he tired of them or crashed them or found he'd been sold a dud but couldn't be bothered to have it fixed. From the beginning there was a formality to be found nowhere else at NEMS: Barrett called him 'Mr Epstein' and he responded naturally with 'Mr Barrett'.

His main car currently was a Rolls-Royce Phantom 5 he'd bought second-hand, from the washing-machine magnate John Bloom despite its many obvious defects. One of Barrett's first outings in it was to drop him at Paul's house in St John's Wood where George would also be present, then pick up a package for them from an address in Soho.

On reaching his destination Barrett could find nowhere to park the hulking Rolls so he asked a policeman to watch it for him while he ran in and collected the package. Not until half-way back to Paul's did he smell the fumes coming from it and realise it contained 'grass'.

After that, he persuaded Brian to change Rolls-Royces from the Phantom 5 to a new Silver Cloud in dark burgundy – the colour favoured by the Royal Family – at the same time exacting a solemn promise that he'd never again have to transport illegal substances in it.

It was only through the car that Barrett realised his new employer's sexual orientation. It was often parked overnight in the mews behind 24 Chapel Street and one morning he found someone had scratched QUEER on its pristine paintwork. Not that the possibility bothered him in the slightest.

Barrett was often to find himself covering for Brian, as when his brother Clive turned up at the house unannounced while he was occupied with a transitory boyfriend. 'I answered the door and said to Clive, "You can't go upstairs, sir. Do you mind waiting in the dining-room?" He said, "Why can't I go up?" and I said, "Mr Epstein is bathing or talking to someone and he'd rather you didn't." He'd never let his brother stay in his house though he had a guest-room which he'd let certain people use.'

Lonnie Trimble was to spend little time at the new address. For two years at the Whaddon House flat he and Brian had successfully combined formality and friendship, but after the move to Chapel Street Trimble began to feel increasingly 'disrespected' – though never on account of his colour.

The breaking point was the stinginess of which Brian could be capable, often with those who least deserved it. Before Christmas in 1966, Trimble had been promised a first-ever pay rise but had received only his previous year's seasonal bonus of a week's money plus a £20 note.

He nonetheless worked on Boxing Day, a public holiday, and also the day after. In the face of such selflessness Brian agreed to give him his rise but with obvious annoyance 'dismissed' him from the room. From then on, he would pass him on the – expensively re-restored – staircase without uttering a word and took to communicating only via scribbled notes.

The last words they exchanged were Trimble's request to take his annual holiday in February and Brian's curt response that he had to take it between May and September like the rest of the

NEMS staff. So one day while Brian was at the office, he typed a formal resignation and, having tried unsuccessfully to change his mind, Bryan Barrett drove him home to Putney.

There the telephone kept ringing and he guessed it would be Brian asking him to stay, but he resisted the temptation to pick up. Had he done so, 24 Chapel Street might well have avoided its tragic destiny.

To take his place Brian followed the current fashion among the rich for employing Spanish married couples to run their homes, seemingly a guarantee of stability and respectability. The couple were named Antonio and Maria Garcia, he the major-domo, she the cook-housekeeper, and they were to occupy his basement for the rest of his life.

His treatment of Lonnie Trimble may have been a symptom of the pressure he felt at NEMS' Argyll Street offices, not only from his ever-lengthening client list but from young performers hopeful of joining it, pushy entrepreneurs with brilliant new ideas for The Beatles and fans simply desirous of breathing the same air they – occasionally – did.

His brisk PA, Wendy Hanson, therefore suggested he move to a small separate office in Stafford Street, just off Piccadilly, taking only her young assistant, Joanne Newfield, there to devote himself to 'top-level management' – i.e., The Beatles and Cilla.

The hideaway was supposed to be known only to Peter Brown and Geoffrey Ellis. 'But Brian spoilt that,' Ellis recalled, 'by immediately ringing up twenty of his closest friends and letting them know where he was.'

It was from Stafford Street that he organised George's marriage to Pattie Boyd in January 1966, having been reassured their wedding-date didn't clash with any Beatles tours.

In deference to the most crowd-averse of the four, he treated the event like a state secret. Top model Pattie wasn't allowed to ask one of her top couturier friends to make her wedding dress for fear that its design would be leaked to the press; instead, she had to put together an outfit from things she already possessed.

* * *

Brian's appetite for new challenges was still insatiable, particularly if they had to do with the stage. His building of a theatre in Kent with his deejay friend Brian Matthew had recently been aborted by the local authority's refusal to grant planning permission, fearing its environs would be invaded by shrieking Beatlemaniacs.

That seemed of little consequence when he acquired the lease of a West End theatre, the Saville, an Art Deco edifice in Shaftesbury Avenue with a distinguished record of both plays and musicals. Being comparatively modern, its 1,400 seats were a sight more comfortable than the iron-and-plush torture chambers traditionally inflicted on West End theatregoers; nonetheless, Brian's first act was to have them all taken out and replaced.

While holidaying with Lionel Bart in the South of France, he had met the pioneering African American writer James Baldwin, who'd found refuge there from the dual stigma of his race and homosexuality in his homeland. Brian revered Baldwin's books, like *Go Tell It on the Mountain* and *Giovanni's Room*, but was shocked by the writer's habit of prefacing some stiletto-sharp observation 'Well, speaking as a faggot . . .'

Baldwin urged him to be as upfront about his sexuality, which was easier in the South of France but unthinkable in London where even the legitimate theatre of which he'd become a part didn't show him its usual tolerance. One day when he and Geoffrey Ellis were lunching at the stagey Mirabelle restaurant, the actor Laurence Harvey passed their table with a group of friends and was heard to remark, 'I didn't know they let queers in here now', although he was hardly one to talk.

The Saville Theatre's first season as a NEMS Enterprise opened with a gala performance of Baldwin's play *The Amen Corner*, attended by luminaries, from the chief executive of EMI, Sir Joseph Lockwood, to the Rolling Stones' manager, Andrew Loog Oldham.

There followed a full programme alternating serious dramas like Arnold Wesker's *The Four Seasons* with lighter productions such as *The Solid Gold Cadillac* co-starring Margaret Rutherford and Sid James, and ten weeks of Gilbert and Sullivan operettas by the D'Oyly Carte Company, all of whom Brian put up at the Savoy Hotel at vast expense throughout the run.

Lionel Bart, meanwhile, had suffered a terrible reversal after writing mould-breaking hit musicals like *Oliver!* and *Maggie May*. Bart's *Twang!!*, a spoof of the Robin Hood story (named after the sound of the outlaw's bowstring), opened to high expectations, its first night attended by Brian and all four Beatles.

Under-rehearsed and riven by backstage politics, it received a merciless critical shafting. When Bart's backers pulled out, he foolhardily used his own money to keep it going and when that was used up sold the rights to *Oliver!* for a fraction of their future value.

The people who'd been wont to help themselves from the bowl of £5 notes left around his house like peanuts now mostly looked the other way. Brian loyally refused to accept that

Twang!! was Twash!! and offered a cash injection but by then a transfusion couldn't have saved it and Bart was bankrupted.

Despite a fair sprinkling of hits, the Saville made little profit from its conventional programming. 'I don't think Brian cared about anything other than having his own theatre where he could sit in the royal box and survey his domain,' his young aide Tony Bramwell would recall.

'It was decorated very tastefully and, instead of chairs, contained sofas covered in zebra skin. Behind was a little anteroom for discreet suppers, stocked with drink. It had its own private entrance from the street and was a fun place to entertain his chums.'

On Sundays, like all its West End rivals, the Saville was closed to plays and shows but Brian discovered that there was nothing to stop it putting on live music. Bramwell, his most knowledgeable employee on the subject, was given the job of turning it into a weekly rock venue.

This was effected with typical Brian extravagance and a resurgence of Epstein luck. He booked one of Motown Records' lesser-known vocal groups, the Four Tops, with airfares and hotels, a total outlay of $30,000 as against a predicted take of £12,000. Then, just prior to their arrival, their new single, 'Reach Out I'll Be There', reached the top of the UK charts and their appearance was a sell-out.

NEMS Enterprises never gave greater value than these Sunday nights at the Saville. For £1 at the door, one could see the likes of Cream, Pink Floyd, The Who, Procol Harum and the Jimi Hendrix Experience, often in company with a Beatle or two out for the evening and digging the sounds just like everyone else.

For the first time in its long history, Shaftesbury Avenue was the apogee of cool. All this while its creator's idea of cool was watching a man in a bejewelled suit and flat shoes kill a beautiful black bull or be half-killed by it.

More fascinating than El Cordobés to Brian now was a 22-year-old English matador named Henry Higgins (like the tetchy dialectologist in *My Fair Lady*), born in Bogotá to a British oil company executive and a Mexican mother and educated on the Isle of Man. Despite his youth, Higgins's courage and grace in the bullring were reckoned the equal of any Spaniard but he couldn't afford the heavy bribes necessary for a ranking among the elite.

Brian got his fellow aficionado, the drama critic Kenneth Tynan, to introduce them and offered Higgins a generous contract but with no strings attached à la Diz Gillespie. He was to attend so many corridas watching his protégé develop that he had a bull named after him – a dubious honour considering the usual fate of its brothers.

He seemed to be fulfilling all his dearest wishes outside the pop sphere – on one occasion, two simultaneously. In February 1966, he produced his first straight play, *A Smashing Day* by the young northern playwright Alan Plater, although not at the Saville but the nearby New Arts Theatre Club.

It was to have been directed by John Fernald, his one-time mentor at the Royal Academy of Dramatic Art, but before rehearsals could start, Fernald fell ill and Brian took over. Open to nascent talent as always, he sent Tony Bramwell to RADA to recruit 'a couple of kids' to play the buskers around whom the plot revolved. Bramwell picked the future stage and screen stars Robert Powell and Ben Kingsley.

'Brian really threw himself into directing *A Smashing Day*,' his young PA Joanne Newfield would recall. 'He was totally involved, right up to the evening of the dress rehearsal. The cast were all waiting in their costumes ... but there was no sign of Brian. He'd forgotten all about it.'

17

'THAT WAS THE START OF HIS DEPRESSION'

Brian's plan for The Beatles in 1966 was to repeat the pattern of the previous two massively successful years. They would make their third feature film along with a soundtrack album, play a series of dates in West Germany and Japan in June and July, briefly pause for breath then return to their dependably adoring American public in August.

The first thing not to happen as per plan was the feature film plus soundtrack album. Mindful of John's – wholly unreasonable – complaint that in *Help!* they'd been little more than extras, Brian had acquired the rights to a bestselling American novel, Richard Condon's *A Talent for Loving*, that seemed to catch the mid-'60s zeitgeist and provide meaty roles for them all. But his boys unanimously rejected it and, furthermore, refused to consider any other potential vehicles for their return to the big screen.

Since early April they'd been working on a new studio album, *Revolver* – 'the acid album', as John called it, with good reason – most of whose tracks were far too complex to be played live by just those four. After the multi-instrumental adventuring of 'Tomorrow Never Knows' or 'Eleanor Rigby', it felt wearisome to have to rehearse simplistic old material and exchange their assorted Carnaby Street finery for the matching stage suits Brian still insisted on.

NEMS had lately purchased the booking and management agency of a former jazz-band leader named Vic Lewis, whose client list included Nina Simone, Carmen McRae and Andy Williams. Part of the deal was that Lewis joined the NEMS board, which meant his being in on the planning of the tour's West German–Japanese segment.

His impressive contribution was to book two shows in Manila to follow the three already confirmed in Tokyo. The Philippines were a long way off the touring map but the $1 million box-office guarantee on offer would make it the highest grossing stop on the entire tour, America included.

A little background research at this point might have saved much trauma later on. The President of the Philippines, Ferdinand Marcos, had come to power a year earlier, mainly by liquidating or incarcerating his political opponents. In a land where direst poverty was the norm, his wife Imelda was a byword for extravagance and insensitivity, known to possess 3,000 pairs of shoes, 15 mink coats, 800 handbags and, as a measure of the public esteem she commanded, a bulletproof brassière.

A larger support team than usual embarked with The Beatles on the rail journey linking their three West German venues. For once Brian was to be with them for the whole tour and, in addition to their roadies Neil Aspinall and Mal Evans, had recruited NEMS' press officer Tony Barrow and Peter Brown. Vic Lewis was to join up in Tokyo for the last stop in Manila.

Aspinall, as usual, carried a large supply of marijuana

pre-rolled into joints and arranged in normal cigarette packets. The incorrigible risk-taker in Brian overpowering the prudent manager had no objection to his boys turning on, indeed was ready and willing to join in (though constitutionally incapable of rolling a joint for himself). There was something of a holiday atmosphere as they lowered the window blinds in their first-class compartments and stuffed towels under the doors to prevent the telltale fumes seeping out.

That light-heartedness vanished in Hamburg where The Beatles were to play for the first time since Brian had turned off the red lights in their lives in January 1963. Before the night's show at the Ernst Merck Halle, an anonymous telegram was delivered to their dressing-room. 'Please don't fly to Tokyo,' it read. 'Your career is in danger.'

No explanation was forthcoming until the party landed at Tokyo airport. It turned out that The Beatles were to be the first pop group to perform at the city's Nippon Budokan arena, a place normally devoted to sumo wrestling and martial arts, which in Japan are religious rites as much as competitive sports. There had been widespread protest at what was seen as its invasion by decadent Western culture, and an association of extreme-right students who saw themselves as inheritors of the samurai tradition were threatening to put more than The Beatles' career in danger.

A stupefying 35,000 police and security personnel had been mobilised to protect the four during their three-day visit. At the Tokyo Hilton, of which they'd been allotted the entire top floor, every alternate room was occupied by armed guards.

Paternal as ever, Brian ordered that they shouldn't be told about the threat in case it put them off their playing, but they could hardly remain unaware of it. They were barred from leaving the hotel to sightsee and taken to the Budokan every day in a high-speed convoy with motorcycle outriders, people lining the streets waving placards saying they were 'bugs needing to be crushed' and snipers unnervingly posted on every flyover. They played on a stage so high, it would have needed siege ladders to storm it while their 9,000-strong audiences were under orders to remain seated and motionless throughout to ensure perfect rifle-sightlines for their protectors.

And after all that, nothing in the least untoward happened.

On their last day in Tokyo, Brian and Peter Brown were having lunch at the Hilton when a man came up and introduced himself as the Philippines' ambassador to Japan. He asked if Brian had received an invitation to The Beatles from its First Lady, Imelda Marcos, to a reception at the presidential palace on the day of their two Manila concerts.

Brian said he'd had no such invitation but explained his policy – in place since their experience with the British Embassy's yahoos in Washington two years before – of turning down all such official functions on their behalf, and then thought no more about it.

When their flight landed at Manila airport the next day, there was none of the usual ritual of screaming fans and popping flashbulbs. Instead, a solitary man in uniform boarded the plane and ordered that only The Beatles disembark with him. At the foot of the stairs, they were surrounded by armed soldiers, told to leave their hand luggage (in which their marijuana supply was hidden) on the tarmac, then put into a waiting limo and driven away.

'No one spoke English and could explain what was happening,' Peter Brown would recall. 'It was the only time they could remember being separated from Brian and Mal and Neil with no support at all. They were vulnerable and helpless like children suddenly separated from their parents . . . Brian was so upset by this point, I thought he would have a stroke.'

His boys had not been taken hostage, as he'd feared, but been driven to a marina in Manila Bay, required to give an unscheduled press conference then taken on board a luxurious boat named the *Marima*. Nor was this any surprise to his new NEMS director and travelling companion, Vic Lewis, who'd booked the Manila concerts.

The *Marima* belonged to a friend of the concert promoter, a media tycoon named Don Manolo Elizalde. In a secret side-deal with Elizalde, Lewis had promised to deliver The Beatles as the *pièce-de-résistance* of his son's twenty-fourth birthday party aboard the vessel; they were to have dinner, party with female guests including the current Miss Philippines and sleep the night on board, in anticipation of which Lewis had cancelled their suites at the Manila Hotel.

Brian retrieved them, with no great show of politeness to the birthday boy's father, and gave Lewis a rocket while blaming himself equally for letting the scam get by him. But much worse was to follow.

At around noon the next day, he was awakened by a pounding on his hotel-room door. Outside were two Filipino army officers who said they'd come to escort The Beatles to Imelda Marcos's reception at Malacañang Palace. Brian replied that he'd declined the invitation on their behalf via the Philippines' ambassador to Japan, and flatly refused to get them up so far ahead of the two shows they were to give a few hours later.

Understandably enough, he felt the need to take back control after the *Marima* episode, but standing up the wife of a South-east Asian dictator was clearly not the wisest move. And all that was being asked of them was to shake a few hands and sign some autographs, probably with interesting food included. If Brian had told them it had to be done, they doubtless would have done it.

All his colleagues were troubled by his decision, but most knew better than to question his judgement in anything Beatle-related. Only Vic Lewis tried, but Lewis's was not a voice carrying great weight at present.

The First Lady's staff had contacted the British Embassy in Manila about the no-show and within minutes a senior diplomat was on the phone to Brian, urging him to get his charges to Malacañang without delay. It was an unmistakable warning that he was courting disaster, but he ignored it.

The Beatles' two concerts at the Rizal Memorial Football Stadium between them attracted almost 100,000 rapturous fans and passed off without the least trouble. Not until later back at the hotel did Brian realise the enormity of his gaffe.

Saturation television coverage of the Imelda Marcos reception showed it to have been a huge affair to which some 200 major political and military figures and their families, including many children, had been invited. There were lingering shots of disappointed little faces as outraged commentators described how the First Lady, and by implication the whole country, had been snubbed by The Beatles.

Reprisals by Marcos loyalists – which it was obligatory to be – soon followed. The next day, when the party were to return to London, they found all police and security cover withdrawn from their hotel. Room-service at first refused to answer their phone calls, then sent them breakfast with stone-cold eggs, congealed milk and filthy cutlery; Neil Aspinall refused to touch his, convinced that somebody had spat on it.

Cool-headed as usual, press officer Tony Barrow arranged for Brian to appear on Manila's main TV channel to explain that it had all been a misunderstanding and no discourtesy to the First Lady intended, but most of what he said was obliterated by a sudden burst of electrical interference. For the channel happened to belong to the would-be hijacker of The Beatles, Don Manolo Elizalde, a fervent Marcos supporter who felt it his patriotic duty to sabotage the transmission. In the same spirit, Elizalde's friend the concert-promoter refused to pay Brian the $500,000 balance owing on the group's two shows, which was to have been in cash.

Their departure from Manila airport was Beatlemania laced with poison, the concourse packed with Marcos enthusiasts, wielding unpleasant-looking sticks and chanting 'Ordinary passenger! Ordinary passenger!', the new status of yesterday's VIPs. Every escalator had been switched off, forcing the two roadies to heave guitars, amps and drums up long flights of stairs. The Beatles, Brian and everyone in their party were repeatedly sworn at, jostled and kicked.

Pre-flight formalities were deliberately prolonged as the minutes ticked away to the departure of their KLM flight. Officials from the Ministry of Finance informed Brian they wouldn't be allowed to leave until he paid a hefty sum in 'income tax' – i.e., a bribe. Yet in all the ransacking of their baggage and repeated body-searches, their pot supply remained undiscovered.

Crossing the open tarmac to their aircraft, everyone was in

fear of sniper-fire from the soldiers guarding the terminal. Peter Brown would never forget the sight of Brian slumping into a window seat, sweating profusely and muttering, 'I'll never forgive myself . . . I put the boys in danger.' Then at the last minute Tony Barrow and Mal Evans were ordered off the plane to deal with some petty immigration query. 'Big Mal' was in floods of tears, thinking he was about to be locked up and would never again see his wife, Lil, and new baby daughter, Julie.

Even after take-off, the unpleasantness continued for only then did Vic Lewis realise that leaving behind the half-million dollars in cash would reduce his percentage of the proceeds as a NEMS director. According to Peter Brown, Lewis was so enraged that he tried to slap Brian's face, but Brown caught hold of his hand just in time.

During the homeward journey, Brian's unabating remorse and self-castigation brought him out in hives, a case worrying enough for the pilot to radio ahead for an ambulance to meet him at Heathrow airport.

'That was the start of his depression,' Brown recalled.

* * *

Some time before the debacle in the Philippines, John and George had asked him to call off the tour's American leg that was scheduled so very soon afterwards. John in fact had been chafing against life on the road since around mid-1964 but endured it for the sake of the others, while George had come to loathe the mindless shrieks that drowned his painstaking musicianship.

Brian had talked both of them round by listing the grosses to be expected from the eighteen shows, including a second at Shea Stadium, the scene of their greatest live triumph. Still, there was an implicit understanding – by the applause-addicted Paul also – that this would be *it*.

The American leg stumbled from the very start. To promote it, Capitol Records released a largely compilation album whose title referenced Paul's most adored ballad: *The Beatles Yesterday and Today*. The four were allowed a say in its cover design and, for a laugh, had themselves photographed wearing white butcher's coats, surrounded by bloody joints of meat and dismembered, naked baby dolls.

What came to be known as the 'Butcher sleeve' caused disgust throughout the American record trade: retailers refused to stock it, radio stations banned it regardless of its content and Capitol hastily recalled 75,000 copies for a bland image to be pasted over it (so creating a sought-after Beatle memento for ever after).

Its authors claimed the bloodbath had been a protest against the Vietnam War, which nightly filled television screens with similar carnage – this in defiance of Brian's long-standing rule that they never get involved with politics. So the old order was already starting to change.

After returning from Manila, he had planned a badly needed rest in Portmeirion, a cosy Welsh seaside village he'd loved since childhood, where his parents and George Martin were to join him. He'd been there only a weekend when Nat Weiss phoned from New York to say that Beatles albums were being publicly burned in Birmingham, Alabama.

Four months earlier, in an interview with the London *Evening Standard*, John had opined that the Beatles had become 'more popular than Jesus' and that Christianity was fated to 'shrink'. In a land where church attendance seemed to be shrinking at

Mach speed, the aperçu had passed unchallenged, as it also did when the interview was syndicated to the *New York Times.*

Now it had been resurrected by an American teen magazine called *Datebook* and put in large type on the cover, unleashing a nationwide storm of protest, above all in the God-fearing Southern states known as the Bible Belt.

Although still not over his attack of hives and suffering from flu, Brian at once chartered a plane to get him to Heathrow for the first available New York flight. There was delay in taking off from Liverpool and to save him from missing the connection at Heathrow his private plane was allowed to land on the runway where New York-bound passengers were boarding and an immigration officer was waiting to inspect his passport on possibly the fastest fast-track ever.

Nat Weiss recalled his extreme agitation when he landed. 'The first question he asked me was, "What'll it cost to cancel the tour?" I said, "a million dollars." He said, "I'll pay it. I'll pay it out of my own pocket because if anything were to happen to any one of them I'd never forgive myself."'

The cool, measured Brian back in control, he called a press conference at which he politely batted aside questions such as, 'They were picketed in Japan and thrown out of the Philippines – is this the end for the Beatles?'

John, he said, had never meant to equate them with the Messiah, but had merely been commenting on the decline of organised worship in Britain. The uniquely Brian touch was to add that if any promoters along the tour route now felt uneasy about putting The Beatles onstage, the cash deposits they'd paid would be fully refunded.

Yet still the furore rumbled on with John and The Beatles

lumped together and denounced from the pulpits of many denominations around the world. The Spanish, South African and Dutch governments issued official condemnations and the Vatican newspaper *L'Osservatore Romano* relayed the view of the Pontiff himself that 'some subjects must not be dealt with profanely even in the world of beatniks'.

In Chicago, the tour's starting-point, Brian and Tony Barrow between them persuaded John to make a personal apology, which he did with enough of his old charm to win over the international media and decide Brian to trust to luck that Beatlemania was still out there.

So it was – but now curdled by anger and reproach. Wherever the group deplaned, they found forests of banners and placards saying BEATLES GO HOME or JESUS DIED FOR YOU TOO JOHN. Radio stations took hammers to their albums on air or sponsored public litter bins inscribed PLACE BEATLE TRASH HERE, in one case hiring a tree-crushing machine to speed up the work. Pastors threatened to excommunicate any among their flocks caught giving ear to the accursed sounds. There was even trading in the 'rights' to mass Beatles record-smashing or burning, usually acquired by supermarkets as attractions to be staged in their parking lots.

In addition to the local police and security operatives – many of them devout Christians so not over-zealous about their duties – Brian hired two government Secret Service agents to accompany the tour for its duration. As when they'd been threatened by militant right-wing students in Tokyo, he didn't tell his boys about the G-men for fear it might worry them more than they already were.

In Memphis, Tennessee, the heart of the Bible Belt, the white

255

supremacist Ku Klux Klan nailed an album to one of its signature burning crosses and a hulking Klansman, minus pointy hood, appeared on local television boasting of its reputation as 'a terror organisation' (which habitually meant terrorising defenceless black women and children) and promising 'surprises' when The Beatles went onstage later that day.

So many hostile crowds lined the route to the Mid-South Coliseum and so many sniper-friendly windows yawned above that their limos were sent ahead empty as decoys and they themselves rode to the venue in a Greyhound bus, crouched double on its floor.

Before the first of the day's two shows there was a bomb scare; demonstrators were reportedly being bussed in by the Klan and albums set aflame in oil drums. At the second, The Beatles had been onstage only a few minutes when a firecracker exploded near them, a noise like a handgun's shallow 'snap-snap-snap'. Tony Barrow never forgot the sheer terror of that moment. 'Every one of us [the tour entourage] and the other three Beatles looked at John, half-expecting to see the guy sinking down.'

Any modern rock band faced with a fraction of the same danger, discomfort and humiliation would have said 'Fuck this' with one voice and caught the next plane home, but The Beatles did everything demanded of them, however monstrous, with barely a murmur. They were like schoolboys, counting the days, hours, minutes and seconds until school was out – for ever.

To cap it all, the tour fell short of the money-spinner Brian had expected. In Los Angeles, Dodger Stadium saw a bigger crowd than a year earlier but the return to Shea Stadium was 11,000 seats undersold and, to keep up appearances, tickets had to be given away – the first time any Beatles show had been 'papered' – and he ended up owing the promoter, Sid Bernstein, $800.

The finale was to be on 29 August 1966 at the Candlestick Park baseball ground in San Francisco. To avoid screaming fans or, as it now might be, protesting Christians, the tour party were based in LA, The Beatles in a rented mansion in Beverly Hills, Brian, naturally, at the grande-lux Beverly Hills Hotel where he was joined by the ever-supportive Nat Weiss.

'Brian said it was the end in San Francisco,' Weiss recalled. 'He was dejected. He said, "This is the last one ever."'

His mood lightened, however, with a phone call from a wholly unexpected quarter. It was Diz Gillespie, the lover he'd thought to have broken up with a year earlier, now all charm and contrition and asking to see him again. Brian was instantly won over and the two enjoyed a seemingly blissful reconciliation beside the Beverly Hills Hotel's VIP pool.

He didn't attend his boys' Candlestick Park show for a reason known only to Nat Weiss. Secretly he hoped it wouldn't really be their last and that they'd relent once the nightmare of the present tour had faded. Downplaying the significance of Candlestick Park was part of that comforting illusion.

Had he been there, he would have seen them give way to something close to nostalgia for the life they were leaving. Paul asked Tony Barrow to record their performance on a cassette-player and John photographed the four of them onstage by pointing the camera at himself, with their audience (and 20,000 unsold seats) as background.

At dinner with Nat Weiss in the hotel that evening, Brian had something more urgent on his mind. He insisted that Diz really loved him, they could start again and it would be different this

257

time. Weiss repeated countless previous warnings that he was 'nothing but trouble'.

When they returned to the suite they were sharing, they found Gillespie had somehow gained entry and taken both their briefcases. Weiss's contained nothing of value but in Brian's were several important contracts, $20,000 in cash, a bottle of Seconal barbiturate, illegal in the US and some pornographic photographs of him with an unknown man. A ransom note from Gillespie demanded 50 per cent of the money or he'd turn the Seconal and photographs over to the police.

Terrified of exposure as always, Brian was ready to pay up, but Weiss was no such pushover. 'My logic was that if someone stole my briefcase, I wanted them arrested,' he recalled. 'And I hated Diz for all that he'd done to Brian. I was really out to get him.'

Sending Brian back to London, he set about pursuing his quarry with the help of a private detective. Having traced Gillespie, the detective inveigled him into a meeting at a bus station where the ransom was supposedly to be handed over. The police were waiting in ambush and Brian's briefcase was recovered with the Seconal bottle empty and $8,000 of the $20,000 missing but the contracts and photographs intact.

Yet when Weiss got it back to him, rather than being mightily relieved, he was distraught to think Diz might have been roughed up by the cops.

18

'PLEASE BANK MY HAPPINESS'

Brian decreed that there should be no formal announcement of the major step-change in The Beatles' career. For three years he had lived with the expectation that sooner or later some new pop mega-attraction was bound to eclipse them. That now seemed to him a certainty if they deserted their live audience and shut themselves away in the recording studio, as they intended.

Only his closest associates like Peter Brown and Geoffrey Ellis knew of his feeling of emptiness now that his boys would no longer be so very like his children. 'What am I going to do now?' he would say with a brave attempt at flippancy. 'Shall I go back to school and learn something new?'

At low moments, it must have seemed that, freed from the shackles of touring – and of each other – they had done their best to get as far from him as possible.

John was making a feature film, *How I Won the War*, in which he'd neither sing nor play a note. Paul was on a road trip through France that turned into a safari to Kenya with his partner, Jane Asher. George had gone to India with Pattie to further his interest in its music, culture and religion. Ringo was hunkered down in deepest Surrey with a year-old son and his wife, Maureen, soon to give birth again.

Yet still the golden bandwagon rolled on. The New York promoter Sid Bernstein, in London to publicise his own (Beatle-inspired) group, the Young Rascals, offered Brian $350,000 for the genuine articles to return to Shea Stadium for two shows in 1967. American television's top comedy series, *The Lucy Show*, offered $100,000 merely to have them stand on a street corner while its star, Lucille Ball, did an amazed double-take.

Brian's explanation for their sudden invisibility was of the vaguest: 'There's no real question of The Beatles retiring. They're simmering down, making films, writing music, making records. That's their future.'

He should have found ample diversion in an organisation that seemingly couldn't stop growing. In addition to NEMS' main office in Argyll Street and his personal bunker in Stafford Street, a new division, NEMS Presentations, based in Cork Street, Mayfair, brought the staff to around eighty. Thanks to Vic Lewis, the executive tier now included Matt Monro's manager, Don Black, the writer of hit movie themes like 'Thunderball' and 'Born Free'.

For a time, it seemed enough for Brian to immerse himself in the Saville Theatre, applying for a licence for late-night film shows and putting on American stars like Fats Domino, Chuck Berry, Lee Dorsey and Little Richard – their first encounter since New Brighton Tower Ballroom in 1962 and their rumoured tryst the night before. Now his offer to manage Richard was purely a reflex since both knew it could never work.

The thrill of discovering and nurturing youthful talent had largely evaporated, at least as far as Britain was concerned. A year earlier, he'd signed another highly talented group, the Moody Blues, with the usual fanfare, yet used them only as a support act on The Beatles' last-ever UK tour, then lost interest and turned them over to NEMS' long-time stalwart, Alistair Taylor.

It was the same with his only folk group, The Silkie, who'd scored a hit with a cover of The Beatles' 'You've Got to Hide Your Love Away' and were to tour the US, appearing on both *The Ed Sullivan Show* and Dick Clark's *American Bandstand*. But Brian refused to pay the $1,000 bribe necessary to get them work permits; the tour was cancelled and they broke up soon afterwards.

His attention was mainly concentrated on a new company, Nemperor Artists, formed with his New York attorney friend Nat Weiss to represent NEMS acts in America and also find new acts there. He was elated when Weiss made the first discovery, a band named Cyrkle whose debut single, 'Red Rubber Ball', co-written by Paul Simon, became an international hit.

* * *

After Diz Gillespie he was never to have anything resembling a long-term relationship. 'The problem was that Brian was not a predatory type of person,' Peter Brown remembered. 'When it came to meeting people, they had to be the moving party. He would never try to seduce a man under any circumstances.

'He was always concerned that someone liked him only because he was Brian Epstein. I saw it happen many times. He would think the relationship was developing and then the person would say, "Now, tell me what [The Beatles] are like, Brian, and when can I meet them?"'

He was still taking appalling personal risks by frequenting gay pubs and known pick-up areas on his own, then bringing some stranger back to Chapel Street in the small hours – frequently more than one. His chauffeur-bodyguard Bryan Barrett recalled him phoning late at night to say that two men were trying to break down his bedroom door after he'd locked it against them. 'I only lived in Westminster, ten minutes away and I crept in behind them and got them out.' Much left unsaid there.

After this he tried to exercise a little more caution, spurred by the awful fate of Joe Meek. The producer-engineer who turned down The Beatles in 1962 had gone on to huge success with the Tornados' 'Telstar', the first single by a British pop group to reach number one in America.

A year later, Meek had relived Brian's worst nightmare by being arrested for 'cottaging' outside a men's toilet. The psychological collapse that followed ended in February 1967 in his home studio when he murdered his landlady with a shotgun after a dispute about his rent, then blew out his own brains.

Barrett became accustomed to Brian's ever-shifting moods in the back of his burgundy Rolls-Royce or blue Bentley Continental; sometimes full of wistful questions about Barrett's three children, sometimes not volunteering a word, always so palpably lonely that one evening Barrett put aside military formality and offered to take him to dinner. However, he vetoed all the plush places Barrett suggested, each time saying, 'So-and-so will be there and I don't want to see them', and the two ended up in a drab steakhouse in Knightsbridge.

Brian's mood swings had a simple explanation, as did his alternating bursts of energy and lapses into inertia. Ever since The Beatles had fed him the amphetamine-based diet pills that kept them going all night at The Cavern, he'd been addicted to oral drugs. It was a way of achieving the kinship with them that was a drug in itself, and of blunting the turmoils and neuroses always at work inside him.

The deadly cycle of 'uppers' and 'downers' had taken full control of his metabolism, the one perpetually creating a need for the other, together blurring the division between day and night. In company he became adept at concealing just how many pills he was taking. His suits were made with special inside pockets to carry them; he'd pretend to cough, then smuggle one between his lips with the hand covering his mouth.

The Swinging Sixties generated pills as colourful as the clothes: Purple Hearts, French Blues, Black Bombers and Yellow Submarines, which his boys mischievously made the title of a children's song on the *Revolver* album. Whatever garish pellet came into vogue, Brian would try. 'He was the Pied Piper of any new drug,' Nat Weiss remembered. 'Unfortunately he was not the best master of his own use of these things.'

Bryan Barrett could already vouch for that, having found him insensible from an accidental overdose and poured salt water down his throat until he vomited up most of it. Not long afterwards Barrett received a late-night phone call from Peter Brown, temporarily living at Chapel Street with Brian, who'd found him in 'a heavy state of unconsciousness'. Brown had already called his doctor and found a note making clear that this time the overdose had been no accident.

Rather than call an ambulance and risk the story getting into the papers, Barrett wrapped him in a blanket and carried him out to the Bentley to rush him to the nearest casualty department. 'Peter Brown was very worried someone might see him. I said, "Who the hell's gonna see him at this time in the morning wrapped in a blanket?"

'They pumped him out and he was moaning and crying on the table. I was watching and he became conscious after a while. He was muttering and mumbling and you could hear what he was saying.' It was the nearest to an explanation of the sudden crisis that anyone would get and forty years later, Barrett still couldn't bring himself to repeat what he'd overheard. A story was fed to the press that the hospital visit had been in daylight hours for a routine check-up.

Recently Brian had given up his Stafford Street bolt-hole and taken to working from home, with his secretary-PA Joanne Newfield coming in every day to a space cleared in the top-floor playroom. Joanne was Jewish as well as efficient in the Wendy Hanson mould and he liked it that her uncle was the big-band leader Joe Loss.

She often found him in good spirits and with a full engagements book, whether presenting the Brian Epstein Trophy for Drama and Public Speaking in his capacity as president of the Finchley Jewish Youth Club, or attending a fancy dress party given by Georgie Fame at the Cromwellian Club in an elaborate clown costume. But there was always a risk of the red-faced tantrums to which he'd always been prone, magnified by the drugs warring inside him. Once, when Joanne made a mistake over a telephone number, he threw a pot full of hot tea at her. 'I was standing there, covered in tea-leaves. I just burst into tears and fled out of the room.

'Another time it was my birthday but he was terrible to me all day. The next day I found this note: "Jo – good morning.

Better late than never. Many happy returns of yesterday. Be a bit tolerant of me at my worst. Really, I don't want to hurt anyone ..."'

Often, when he'd resorted to a downer like Seconal or Nembutal, she wouldn't see him until early afternoon. 'As I passed his bedroom on my way up there would be notes left for me under the door. "Wake me at three o'clock with breakfast" – that meant three o'clock in the afternoon.'

Life could switch back to normality, as when his mother came to stay. Paradoxically, spells of normal illness put him, temporarily, back on the rails. 'He had a bout of jaundice while Queenie was there,' Joanne said. 'He got into a good routine then and really seemed to enjoy it. I remember on Saturday afternoon how thrilled he was that he and Peter Brown had been out to buy fruit. Brian thought that was wonderful. He'd done something normal – just the same as other people did.

'He did once confide in me how hopeless his private life was. "I'm no good with women and I'm no good with men," he told me. He was in absolute despair about it.

'His doctor told me once that he was like a terrible collision inside himself. He could only be terribly happy or terribly unhappy. If there was any depression or misery, Brian would be drawn helplessly into it. The Beatles caused that happiness and they caused that unhappiness. I don't think there'd been any hope for him since the day he met them.'

In October 1966 Alma Cogan, 'The Girl with the Giggle in Her Voice' whom Brian had once thought of marrying – and who would have changed his life immeasurably for the better if he'd done so – died from ovarian cancer aged thirty-four.

'Brian was at Alma's Shiva [memorial prayers],' her sister

Sandra told me. 'He came in very quietly and left before the end, but he wrote my mother a beautiful letter afterwards.'

Publicly, too, he was always there to strike the right note on his boys' behalf. When the Welsh mining village of Aberfan was engulfed by a giant coal-tip on 21 October, killing 144 people, most of them schoolchildren, he donated £1,000 to the disaster fund in The Beatles' name.

Early in November an American filmmaker named Tony Cox secured a booking at the Saville for his wife, the Japanese American performance artist Yoko Ono. Her show relied heavily on audience participation, as when she invited several people onstage, gave them fishing rods and challenged them to hook objects held up by their companions in the front stalls.

A couple of weeks later, at her first London exhibition, Yoko hooked John Lennon. But John, fearing for his Beatle image, wasn't to take things further for another eighteen months, by which time it wouldn't be Brian's problem.

*   *   *

Back in Liverpool, Harry and Queenie Epstein had left their spacious Queens Drive house some time since and downsized to a bungalow named 'Treetops' in Woolton, a couple of miles away. Just before Christmas, while they were dressing to go out for the evening, Harry suffered a heart attack and was taken to Sefton General Hospital. Brian immediately rushed to the bedside of the man whom, at the age of thirty-one, he still called 'Daddy'. Harry needed two stays in hospital totalling eleven weeks before being discharged with a stern warning to take things easier in future.

Father and elder son grew unwontedly close during this time, Brian even daring to buy the conservative Harry a selection of shirts and ties in modish Flower Power patterns. His visits were naturally of great interest to the female nursing staff though he would have preferred to keep a low profile. Harry always told him to 'wave to the ladies', the first real evidence of paternal pride he'd ever known.

After their diverse journeys, The Beatles had reassembled at Abbey Road studios with George Martin and were working on a new album said to be a celebration of their Liverpool childhoods. Brian – still keeping a respectful distance – hoped it would make up for their perceived abandonment of the city three years earlier.

One of the tracks that leaked out to him was Paul's 'Penny Lane' about a locale no less familiar to him than to its composer. As a teenager working with his father at I. Epstein's Walton store, he used to take a tram from the Penny Lane roundabout on mornings when he'd overslept and Harry had impatiently gone on ahead in the family Triumph Renown.

The perspicacious Wendy Hanson suggested he should fill the vacuum in his life by making the Saville a showcase for Britain's most exciting young playwrights. Brian jumped at this second chance of theatre production after the debacle of *A Smashing Day* and agreed with Wendy that he'd have to give up drugs if he didn't want to repeat it.

He insisted he could only do so at home, so 24 Chapel Street was swept clean of all pills and expensive round-the-clock nursing care set up to keep him on the new regimen. He seemed to be doing well until one afternoon when he persuaded the nurse on duty to let him go out for a walk, then disappeared for forty-eight hours. That was the end of the exciting young playwrights season.

267

Drugs made him lackadaisical even about so important a matter as The Beatles' third feature film for United Artists in succession to the worldwide smash hits *A Hard Day's Night* and *Help!*. Their interest in ensemble screen-acting having waned, this was to be a feature-length animation produced by an American named Al Brodax whose King Features company had made a hugely successful series of Beatles cartoon 'shorts' for ABC television.

Nothing being too good for The Beatles, Brodax commissioned around a dozen treatments for the film from distinguished writers including Joseph (*Catch-22*) Heller. Flying to London to advance the project, Brodax found himself in a Catch-22 of his own when Brian kept him waiting for ten days yet still dodged being tied down to a meeting.

In desperation, he sought help from Wendy Hanson who simply booked him a table next to Brian's regular one at the costly Les Ambassadeurs club in Hamilton Place. The formula agreed on was that The Beatles would be cartoon characters, voiced by soundalike actors, in a fantasy woven around and titled by their covert drug ad, 'Yellow Submarine'.

Brian, alas, wouldn't live to see it hailed as a masterpiece ranking with Walt Disney's *Fantasia*.

* * *

Since Wendy had first gone to work for him at the New York Plaza in 1964 she'd quit numerous times but always given way to his pleas – or The Beatles' – not to go. Then one evening he phoned her at home at 10 p.m. having lost the name and address she'd given him of a recording studio where he'd been expected four hours earlier.

268

When she protested at his absent-mindedness and the lateness of the hour, Brian retorted that it was her duty to be on call for anything at any time. Wendy said she was tired of being his nanny. She didn't relent the way she always had before, so he insisted she work out her full notice, even doing his Christmas shopping for him the way she always did, but then wrote her the most gracious of goodbye letters.

He had always been a compulsive gambler, whether with horse racing – preferably at Royal Ascot when he could don a grey tailcoat and top hat – or playing roulette with Elvis when the Colonel finally allowed them to meet, or backstage card games with his boys when he'd casually wager his gold Dunhill cigarette-lighter in pursuit of the smallest pot.

Now the new tracts of time open to him inexorably drew him to Mayfair's gaming clubs. Although Bryan Barrett was supposedly his bodyguard as well as chauffeur, Barrett had a healthy aversion to such places and refused to enter them, instead dropping Brian outside, then reluctantly giving the car keys to the doorman so that he could drive himself home later if he wasn't too stoned.

His favourite such haunt was the Clermont Club in Berkeley Square, an establishment catering to the aristocracy with a clientele said to include five dukes, five marquesses and twenty earls. Its owner, John Aspinall, presided over a 'Clermont Set' whose leading light, John Bingham, the seventh Earl of Lucan, a descendant of the man who led the cavalry during the Charge of the Light Brigade, would one day murder his children's nanny, seemingly mistaking her for his wife, and disappear from the face of the earth.

Since Aspinall was an undisguised anti-Semite, there could be no question of Brian joining the Clermont Set, but there was no objection to his money. He invariably played chemin-de-fer, a game for impatient thrill-seekers favoured by some of the club's highest rollers, Lord Lucan among them. As much as £50,000 might be won or lost in the space of a few minutes.

Sometimes he won a little – and his PA Joanne would find the money outside his bedroom door the next morning with a note saying, 'Jo, please bank my happiness' – but usually he lost on an epic scale.

Honest to the core, and with a touching belief in the straightness of the aristocracy, it never crossed his mind that the Clermont's 'chemmy' might be rigged against him personally. Moreover, it would have seemed the purest fiction had anyone warned him Aspinall was in cahoots with the arch-criminal Kray Twins to pile up his debts until he'd have no choice but to sell his boys to the Krays.

But it was fact.

At the time, still greater losses were weighing on his mind. The lawsuit against NEMS by Seltaeb, the US-based Beatles merchandising company, had by now been dragging on in New York for three years, expanding the latter's claim for damages from $5 million to $25 million and accumulating three tons of documents.

Brian had, in Geoffrey Ellis's phrase, adopted an 'ostrich' attitude to the case, avoiding any involvement – beyond hiring America's most famous trial lawyer, Louis Nizer, to represent NEMS – and failing to appear at any of its numerous pretrial hearings. But he was obliged to attend the culminating one, accompanied by his lawyer, David Jacobs, and Ellis.

For two gruelling days, he had to sit in the New York

Supreme Court, facing questions from Seltaeb's counsel to which his only answers could be that he didn't know or couldn't remember, and irked by the court's continual use of his hated middle name, Samuel. According to Ellis, he'd finally owned up to The Beatles about what had happened and they had been 'understanding', although perhaps not aware of just how much it had cost them.

He'd had no personal contact with any of the American manufacturers affected by his licensing muddle, but Seltaeb's British managing director, Nicky Byrne, still based in the US, knew several for whom cancellation of their orders for Beatle ware had led to financial ruin. One in particular had suffered a fatal heart attack from the stress and his grief-stricken son had turned up at Byrne's office, vowing revenge.

'This guy said he was going to take out a contract on Brian,' Byrne recalled. 'I thought it was just American bullshit so I jokingly said, "Wait until I've finished with him in the courts."'

* * *

The time had come to renegotiate the four-year contract The Beatles had signed with the Parlophone label in May 1962 at what now seemed the laughable royalty rate of one pre-decimal penny per double-sided record. Those pennies had of course turned into a phenomenal number of pounds and George Martin proved to be a producer beyond price. Nonetheless, Brian had no intention of letting his boys be taken for granted.

The deal to be made now was jointly with EMI and its US subsidiary, Capitol. Before weighing their offer, he put out feelers to other major American labels, expecting to be inundated by multimillion-dollar bids.

But none came. Columbia opined that after record sales of 180 million, The Beatles had peaked and could only go downhill (a view also held secretly by EMI's chairman, Sir Joseph Lockwood).

Atlantic, under its co-founder Ahmet Ertegun and legendary chief producer Jerry Wexler, saw no place for them in a catalogue devoted to R&B and soul. RCA, 'the Elvis label', sought to prove their suitability by showing Brian an album of bland Beatles cover-versions that made him walk out of the meeting, fuming that they were 'cabbage-heads'. So it was to be EMI/Capitol again, with his one-time adversary Alan Livingston raising the royalty to an unprecedented 9 per cent, adding a $2 million bonus and guaranteeing non-interference in The Beatles' album-cover choices, even should they ever repeat their blood-soaked 'Butcher' tableau for *The Beatles Yesterday and Today.*

Brian was absolutely certain the Beatles hadn't peaked but less so about his own position when his management contract with them expired, as it was to do four months after their recording one, in September 1967.

Hence the nearest he ever came to sharp practice in his dealings with them, seemingly born of a fear that they mightn't be with him for much longer. The recording contract contained a clause stipulating that NEMS Enterprises fixed 25 per cent of their royalties, both as a group and individually, be paid directly to the company for nine years (i.e., until 1976) regardless of whether he continued to manage them.

Having negotiated the clause, he worried about it so much that he developed glandular fever and had to let Peter Brown take the contract to them for signature. But, as usual, they signed without reading.

Few people apart from Brown and the ever-discreet Geoffrey Ellis were privy to his thoughts at this time when he seemed to waver between exhaustion and further ambition. One notable exception was Larry Parnes, the founding British pop mogul he'd always regarded as a mentor more than a competitor.

Invited to tea at Chapel Street, 'Mister Parnes Shillings and Pence' found Brian not quite over glandular fever, in bed in pyjamas and dressing-gown and with a yellowish tinge to his skin. He said he was too worn out to cope with NEMS any more and could leave if only Parnes would join the company in a senior executive role. But Parnes by that time wanted out of the pop business where his once numerous 'stable' had shrunk almost to nothing, and was planning to follow Brian into the theatre world.

'Don't step back from a business you've spent all these years creating because without you it will fragment and break up,' he advised but could see his words carried little weight. He therefore did not share the general surprise when, soon afterwards, Brian announced a merger of NEMS with the Robert Stigwood Organisation.

Australia born, Stigwood had emigrated to Britain in 1960 and found a way into the pop business during the pre-Beatles era when male vocalists had only to be good-looking. Indeed, he'd been behind Brian's touchstone single, 'Johnny Remember Me' by a barely in-tune actor named John Leyton, for which he'd arranged exposure on a new female-interest television soap, thereby ensuring it would reach number one.

Stigwood was Brian's age, shared his sexual orientation and

was known as 'Stiggy' to his 'Eppy' but otherwise they could not have differed more. Stigwood had always teetered on the edge of insolvency (which didn't curb a lavish lifestyle almost equalling Brian's) and done business in ways that frequently caused his associates to lay violent hands on him.

After a Rolling Stones tour of the UK he'd organised, the band received so little payment that Keith Richards beat him up in front of the high-fashion crowd at the Ad Lib club. 'He got the knee for every grand he owed us,' Richards recalled. 'Sixteen of them.' Scarier still – so the story went – was the penalty for trying to entice the Small Faces away from their manager Don Arden, the so-called 'Al Capone of Pop' (with whom Brian had clashed long ago over Little Richard at New Brighton's Tower Ballroom.) Turning up at Stigwood's office, accompanied by four heavies, Arden had scooped him from behind his desk and dangled him out of the fourth-floor window by his ankles.

For Brian this shady side was cancelled out by the names Stigwood could bring to NEMS for management or agency or the use of his Reaction record label, notably Cream and The Who. The arrangement was that they'd be joint managing directors for six months, then Stigwood would have the option to buy a majority shareholding for half a million pounds that would put The Beatles and Cilla Black to some degree in his control. 'Brian told me he wanted to get out of the business altogether,' Stigwood recalled. 'He was going to live in Spain and train bullfighters.'

But to The Beatles, the thought of exchanging Eppy for Stiggy was as appalling as if someone had suggested they be managed by the Kray Twins. Paul spoke for all four in saying that if it happened, they'd retaliate by recording nothing but 'God Save The Queen' backwards.

Just when Brian felt they no longer needed him came this unequivocal sign of how much they still did.

19

'EPPY IS STILL TOGETHER'

Brian had come late to LSD. He didn't get around to trying it until the winter of 1966–67, by which time it had become illegal and transformed pop music, that of his boys above all.

His initiation into its 'mind-expanding' properties had none of the shock or trauma John and George had experienced eighteen months earlier when unsuspectingly dosed with it at a dinner party given by their dentist. Brian took it of his own volition together with Peter Brown during a Saturday night in at Chapel Street.

That first trip, 'too important and powerful to convey in words', nonetheless didn't make him feel he could 'fly or jump hedges'. Likewise, the after-effects, so often bleakly horrific, were minimal compared with his hangovers from brandy or pill-popping. Overall, he felt that acid allowed him to know himself better and made him less prone to blushing temper tantrums. Few of its other converts would claim to have been shown such mercy.

At around the same time, Brown convinced him he should try to get out of London at weekends when loneliness and temptation combined most perilously. While most people of his means would have been content with a rented apartment or cottage, Brian demanded nothing less than a full-blown 'country seat'.

In February 1967 he paid £25,000 for Kingsley Hill, near Warbleton, Sussex, an eighteenth-century timber-framed house that Winston Churchill had used to confer with his service chiefs during the Second World War. Its location deep in prime Sussex countryside was not totally alien to Brian. His old friend John Pritchard, formerly conductor of the Liverpool Philharmonic Orchestra, lived in the neighbouring village of Herstmonceux, and Glyndebourne, whose summer opera festival he'd often attended, was a short drive away. A little further afield David Jacobs had a seaside home in Hove, where the newlywed Ringo Starrs had secretly honeymooned.

Kingsley Hill was a Grade II-listed gem with its oak beams and open fireplaces, and the modern touch of an extensive space under its eaves rather like the playroom at Chapel Street. While Jacobs handled the purchase, Brian and Geoffrey Ellis stayed with him and combed neighbouring Brighton's antiques district, The Lanes, for furniture and ornaments.

The only structural alteration Brian made to the house was to its classically elegant living room where, seemingly nostalgic for simpler times in Liverpool, he installed a replica of one of the audio-booths in his record department at NEMS' Whitechapel store.

The Beatles were early visitors, and signalled their approval by painting the roof space in the same psychedelic colours John had just decided on for his white Rolls-Royce. As a remembrance of themselves, they also tied a beetle-like insect in gold-coloured metal to one of the beams.

Where business was concerned, Brian stuck to his resolution to give them space to record with George Martin, whom he knew to be the safest possible pair of hands. Yet the pressure on them to put out a new single every three months remained as unrelenting as ever.

They had soon gone off the idea of an album inspired by their Liverpool childhoods and, with nothing else in the can, Martin had no choice but to release two of its tracks, Paul's 'Penny Lane' and John's 'Strawberry Fields Forever' as the greatest value double A-sided single of all time (which, ironically, became their first not to reach number one in the UK).

Brian was sent a test-pressing and praised both songs equally as 'Wonderful – the best ever'. Unfortunately, one of the strangers he was wont to take back to Chapel Street stole the pressing and, not content with that, left the familiar sentiment BRIAN EPSTEIN IS A QUEER scrawled on the garage door.

His boys' new idea was to step outside their own beleaguered selves and make a concept album portraying nameless members of a Victorian military band, with the help of stimulants no real Victorian military band ever enjoyed. Absorbed in this new project, they had even less time than usual to think about Brian – as both George and John would admit when it was too late.

'We never knew what he was up to, really,' George said. 'You'd just hear stories that he'd been robbed or he was beaten up by somebody. That happened to him when he took acid once, so I believe. I saw him a day or so afterwards. He'd been up in his room and he had all the newspapers and he'd ripped them into little pieces.'

'He had hellish tempers and fits and lock-outs and he'd vanish for days,' John said. 'We weren't too aware of it . . . He'd come

279

to a crisis now and then . . . because he'd been on sleeping pills for days on end and wouldn't be awake for days. Or beaten up by some docker in the Old Kent Road. Suddenly the whole business would stop because Brian would be missing.'

So now at Abbey Road studios, as a masterpiece palpably took shape, he would drop by half-apologetically with something for them to sign or approve then make himself scarce, unaware – as Sir Paul McCartney remembers – that they were pleased to see him and happy for him to be around as long as he liked. Since they were already in character as the notional Sergeant Pepper's bandsmen with military-looking moustaches and Brian was still clean-shaven, they straggle-haired and himself with a belated Beatle cut, he suddenly looked the youngest of them all.

By now he had come to recognise that the pills were a problem – as were the drinking, the gambling, the insomnia and depression – and began having treatment at The Priory, a private psychiatric hospital in Roehampton much frequented by show-business legends and wealthier members of the aristocracy. But he would always discharge himself after a few days, pronouncing himself cured, then return to his old habits.

* * *

Meanwhile all was far from well with the NEMS–Robert Stigwood merger. The intended super-company had instead become two mutually hostile camps, one reflecting Brian's scrupulous and gentlemanly way of doing things, the other Stigwood's dishonesty, disreputability and general dangle-out-of-window-worthiness. But there could be no doubting his eye for talent nor his forward vision.

Brian had recently been approached by three brothers, Barry, Robin and Maurice Gibb, British-born but raised in Australia, as a potential manager for their group, the Bee Gees. Seeing nothing special, he'd passed them to Stigwood, who instantly signed them to a five-year contract.

The Bee Gees' dirgey single 'New York Mining Disaster 1941' was widely played by deejays mistaking them for The Beatles, and made the British Top 20. That gave an extra edge to Brian's hostility, undiminished when each of the toothy brethren proved a talented songwriter.

Altogether it was a relief to get away to New York, as he regularly did, and the straightforward dealings of Nemperor Artists, the NEMS satellite-cum-independent talent agency he'd virtually given to his friend Nat Weiss. He was thinking of moving there permanently, for choice into a luxury high-rise called the St Tropez with a panoramic view of the East River.

Weiss had effectively become *his* manager, treating him with some of the same paternal solicitude he'd once lavished on The Beatles, whether making his travel and hotel arrangements for a (solitary) vacation in Mexico, settling the bills for the numerous town cars he would rent in Manhattan, then simply jettison when he'd done with them, or negotiating with the 'hard hat construction-worker types' he temporarily befriended over the price of their discretion.

For Brian, Weiss's greatest coup was not signing this or that new talent to Nemperor Artists but discovering the great matador Luis Miguel Dominguín was in town and arranging for the two of them to meet for cocktails and dinner. He was as overcome as any Beatles fan and only just restrained himself from asking for Dominguín's autograph.

Since The Beatles' withdrawal into the studio and consequent public silence, rumours had been rife that they might be breaking up or involved in some major disagreement with Brian, or both. On his visit that spring, Nat Weiss urged him to put an end to all such speculation.

Weiss arranged for him to appear on New York's leading pop radio station, WOL FM, at its evening peak hour and talk to its star deejay, Murray 'The K' Kaufman, who'd attached himself, limpet-like, to The Beatles on their triumphant advent in 1964.

Arriving at Brian's hotel to escort him to the studio, Weiss found he'd taken so many Seconals that he was barely conscious. Somehow his friend managed to revive him and deliver him to WOL FM with seconds to spare.

On the private tape Weiss made of the hour-long conversation, he's at first barely coherent as he says what everyone – he most of all – wants to hear. He and his boys are still as close as ever. 'There hasn't been so much as . . . a row.'

Gradually his head clears on the subject dearest to his heart. 'At the moment they're doing great things in the studio. They take longer nowadays, of their own volition, to make records. They're hyper-critical of their own work. Paul rang me the other day and said that he wanted to make just one small change to a track.

'I hope "Penny Lane" and "Strawberry Fields" are going to prove a thing or two. And certainly – *certainly* – the new album [*Sgt. Pepper's Lonely Hearts Club Band*] is going to prove more than a thing or two.'

'So there we go,' Murray the K signs off, clearly not quite convinced. 'It's good to know The Beatles are still together. Eppy is still together.'

Reluctantly returning home a few days later, he had a sudden premonition of death. 'He was certain his plane would crash,' Weiss recalled. 'I persuaded him to take the flight – which in fact was delayed a long while on the runway at Kennedy.'

Nonetheless, he insisted on writing down his 'last wish' in the airport coffee shop and giving it to Weiss to pass on in case he shouldn't survive. It was an instruction for the packaging of the new album that hadn't a hope of being followed: 'Brown paper bags for "Sgt. Pepper".'

Back in London he had to deal with a complication that would never have arisen but for the pills that clouded his memory.

The Beatles' third cinema film was supposedly to be *Yellow Submarine*, the feature-length animation for which the American producer Al Brodax had received the go-ahead a year earlier. Yet now, seemingly forgetful of *Yellow Submarine*, Brian joined Walter Shenson, the producer of *A Hard Day's Night* and *Help!*, in trying to set up *another* Beatles film, its subject matter still undecided.

A succession of top screenwriters pitched scripts, one a remake of *The Three Musketeers*, another a pastiche Western. The most promising imagined them as four different facets of the same person – essentially what they were as a music group – but the dialogue as it stood was unsatisfactory. Rather than try yet another screenwriter, Brian and Shenson decided to use one of the current crop of brilliant young British dramatists to 'punch up' the words.

In early 1967, the most brilliant was Joe Orton, a working-class boy from Leicester whose bleak comedies like *Entertaining Mr Sloane* and *Loot* were about social and sexual anarchy let loose in prim front parlours and kitchenettes. Orton, a besotted

Beatles fan, instantly accepted the commission and was invited to dinner at Chapel Street with Brian and Paul McCartney, the playgoer of the group who turned out to have invested £1,000 in *Loot*.

Afterwards Orton noted in his diary with a, for then, routine dash of prejudice: 'I'd expected Epstein to be florid, Jewish, dark-haired and overbearing. Instead I was face to face with a mousey-haired, slight young man. Washed out in a way [the mark of chronic pill-taking]. He had a suburban accent.'

Puzzlingly, Brian, that wishful man of the theatre, made no attempt to capitalise on meeting Orton, say by asking him to write something especially for the Saville or inviting him to first nights or parties. His being gay, gamin and wildly promiscuous seemed of no interest either.

His agent, the formidable Peggy Ramsay, negotiated the munificent fee of £10,000 and for two months Orton worked on the script, now titled *Up Against It*, in the Islington bed-sitting room he shared with his long-time lover, Kenneth Halliwell.

The result was his bizarrest flight of fancy to date, casting The Beatles variously as murderers, adulterers, drag-artists, assassins, arsonists, polygamists, saboteurs and convicts amid scenes of civil war, mass-murder and copulation. It was all clearly too ripe even for their new experimental mode, but Brian's usual punctiliousness failed to operate: after a long silence Orton's script was returned without comment. 'An amateur and a fool,' wrote Orton. 'Probably he will never say Yes. Equally he hasn't the courage to say No. A thoroughly weak, flaccid type.'

Up Against It was subsequently acquired by another producer who provisionally cast Mick Jagger to co-star. The director of *A Hard Day's Night* and *Help!* Richard Lester was invited on board and a meeting between Orton and Lester scheduled at Twickenham film studios.

Orton never kept the appointment. The night before, in their bedsitter, Kenneth Halliwell beat him to death with a hammer in a jealous rage, then took his own life with an overdose of Nembutal.

* * *

The five months of recording *Sgt. Pepper's Lonely Hearts Club Band* might have separated The Beatles from Brian but its pre-production and release made them one again.

Its cover was at the furthest possible remove from his 'brown paper bags', a Pop Art fantasy showing the band as sateen hussars, John yellow, Paul blue, George orange and Ringo pink amid a collage of celebrity images from both low and high culture, from Marilyn Monroe to Karl Marx, Bob Dylan to James Joyce, Oscar Wilde to Marlon Brando.

EMI would allow the cover only if permissions were obtained from those among the chosen sixty-two icons who were still alive. The one person capable of tracing, contacting and shmoozing them into acquiescence was Brian's former PA, Wendy Hanson, whom he traced, contacted and shmoozed into returning to NEMS for the nightmare task.

Both his homes were to be co-opted in promoting the album, Chapel Street for its international press launch on 19 May, Kingsley Hill for a celebration party on the twenty-eighth. The fact that he was currently back at The Priory as an in-patient presented no obstacle for its non-institutional regime allowed him to come and go as he pleased during the day.

He could therefore attend the press launch at Chapel

Street – where Paul and an American photographer named Linda Eastman were observed in earnest conversation – without any journalist suspecting he'd be returning to a hospital bed that night. Two more exeats followed on successive days: to visit Ringo and his family at home in Surrey and back to Chapel Street for lunch with Harry and Queenie.

Sgt. Pepper's Lonely Hearts Club Band was released on 1 June. It topped the UK album charts for twenty-seven weeks, selling half a million in its first month, and in America stayed number one for nineteen weeks, selling 2.5 million by August.

In Britain it marked the beginning of the Summer of Love, the apogee of the hippie and Flower Power era and seeming affirmation of the power of young people and their music to change the world for the better. Millions would always recall exactly where they were and what they were doing when they first heard it, as less fortunate generations past and to come recalled outbreaks of war, the assassination of public figures or great natural disasters.

Brian's guests at Kingsley Hill two days earlier for what was equally a belated housewarming included Mick Jagger and Marianne Faithfull, Lionel Bart, Nat Weiss, the classical conductor John Pritchard and the zany deejay Kenny Everett. The Beatles' former press officer, Derek Taylor, was flown over from California, where he'd been co-organising the Monterey Pop Festival, with his seven months-pregnant wife Joan. An invitation had even been sent to Private Brian Joyce (c/o Chelsea Barracks London SW1), the young Coldstream Guardsman with whom Brian still kept up a platonic friendship despite often wishing it were more.

Three Beatles only were present, Paul having preferred to be with Jane Asher after her return from a trip to America. That effectively blighted Brian's day, for Paul was still the one he wanted most to impress.

Lavish supplies of acid had been shipped from the drug's master chemist in San Francisco, Owsley Stanley, and brought down to rural Sussex in John's psychedelically decorated Rolls-Royce. Everyone partook greedily of it, even Derek Taylor's heavily pregnant wife and John's neglected one, Cynthia, who'd vowed never to touch it again after being covertly dosed with it at the dentist's dinner party. The resulting trip so magnified her unhappiness that she briefly contemplated throwing herself from an upstairs window onto the paving stones below.

All this was astonishingly foolhardy of Brian. The police were cracking down hard on pop musicians who did drugs; here they could have netted three of his boys in one swoop and himself for allowing his premises to be used for the purpose.

Especially vulnerable was Mick Jagger, someone they were longing to put behind bars and had every prospect of doing so. Three months earlier on the other side of Sussex, Jagger and his fellow Rolling Stone, Keith Richards, had been busted together for minuscule offences and were currently awaiting trial.

But, in a final stroke of Epstein luck, the Law never showed.

* * *

For three years Brian had striven with only patchy success to build a profile as a TV presenter or record producer-performer or theatre director; however, in the aftermath of *Sgt. Pepper* he found himself acquiring a substantial role almost without trying.

On 5 June, Israel launched a pre-emptive strike against the surrounding Arab states that had menaced it since its creation in

1948. Though its victory in this six-day war was never in doubt, many leading Jewish figures in the entertainment industry sent it hefty financial aid.

As a victim of anti-Semitism his whole life, Brian might have been expected to be in the front rank of donors yet he declined to contribute a penny, thereby incurring sharp criticism from senior members of his faith. 'I refuse to help Israel's war effort because I'm as sorry for a wounded Arab as I am for a wounded Israeli,' he explained. 'People are fundamentally all the same and I can't discriminate ... I believe in and want to help as far as I can to understand mankind and every colour, creed, religion and nationality.'

It was the first in a series of public pronouncements that won him increasing attention as the Summer of Love progressed with its plentiful interleaving of the opposite. On 15 June, Paul gave an interview to Independent Television News, admitting he'd taken LSD 'about five times' before it was made illegal and creating almost as great a furore as John's 'more popular than Jesus' comment a year earlier.

For Brian it was an opportunity to stand shoulder-to-shoulder with the Beatle who'd always seemed to need him least, and damn the consequences. In a series of detailed interviews with *Melody Maker*'s Mike Hennessey, he admitted taking LSD himself when it *was* illegal as well as smoking pot 'from time to time'.

His acid trips had had only positive effects, he said, reducing both his ego and tendency to bad temper, nor had he ever feared becoming addicted to it or marijuana either: 'I am in no way addicted to alcohol and seldom smoke cigarettes.' The pills didn't get a mention though.

Here, too, he made his first, oblique acknowledgement of

his homosexuality in view of the pending Act of Parliament to partly decriminalise it. 'I think society's whole attitude to soft drugs will eventually change. There is a parallel with homosexuality when that was a cardinal sin. Isn't it silly we have had to wait all this time for the reforming legislation to go through?'

No topic, in fact, was off the table. What did he fear most in life, Hennessey asked.

'Loneliness,' he replied. 'I hope I'll never be lonely. Although actually one inflicts loneliness on oneself to a certain extent.'

The Summer of Love was taking root far outside its country of origin. On 25 June, The Beatles starred in *Our World*, a BBC television programme using the new satellite technology to disseminate images from twenty-four different countries – apart from them, rather boring ones – as a symbol of global togetherness.

A decade earlier, Paul had first beheld John performing to an audience of around forty at a church garden fete; now the four would have one of around 40 million. It was an opportunity to bestow a first honour on the young man who'd turned them into ambassadors for Britain on such a scale – but of course was not taken.

Their principal engineer at Abbey Road, Geoff Emerick, recalled that when Brian took the idea to them during the *Sgt. Pepper* sessions, they were unenthusiastic about a seeming breach of their ban on performing live. He not only talked them round but persuaded them the broadcast deserved more than just a *Pepper* track, however wondrous; hence John's 'All You Need is Love'.

As the album settled down to its eternal life, his focus returned to NEMS and the new regime he'd installed. Although he and Robert Stigwood were theoretically joint managing directors, Vic Lewis was still on the board and invariably sided with Stigwood to outvote him.

He was therefore powerless to stop NEMS promoting a British tour by The Monkees, who'd been recruited for an American TV series about a wacky Beatley group and blatantly copied his boys except in musical brilliance.

His disengagement from the company was most keenly felt by Cilla Black, who had once rivalled The Beatles in his affections and whose image he'd crafted even more lovingly than theirs.

Cilla was currently co-starring with Frankie Howerd in a hit West End show, *Way Out in Piccadilly*, and took it deeply amiss that Brian had dropped by to check on her only a couple of times in the entire run. Plus, she was furious with him for his pot-smoking confession when he didn't like her even to smoke cigarettes in public.

A lunch was hastily arranged with Cilla and husband Bobby at which Brian managed to reassure her of his wholehearted attention and commitment, and that no one would automatically think she too smoked pot, as she'd feared.

He had long felt that her personality made her a 'natural' for television and the last significant deal he ever did was with the BBC's Head of Light Entertainment, Bill Cotton, concerning the first of many series that would make her one of its best-loved faces.

* * *

At the time, The Beatles were about to receive a payout of around £2m in record royalties which, under the Labour government's 'supertax' regime, would virtually disappear if each paid his share as a private citizen. Their accountants' advice was to sink the money collectively into a business, so incurring far less punitive corporation tax. Brian felt they should remain creators rather than try to become businessmen but he went along with the idea, seeing it as a further way of keeping Robert Stigwood at arm's length from them. The company name Apple – Paul's suggestion – was registered in May 1967, with Brian and his brother Clive joining them as directors but with no clear idea yet of what its business would be.

Given Brian's background and original talent, something in retailing seemed the obvious course. He suggested a chain of shops selling nothing but greetings-cards like those to be seen nowadays at every major train station, but they thought that much too straightforward and uncool.

While the disposition of their millions was being debated, the four had the semblance of hippies to end all hippies, even considered taking the ultimate hippie step of living communally with their wives, partner and children, going 'back to Nature' in every way, except for their money and their roadies.

Their idea was to purchase some idyllic English village and live in adjacent houses around its postcard-perfect village green. Brian affected tolerant amusement but in reality any sign of them acting independently must have caused him agony. He now felt sure that when his management contract expired in September, it would not be renewed – though so far he'd taken only Larry Parnes into his confidence about the matter.

'He said the Beatles were leaving him,' Parnes recalled. 'They were giving him notice.'

As a grace-note to the Summer of Love, the 1967 Sexual Offences Act, ratified that July in England and Wales, de-criminalised homosexual acts between consenting males over twenty-one but left those with Brian's preferences still on the wrong side of the law. And no amount of legislation ever would eradicate the homophobia that had been his birthright.

When Nat Weiss next came to London, he was back in The Priory, this time with no day-release option. Weiss visited him, accompanied by Robert Stigwood, for whom it was clearly an irksome duty since he left after a few minutes. According to Weiss, Brian by now rued the day he'd merged operations with Stigwood and felt the company was slipping away from him. 'He said he was always telling Robert to do things [at NEMS] that Robert obviously had no intention of doing.'

One of his boys, at least, had realised that all was not well with him – the one who, as a rule, seemed least likely to care. 'When I was there, a big bouquet of flowers arrived from John Lennon,' Weiss told me. 'The card from John said, "You know I love you – I really mean that." When Brian read it, he just broke down.

'He begged me to stay on until he got out of the clinic but I needed to get back to New York to look after Nemperor Artists. That was the last time I ever saw him.'

20

'Beware the Ides of March'

For the past three months Harry and Queenie Epstein had been renting a flat in Bournemouth on the South Coast to allow Harry a complete recovery from his heart attack. They liked the placid seaside town so much that they were thinking of moving there and Harry even talked about opening a small shop as a hobby for his retirement.

It was never to happen. On 17 July, Queenie awoke to find him dead from a second heart attack, aged sixty-three.

Brian had just returned from Knokke Le Zoute in Belgium where several NEMS artists had been competing in the Knokke Song Festival – a wearisome chore since it was nowhere near as prestigious as the Eurovision Song Contest – when the distraught phone call came from his brother Clive.

For a while, the shock was delayed by the responsibility he naturally assumed in dealing with the formalities that follow any sudden death: arranging for Harry to be brought home to Liverpool and organising a funeral befitting so prominent a member of its business community. It wasn't until the car journey from Long Lane Jewish cemetery after the interment that he remembered 'Daddy's' softer side and wept uncontrollably.

293

Harry had been the only man Queenie ever loved and, although still only fifty-two, she now regarded her life as over. Brian set out to convince her it could still be worth living; he returned to Liverpool to see her every weekend, engaged a live-in housekeeper to keep her company when he wasn't there and phoned her religiously at the same time every evening.

His public profile received a further boost in the wake of an episode which, more than any other, revealed Britain's bountiful Summer of Love to be a sham and a delusion.

In June, Mick Jagger and Keith Richards had paid the penalty for their long hair and risqué lyrics with a ludicrous show trial and prison sentences for microscopic drug offences, though both were then freed pending their appeals.

Their case reignited the fierce debate between those who saw pot as an instrument of the Devil and those for whom it was a harmless recreation – by now no longer just hippies. On 24 July *The Times* carried a full-page advertisement in the form of a letter from sixty-four prominent figures in the arts, media, science and medicine, asserting 'that the law against marijuana is immoral in principle and unworkable in practice'.

Its signatories included Brian and The Beatles, each of their names followed by MBE, his by nothing. *The Times* had had last-minute qualms about the ad and insisted its cost, £1,800, be paid upfront. Brian messengered them a personal cheque.

The next day – which happened to mark the end of the week-long Shiva for his father – he wrote to thank Nat Weiss in New York, for Weiss's message of condolence. Comforting Queenie, he said, had comforted him with the realisation that someone could need him so much. He confessed that 'the un-worldly Jewish circle of my parents' and brother's friends' was not as boring as he'd always thought as they rallied round with food and love: 'provincial maybe, but warm, sincere and basic'.

He was looking forward to returning to New York on 2 September. As well as running Nemperor Artists, Weiss was attempting to revive his performing career and was negotiating for him to present a series of television talk shows for the Canadian Broadcasting Company. That meant the two of them calling on CBC in Toronto before going on to Los Angeles to check out a potential new signing named Harry Nilsson.

The letter mentioned 'a divine time' when all four Beatles, their wives, partner and roadies had spent a weekend at Kingsley Hill where they'd been joined on the Sunday by Mick Jagger and Marianne Faithfull.

'Poor Mick', wrote Brian, unable to resist, adding 'he looked beautiful ... I hope he gets off when the appeal [against his prison sentence] comes up at the end of the month. Of course the whole thing from the beginning was stupidly handled.' A moment of untypical *Schadenfreude* this, since the Stones' manager was NEMS' former PR man, Andrew Oldham.

His latest news about the boys was that in their quest for communal living and a refuge from their fans they'd 'gone to Greece to buy an island'. The role he might have played in the search had been pre-empted by John's Greek protégé, 'Magic' Alex Mardas; it had progressed as far as negotiations with the country's fascist military government over residency permits and securing the British Treasury's permission to transfer the necessary funds abroad.

'I think it's a dotty idea,' Brian told Weiss, seemingly not feeling not at all excluded, 'but they're no longer children and must have their own sweet way.'

As always, his innermost thoughts tended to surface while he was being driven somewhere by Bryan Barrett. 'Beware the Ides of March,' Barrett once heard him murmur, quoting the soothsayer in Shakespeare's *Julius Caesar* who warns Caesar of his imminent carve-up in the Senate. And another time, clearly reflecting on The Beatles: 'I feel as though I'm Svengali who's created a monster.'

A particular train of thought startled even his phlegmatic chauffeur: he asked Barrett to arrange the murder of his oldest friend Peter Brown and how much it would cost, though without giving any reason. 'I told him there were ways of getting it done,' Barrett recalled. '[I said] "money speaks, sir, but do you really want to do it?"' There, to his relief, the matter rested.

One evening at Robert Stigwood's flat, Brian met a young newcomer to the management game who out-poshed him with a double-barrelled, hyphenated surname: Simon Napier-Bell. He too was gay, with an openness following the new Sexual Offences Act that was still denied to Brian.

Napier-Bell would later recall a bizarre night out with Stigwood and Brian at Battersea Funfair, where they'd gone seeking 'action' but ended up sampling some of the rides and sideshows. Among the latter was a distorting mirror warranted to 'turn a man into a woman' that the others persuaded Brian to try. His reflection, said Napier-Bell, was unnervingly feminine.

Brian later phoned him and asked him out to dinner, which he welcomed as an opportunity to pick up tips about the business from a master. However, it soon became plain this was not the whole idea and Napier-Bell had no wish to take things further.

Afterwards he received several invitations to Kingsley Hill

for the weekend, but managed to turn them down without giving offence.

* * *

On 14 August Queenie Epstein arrived at Chapel Street for a ten-day visit. She'd recently seen Brian only in mourning black, so was disconcerted by his new look as an upmarket hippie, the mode which had made straight and gay men indistinguishable. But she said nothing, only wondered what his father would have thought of his frill-fronted, puffy sleeved yellow shirt, black and white-striped hipster trousers and hair now almost as long as his boys'.

For those ten days, he abstained from all pills and nocturnal forays and reshuffled his wildly disordered nights and days with the dual object of entertaining his mother and convincing her that all was fine with him.

The result was the most stable routine he'd followed for years. Each morning, she would come into his bedroom and draw the curtains just as she used to when he was a child; they'd have breakfast together, then Brian would go off to his former Stafford Street office – reinstated as part of the deception – back in a maternally reassuring business suit.

In the evening he'd take her to some trendy restaurant he knew she'd love, like Robert Carrier's in Islington, or they'd revive their shared passion for the cinema, both of them particularly loving *A Man for All Seasons* starring Paul Scofield and Susannah York, a student with Brian at RADA. During this week with Queenie, the chronic insomniac and small-hours gambler seldom went to bed later than eleven.

Brian had never been able to talk to his father about his sexual orientation. Over time Harry had learned to live with it rather like an ineradicable stain on the carpet; he maintained that he wouldn't expect to know about his son's private life if it were a heterosexual one, and the same applied here.

But Queenie had conscientiously read up on the subject, as far as she was able, and would sit for hours with Brian in their new shared loneliness, holding both his hands and doing her best to understand what he did so imperfectly himself. He'd persuaded her to move down to London some time previously, and to keep her close to him was buying her a flat at Whaddon House, his former domicile in Knightsbridge.

On 23 August he wrote again to Nat Weiss about his imminent New York visit, asking Weiss to arrange a yachting trip with 'all manner of pretty persons aboard' – implicitly non-female ones – and a reunion with his old Liverpool Playhouse friend Bryan Bedford who'd be 'appearing in something with Peter Ustinov at Lincoln Center'. Plus, it would be 'fun' to go to a Judy Garland concert. 'If tickets are difficult, try her people. I *do* know her.'

'Till the 2nd,' he ended with a hippie flourish, 'love, flowers, bells, be happy and look forward to the future. With love Brian.'

On the morning of Queenie's last day at Chapel Street, he met with all four Beatles to hear about the new film they were planning, this time without a professional director. He said their *Magical Mystery Tour* sounded a wonderful idea, one perhaps even surpassing *Sgt. Pepper's Lonely Hearts Club Band*.

In the afternoon, Paul dropped by with his Old English sheepdog Martha and asked Brian's PA Joanne to look after her while he and Jane Asher joined John, George and their wives at a lecture to be given by the Indian guru Maharishi Mahesh Yogi at the London Hilton hotel.

The next day, as Britain was winding down to the August Bank Holiday long weekend, it was reported they'd become followers of the Maharishi's Transcendental Meditation movement, allured by its promise of 'inner peace', and had agreed to an immediate induction at a seminar for his followers in Bangor, North Wales.

Brian, who stood in greater need of inner peace than most, said he'd try to join them there later, but in fact had other, non-spiritual plans for the weekend. After the strain of ten days' good behaviour for his mother's benefit, in Peter Brown's words, 'he felt like playing'. And the most private place to do it was Kingsley Hill.

That Friday, The Beatles' party, plus the late addition of their friends Mick Jagger and Marianne Faithfull, battled through gawping holiday crowds at London Euston station to catch the Maharishi's ordinary, grimy train service to North Wales. It was the first time for years that any of them had travelled other than First Class, with a heavy security screen; John compared it to 'going out without our trousers'. Nothing could have been more unlike the way Brian always organised things.

The master arranger, meanwhile, was en route for Kingsley Hill to make advance preparations for his Bank Holiday house guests. At the last minute he'd invited Joanne and her friend, the singer Lulu, to join them, but both had prior social commitments.

'He drove off on his own that Friday afternoon,' Joanne would recall. 'He seemed really bright and happy and the weather was beautiful. The Bentley was parked outside the house with its top down. I walked him to the car and as he pulled away, he turned and waved to me. That was the last time I saw Brian alive.'

* * *

He'd looked forward to another 'divine time' in Sussex, but it was not to be.

There was someone he particularly hoped to see at Kingsley Hill – never named but most likely Simon Napier-Bell. On arriving there, his sunny mood vanished with the news that this most desirable invitee wouldn't be making an appearance. So for the three long days of the holiday, his only companions were to be two old friends, Peter Brown and Geoffrey Ellis, and the chances of the excitement he craved were therefore negligible.

For 'excitement', of course, read 'danger'. All through dinner with Brown and Ellis that evening he was irritable and abstracted and directly afterwards began phoning various agencies in London that peddled young men for sex, still under the Victorian name of 'rent boys' and below the age of consent prescribed by the Sexual Offences Act.

When there proved to be no availability anywhere, he announced he was returning to London at once, leaving his friends to make use of his house as they pleased. Neither was offended nor surprised; they had experienced such mini-tantrums many times before. Brown followed him out to the Bentley and suggested that after all the wine and port he'd consumed, perhaps he oughtn't to drive.

His answer suggested he might only be going for a spin in the lingering twilight to put himself in a better mood. 'He said he'd be all right, I should go to bed and that we would all be together the next morning for breakfast,' Brown would recall. 'I had no belief in that at all. I hadn't seen Brian at breakfast for years.'

After he'd gone, one of the agencies he had contacted did manage to meet his order for three young men and dispatched them the fifty-five miles to Kingsley Hill in a black London taxi where they found there was still a demand for their services.

Late the following afternoon, Brian phoned Brown from Chapel Street to apologise for his bad manners the evening before. Brown gathered that on reaching London, he'd cruised the West End for a while, but had gone home alone, taken a sleeping pill and gone to bed. He still sounded so woozy that Brown begged him not to drive back to Sussex if he intended to return but to take a train instead.

That evening, Queenie Epstein contacted Brown to say Brian hadn't phoned her as he normally did without fail at bang-on the agreed time. Having learned he was at Chapel Street, she spoke to his Spanish butler, Antonio Garcia, who told her he was asleep. To the end of her life, Queenie would reproach herself for her answer: 'Don't wake him.'

On Sunday, Joanne Newfield was having lunch with her mother in Stanmore, her reason for missing the Kingsley Hill house party, when Garcia phoned her to say that Brian's Bentley was still parked outside 24 Chapel Street where he'd left it sometime during the early hours of Saturday morning and he was apparently still asleep.

Joanne wasn't especially perturbed since he often 'checked out', as he called it, for days at a time; nonetheless, she hurried straight over there. She had her own front-door key and as she let herself into the house, she would recall, she sensed that something wasn't right.

With Garcia and his wife Maria, annoyance at this interruption of their Bank Holiday off duty had become genuine anxiety. Garcia had last spoken to Brian when serving him 'breakfast' at around 5 p.m. the previous day, at which time he'd been sitting up in bed, talking on the telephone. Since then his bedroom door had been locked and he hadn't responded to knocks or buzzes of his bedside intercom.

Joanne's knocks and buzzes proving equally fruitless, she telephoned Peter Brown in Sussex to apprise him of the situation and get permission to break down the door. Brown was at first reluctant to give it; there had been so many similar scares that turned out to be false alarms with Brian at his most imperious demanding what all the fuss was about.

Brian's doctor, Norman Cowan, was away on holiday, so Brown gave Joanne the phone number of his own, John Gallwey, who agreed to come at once. Gallwey was in no doubt that the door should be forced and did so himself, helped by Garcia, with Joanne and Maria watching and Brown still hanging on the phone.

There was a small outer lobby to the bedroom, which was in semi-darkness with all the curtains drawn as if waiting for Queenie to open them. Brian, clad in pyjamas, lay on his side on top of the bed, whose coverlet was strewn with opened correspondence, a script for the *Yellow Submarine* film and a novel he'd evidently been reading, *The Rabbi* by Noah Gordon, left open at his place. Beside him was a plate with two chocolate digestive biscuits; on the shelved bedside table were an empty coffee mug and soft-drink bottle and several vials of pills.

Joanne approached and shook him, but there was no response. 'Even though I knew he was dead, I pretended to the others that he wasn't,' she recalled. "It's all right," I kept saying, "he's just asleep . . . he's fine."

'The doctor led me out of the room then. Maria was there screaming "Why? Why?" Peter Brown was still holding on the phone.'

Joanne had also summoned Alistair Taylor, Brian's fellow Liverpudlian and longest-serving employee, who was just back from a trip to America on NEMS business. Another old hand at Epstein false alarms, Taylor had told his wife, Lesley, that he didn't expect to be too long.

He was struck by how 'normal' Brian looked, immaculate even in pyjamas, with the voluminous correspondence, rather highbrow reading-matter and chocolate digestives. Nonetheless, realising the police would have to be involved, he did a quick scan of the room for drugs, ignoring the pills – which he presumed had been on prescription – and removing only a single joint he knew Brian would have been incapable of rolling himself.

At this moment of shock and confusion, Joanne took a phone call supposedly from the *Daily Express* in Fleet Street. That in itself was no surprise but the timing was. 'We'd broken down the bedroom door at about two o'clock and by about three this reporter was saying, "We've heard that Brian Epstein's terribly ill – is there any truth in it?" Only six of us knew what had happened and none of us would have contacted the press. How they'd found out was a complete mystery.'

Although the police were close at hand, in Rochester Row, Victoria, some little time elapsed before they were called. First, Peter Brown had to drive up from Sussex with Geoffrey Ellis to take stock of the situation and then break the news to Clive

Epstein. Joanne heard Clive's voice down the line shout, 'You're lying! You're lying!' in the double agony of losing a brother and having to tell their mother. And with a post-mortem inevitable, David Jacobs, had to travel from his home in almost-as-distant Hove to take charge of matters far removed from his usual cocktail-partying milieu.

When the Law did arrive, it was in strength led by a uniformed inspector, George Howlett, who made a preliminary examination of Brian's body and did a count of the pill bottles and vials on his bedside table, in his bathroom cabinet and briefcase. Including empties, there were thirty.

By early evening, a crowd had gathered outside 24 Chapel Street to see the body taken away in a makeshift police coffin. Joanne physically attacked a press photographer who focused on it because 'I couldn't bear the thought of people seeing Brian in a thing like that.'

A prerequisite of The Beatles' meditation retreat with the Maharishi at a Welsh teacher-training college was total isolation from the outside world. But on Bank Holiday Monday, as they strolled in the grounds with their guru, a telephone began ringing so insistently that Paul gave in and ran to answer it.

'Yeah,' he was heard to say, 'yeah ... yeah', like in the song, and then: 'Christ, *NO!*'

21

'HIS LAST STARTLING WORDS'

'EPSTEIN (THE BEATLE-MAKING PRINCE OF POP) DIES AT 32' was the London *Daily Mirror*'s front-page banner head-line on 1 September 1967. Were the newly departed allowed a peep at their own valedictions, one feels that Brian would have liked that.

The rival tabloid *Sunday People* had interviewed him a short while previously but not yet run the story, which now could be presented as 'his last startling words'.

Startling indeed: he'd admitted that six months earlier, de-pression had almost driven him to suicide and that, although he would have liked to be married – even citing Mick Jagger's partner, Marianne Faithfull, as his first choice – 'I have found women vulnerable in the affectionate aspect of life so therefore my trust has been placed in men.' It was the nearest he'd ever come to coming out.

George Martin heard the news in Wiltshire, where he'd been spending the Bank Holiday at his country cottage with his wife, Judy, and their newborn daughter, Lucy. As he was parking his car, a stranger approached and told him abruptly, 'Your friend is dead.'

After Lucy's birth on 9 August Brian had sent a giant teddy bear made of flowers to the hospital. And when the Martins had taken the baby home to their London house, a bouquet from him to Judy was waiting on the doorstep.

In New York, Nat Weiss was making final preparations for Brian's arrival the next day: his usual suite at the Waldorf Tower, the stretch limo from the airport with a cassette of new American pop hits he had pre-selected.

Weiss dropped everything and booked the next available flight to London. As he rushed out of his apartment, something made him slip Brian's last letter – the one ending 'love, flowers, bells, be happy and look forward to the future' – into his briefcase.

At the Saville Theatre, where Jimi Hendrix was booked for two performances, the outgoing audience from the first heard the news from the incoming one. There was some talk of cancelling that show but the manager, John Lydon, decided it was the last thing Brian would have wanted. So even in death he represented customer satisfaction.

Elvis Presley, his ideal of ultimate, unsurpassable fame before he strayed into The Cavern, sent the Beatles a message saying, 'Deepest condolences on the loss of a good friend to you and all of us.'

Among the welter of obituaries – none fully grasping the magnitude of Brian's achievement – the most perceptive was by Mike Sarne, who'd briefly been famous in the early '60s (under Robert Stigwood's management) as the first British pop star to be university-educated.

Writing in the *Jewish Chronicle*, Sarne characterised him as 'never completely au courant with the music he was so much

306

involved in. He was always a little surprised by success despite the fact that he worked so hard for it ... In the end [he] was a confused, slightly melancholy figure, at odds with his artistic inadequacy and his decency and good sense.'

The man who'd sent other people so many flowers was finally to receive some payback. On the day after his death, some stealthy mourner left five red carnations in a row on the top front doorstep of 24 Chapel Street, their only message a sheet of paper saying, 'We love you too.'

With his preference for understatement as well as his need of love, Brian would most certainly have liked that.

* * *

Like his father six weeks earlier, he was taken home to Liverpool for a funeral at Greenbank Park synagogue – although Harry's obsequies hadn't had the shadow of a post-mortem and inquest hanging over them. It was a private family ceremony with only a select few outsiders: Cilla Black, Gerry Marsden, Peter Brown and Nat Weiss. By agreement with Queenie and Clive, The Beatles didn't attend, in order to prevent it from turning into a screaming riot.

Even here, Brian received less than his due. Rather than extolling his achievements, from Beatlemania back to his word-perfect bar mitzvah performance, the officiating rabbi, Dr Norman Solomon, clearly no pop fan, described him as 'a symbol of the malaise of our generation'.

At Long Lane cemetery, to his mother's further distress, he was not interred beside Harry but on a different avenue some way off. Strict Jewish funerary procedure was observed with only the male mourners following the coffin on foot to the

307

graveside for its ritual sprinkling of earth before full burial took place.

Queenie remained impressively calm but Cilla – doubtless recalling her gripes about Brian and the television career he'd then handed her – broke down in tears and needed Valium to get her through the rest of the day.

Normally, flowers have no role in Jewish cemeteries, where remembrance is signified by small stones placed on the graves. However, George, the hippiest Beatle, had given Nat Weiss a single sunflower as his tribute to Brian, full of cosmic significance but rather crushed by the journey from London, which Weiss discreetly threw onto his coffin.

For several days after his death there were newspaper stories of police 'probes' into his last hours and of the pills removed from 24 Chapel Street. These probes seemingly revealed nothing of interest and were soon discontinued; nonetheless, a rumour took root – and still lingers to this day – that Brian had taken his own life, unable to face it without The Beatles.

True, he had thought of doing so many times apart from the one mentioned in that *Sunday People* interview. When his PA, Joanne Newfield, was given the distasteful job of clearing out his bedroom following the removal of his body, she found two suicide notes, possibly versions of the same one, that had never been put to use.

Yet, as his last letter to Nat Weiss showed, he'd become reconciled to a less paternalistic role where The Beatles were concerned ('They're no longer children and must have their own sweet way') and was eagerly anticipating new challenges with Nemperor Artists.

That apart, there were two equally compelling reasons why,

however despairing or attention-seeking, Brian would never have taken such a step. In Judaism, which he respected so deeply, suicide is a sin. And at the moment when she needed him most, he could never have deserted his mother.

* * *

The inquest took place on 8 September at Westminster Coroner's Court and was, by any measure, a perfunctory and sloppy affair. A notable exception to the newspaper reporters who packed the court was Brian's former 'houseman', Lonnie Trimble, who still felt great affection for him and had been mortified to hear of his passing.

Trimble sat through the entire hearing, afterwards remarking cryptically that 'there were a hell of a lot of lies told' but otherwise maintaining the perfect discretion on which Brian could always count.

Doctor John Flood, a psychiatrist at The Priory hospital, testified to having first seen Brian three months earlier, when his main symptoms were insomnia, depression and 'excessive irritability'. He'd claimed not to have slept for two or three nights previously despite taking large doses of sleeping pills.

It had emerged that for eighteen months to two years he'd been 'quite significantly depressed' and had previously been in the care of two other psychiatrists but hadn't persisted with them. There had been times however when he'd been 'relatively well'.

For the past five years he'd been taking large quantities of amphetamines, had regularly used marijuana and 'experimented' with heroin without becoming addicted. He also drank excessively and had a tendency to take excessive doses of any drug although, in the psychiatrist's view, was not classifiable as a drug addict. In addition, he'd shown signs of 'emotional instability . . . He was homosexual and unable to come to terms with this problem.'

Flood had immediately admitted him to The Priory for a two-week course of sleep therapy and antidepressants that had brought about a marked improvement until the death of his father knocked him back again.

His last consultation had been in July, during his day-release visits at the time of the *Sgt. Pepper* album when he'd admitted to once more taking large quantities of sleeping pills and alcohol, and Flood had delivered a stern warning about the dangers of mixing the two, especially if the pills were barbiturates.

Peter Brown described the events at Kingsley Hill, Brian's arrival 'relaxed and happy', his change of mood and abrupt exit, but omitting the taxi-load of too-youthful male sex-workers who'd subsequently appeared there.

Inspector George Howlett, the only police witness from those who'd gone to Chapel Street, recalled making a preliminary examination of his body while it still lay as it had been discovered, and gathering up the thirty bottles and vials of pills from his bedroom, bathroom and briefcase.

The pathologist who carried out the post-mortem, Dr Donald Teare, pronounced him to have overdosed on a drug named Carbital, a barbiturate composed of pentobarbital and bromide commonly used to treat insomnia. It had not been a massive overdose but what pharmacists term 'a low lethal one', suggesting that he'd been using the medication for some time. The pentobarbital tended to wear off first, causing bromide 'intoxication', which might make someone mistakenly duplicate the dose and so cross the safety line. No trace of any other drug had been found in him.

His regular doctor, Norman Cowan, confirmed having prescribed two Carbital nightly in the knowledge that it was 'a very safe hypnotic, widely used'. When Cowan had last seen him, on 16 August, moreover, he'd been 'in excellent health – I had never seen him better'.

That made three witnesses to Brian's ability to function normally for much of the time, however great the psychological or chemical stress on him. Yet the coroner, Gavin Thurston, seemed to have decided from the outset that he was a near-basket case, worn down by business worries and sleeplessness, and doggedly stuck to that view, despite all evidence to the contrary.

Before the hearing, Nat Weiss had submitted the 'love, flowers, bells' letter he'd brought from New York as proof of Brian's positive state of mind just before his death, but Thurston had dismissed it as irrelevant.

Nor did he think it necessary to hear from anyone involved in the discovery of the body except the butler, Antonio Garcia; not Joanne Newfield or Alistair Taylor or Peter Brown's doctor, John Gallwey, who'd helped break down his bedroom door before pronouncing him dead, or Garcia's wife, Maria, who'd been another eyewitness.

This urge to get the job done as quickly as possible without undue complications would be more glaringly evident three years later when Thurston conducted the inquest on Jimi Hendrix, calling almost no material witnesses and recording an open – i.e. indeterminate – verdict that would leave Hendrix's death forever a mystery.

So here he seemed blind to an obvious question: if Brian really had been so befogged by the Carbital as he lay on his bed, how could he have been simultaneously dealing with business correspondence and reading a film script and a novel and have fancied a chocolate digestive biscuit? In any case, he was the last person likely to miscalculate the dosage of anything from a heroin jack to an aspirin. As his brother Clive later told me, 'Brian always knew just what he was taking.'

A sceptical eye should also be cast on the findings of the pathologist Donald Teare, who would similarly partner Thurston in the Jimi Hendrix inquest in 1970. At the time one of only three pathologists covering the whole of London, Teare had a serious blot on his record that had in no way damaged his career.

In 1949, Teare's failure to spot a crucial piece of evidence was instrumental in the hanging of an illiterate Welsh lorry-driver named Timothy Evans for the murder of his wife and baby daughter, to which the serial killer John Christie would confess in 1953.

Gavin Thurston's summary of the proceedings suggested he had just awakened from a light doze. 'We have a picture here of a man who we heard was sensitive, inclined to be anxious and having a lot of trouble with sleeping. And on this occasion he took a singularly unwise dose of Carbitral.'

The verdict was accidental death from an 'incautious' self-overdose. Yet, unremarked by the coroner and mentioned, briefly, in only one newspaper report, was a piece of evidence suggesting something rather less straightforward.

It was Inspector Howlett's recollection that when he'd made his preliminary examination of Brian at 24 Chapel Street, 'some blood appeared to come from the nose and when I moved the body, more came out'.

* * *

On 17 October, a memorial service for Brian was held at the New London synagogue in Abbey Road, a minute's walk away from the recording studios to which he'd delivered authentic magic time after time.

All his principal discoveries, The Beatles, Gerry Marsden, Cilla Black and Billy J. Kramer, were present, together with older men whose fortunes he'd transformed, like George Martin and Dick James, early Liverpool allies like Bill Harry, Frieda Kelly and Bob Wooler, and representatives of the Finchley Jewish Youth Club, of which he'd been a conscientious president.

The Beatles wore black paper yarmulkes which kept slipping off their shaggy hair. Wendy Hanson's last duty for Brian was catching these and plonking them back on the appropriate head.

In contrast with his funeral, the rabbi, Dr Louis Jacobs, was eulogistic, praising him for 'encouraging young people to sing of love and peace rather than war and hate' and referencing his career in a quotation from the Old Testament Book of Proverbs: 'Seest thou a man diligent in his business? He shall stand before kings.'

Although Brian had indubitably stood before kings of a sort, he had been less than diligent where his private business was concerned. A few weeks before his death, he had claimed to be worth £7 million, yet the true figure was only £486,000. His 25 per cent commission of the £25 million the Beatles had earned by then had been mostly eaten up by his lavish lifestyle; he'd spent money as if there was no tomorrow and there hadn't been.

Strangely for somebody so meticulous (and with so many lawyers), he died intestate. Peter Brown claimed that he'd shown him a will to replace the angst-ridden one he'd drafted as a teenager, but it was never found. His mother and brother therefore inherited everything.

Clive Epstein took the helm at NEMS with the same reluctance that shy King George VI succeeded his charismatic brother Edward VIII after the latter's abdication in 1936. At Queenie's request, Brown lived for a time at 24 Chapel Street, his resemblance to Brian and her reliance on him seeming to guarantee him the role he'd understudied for so long.

At the office, he took over Brian's desk and personal assistant – even some of Brian's mannerisms. 'Brian used to have this habit of dropping all the music papers on the floor and saying, "I've finished with these now,"' Joanne Newfield recalled. 'Peter did exactly the same thing and used exactly the same words.'

Robert Stigwood walked away from NEMS with an undisclosed golden handshake and the pick of its artists, most valuably the Bee Gees. Brian's share of the company passed to Queenie; its name changed to Nemperor Holdings; it was sold on to an investment company two years later.

Stigwood would go on to huge success through the 1970s, managing major artists like Eric Clapton, scoring multiple hits on his RSO record label and producing blockbuster films like *Saturday Night Fever, Grease, Jesus Christ Superstar* and *Evita*. Statistically speaking, he could be termed another Brian Epstein but personality-wise one element would always be lacking: class.

* * *

It didn't take long for the Beatles to realise what they had lost.

After Brian's memorial there had been an emergency band-meeting where pragmatic Paul convinced the others that, however they felt, they should go ahead with their (or, rather, his) *Magical Mystery Tour* film.

But the intended carefree jaunt into the West Country on an old-fashioned motor bus with a cast of English eccentrics, like a mobile version of the *Sgt. Pepper* cover, turned into a woeful shambles. At least once a day after some fresh disaster, the same lament was heard among the several Beatle aides trying in vain to fill one pair of beautifully polished shoes:

'Brian would never have let it happen.'

22

'IT'S EASY TO KILL SOMEONE AND MAKE IT LOOK LIKE AN OVERDOSE'

After Brian, everything with The Beatles started to go downhill. *Magical Mystery Tour,* that chaotic home movie, became their first flop, although it was later to be cited as a precursor to absurdist comedy shows like *Monty Python's Flying Circus* and *Saturday Night Live.* It didn't help that it had been shot in colour when the overwhelming majority of television sets in Britain were still black-and-white. That was something which, assuredly, Brian would never have let happen.

Soon tiring of Indian mysticism (George excepted), they switched vertiginously to commerce with their Apple organisation, centred in an elegant Georgian town house in Savile Row, Mayfair. What Brian had envisaged as a single, manageable retail business mutated into several in alien fields like electronics and men's tailoring, run by friends living high on the hog at their vast expense. So much for the longstanding belief that The Beatles were infallible.

* * *

What Brian couldn't have prevented was John's extramarital affair with Yoko Ono, his increasing role as merely an assistant to Yoko's performance art stunts and the resulting collapse of the greatest songwriting partnership of all time. Apart from *Abbey Road*, made in 1969 by which time the four were barely on speaking-terms, they would create no more albums to enchant the world.

The search for a replacement for Brian, largely carried on by Paul as group-leader without portfolio, lasted two years and succeeded in establishing that another such being did not exist. The only halfway-plausible candidate was the New York showbusiness lawyer Lee Eastman, father of Paul's soon-to-be bride Linda, who by a strange coincidence had been born Leopold Epstein but changed his name to sound more WASPy.

Eastman's firm was already acting for The Beatles when John fell under the spell of the corkscrew-crooked Allen Klein, their overt stalker since 1965, and unilaterally appointed Klein to manage him. He persuaded George and Ringo to do likewise but Paul, wisely, refused. The four thereby lost the asset that had been second in importance after Brian: their total unity.

By 1969, they had effectively broken up, although this wouldn't become plain until Paul's High Court action to dissolve their partnership in 1971. The legalities, comparable to those of the Treaty of Versailles, were not completed until 1974.

* * *

I began researching my Beatles biography *Shout!* in late 1978, an epoch far removed from the carefree, Beatle-besotted 1960s. It was the nadir of Britain's so-called Winter of Discontent when strikes – or 'industrial action' as they'd been rebranded – crippled almost every public service, festering garbage sacks grew mountain-high and the sick shivered on stretchers in the freezing cold as ambulance crews searched for hospitals willing to accept them.

It was also the height of the Punk Revolution, whose raucous new demigods with Mohican haircuts and safety-pins through their cheeks demolished the notion that pop stardom might be about musical talent, originality or – God forbid! – charm.

The Beatles were still listened to and enjoyed, but their career had passed into legend like something from the Norse Sagas, to which, seemingly, nothing further could possibly be added. Nor were they considered a suitable subject for a serious biography as opposed to the pulpy paperbacks being churned out for their now ageing and embattled fans.

After a few weeks of floundering panic as I contemplated the millions of words already written about them and forgotten, I realised the only place to start my research was Liverpool, a city I'd visited only once before.

By then, it was but a shadow of the stately Victorian metropolis they and Brian had known as children. Its transatlantic luxury liner traffic had long since disappeared, shipbuilding on the River Mersey had shrunk almost to nothing and the City Council tottered permanently on the edge of bankruptcy.

Yet thus far almost nothing had been done to monetise its colossal legacy. The Cavern had been bulldozed in 1974 to make way for a car park. All that commemorated it in cobbled Mathew Street was a rather melancholy bronze bas-relief by local sculptor Arthur Dooley, depicting 'Four Lads Who Shook the World' but not mentioning who had brought about that shaking.

There were still many people around who'd played major roles in The Beatles' evolution –– such as their sacked drummer, Pete Best, their first approximation to a manager, Allan Williams, and The Cavern deejay, Bob Wooler – but been left behind when Brian transferred operations to London. I soon came to recognise those Liverpool eyes, still full of fathomless disappointment two decades later.

The pun-loving Wooler had an especially desolate look: he'd nicknamed Brian The Nemperor only to see 'Nemperor' become the London company's cable address, the name of Brian's American company with Nat Weiss (Nemperor Artists), even of the one that replaced NEMS when it passed to Queenie Epstein (Nemperor Holdings), all without acknowledgement, let alone payment.

Clive Epstein had by then long relinquished his unwanted chairmanship of Nemperor Holdings and gone into artist management, although more tentatively than his older brother. Portly and less than comfortable in his skin, Clive had none of Brian's energy or charisma but he was very helpful to me, driving me around in his Jaguar while giving me a potted history of the Epstein family business and an unenvious account of Brian's success in it for years prior to that lunchtime epiphany at The Cavern.

Most importantly, he allowed me access to Queenie, now exceedingly frail and with failing eyesight, who'd never spoken about Brian to a writer before. We met for afternoon tea in the Adelphi Hotel's Palm Court, which he'd once regarded as the ultimate in luxury and sophistication.

To begin with, I had to tread as carefully as if on our bone-china teacups, but gradually Queenie opened up, recalling how even as a small boy he'd advise her which dresses to wear on her evenings out with Harry, and the 'beautiful little cream and maroon Hillman Continental' they'd bought him for his twenty-first birthday.

Though still palpably in shock from his death, she admitted it had at least made her more open-minded about his sexuality; in its aftermath, the greatest kindness she'd received had been from those she termed 'Brian's people'.

One of Brian's people, albeit from a long way back, had increasingly come into Queenie's orbit since his death. This was Joe Flannery who, in their teens, had provided his one and only stable gay relationship, and remained as much in love with him as ever. On his birthday every year, by special rabbinical dispensation Joe brought a bunch of flowers to his grave at Long Lane cemetery.

Latterly he'd gone into partnership with Clive Epstein in a management agency named Carlton Brooke solely because of Clive's faint resemblance to Brian. 'Every time I hear him talking on the phone, I have to stop myself from saying, "I love you."'

* * *

Since I wasn't an authorised biographer, tracing possible sources of new information about The Beatles was a time-consuming and often frustrating process. In those days before the rise of social media and virtual disappearance of personal privacy, tracking down a potential contact with the primitive tools of phone calls and letters could take weeks or even months, never knowing if they'd agree to be interviewed or, if they did, whether it would be worth the trouble. My obsession with finding some obscure art-school crony of John's or ex-PA of George's felt like a fever of which I hoped one day to wake up cured.

I also first became aware of what I call biographer's luck, that with future books I'd come to expect and even depend on. With *Shout!* it took some time to materialise but when it did, it was astounding.

Top of my interview wish-list was Nicky Byrne, to whose Seltaeb company Brian had given the licensing of Beatles merchandise in America for a ludicrous 90–10 split in its favour. Byrne had last been heard of suing Brian and NEMS for $25 million in the New York Supreme Court, but since then seemed to have vanished.

I mentioned the problem to my next-door neighbour, the artist Adrian George, resigned to never locating Byrne and having somehow to camouflage the lack of his first-hand testimony in my book.

A couple of nights later, Adrian and his journalist partner Glenys Roberts attended a Tony Bennett concert at the Royal Albert Hall. Glenys being acquainted with Bennett, they paid him an after-show visit in his dressing-room, where he had an easel set up and relaxed between shows by painting watercolours. Whenever he was in London, he said, he liked to paint in company with a woman friend whose husband, Nicky, had once had something to do with The Beatles . . .

Byrne proved to be a small, jaunty man with somewhat the air of a minor duke in a P. G. Wodehouse story. Two decades on, there was little sign of the lifestyle he'd enjoyed while selling The Beatles to America: the private helicopter, the two chauffeured Cadillacs on stand-by around the clock, the unlimited charge accounts at top Fifth Avenue stores. He and his painter wife were 'house-sitting', as he put it, for a friend in Wimbledon, suggesting they currently had no home of their own.

He was, of course, a hostile witness who still resented Brian's capsizing of the Seltaeb merchandising bonanza in America before it had achieved a fraction of its true potential. In the aftermath, Byrne had dealt directly with some of the retail chains and manufacturers to have lost heavily without hope of redress.

The one exception was the manufacturer's son whose father had suffered a fatal heart attack because of the stress and who'd threatened to take out a contract on Brian as the person directly responsible. 'Wait until I've finished with him in the courts,' Byrne had bantered, thinking it just talk.

In the end, he told me, he'd settled his $25 million lawsuit against NEMS for just $10,000. After receiving an offer to manage the Four Seasons (the band not the hotel) but declining it because of the New Jersey Mafia's involvement in their career, he'd decided to buy a boat and sail away to a new life in the Bahamas.

Just before leaving New York, he said he'd received a mysterious telephone call. 'This man's voice, very low, very polite, said, "Mr Byrne, I understand that your suit against Brian Epstein is settled, is that right?" I said, "Yes – and what's it got to do with you?" But whoever it was just hung up.

'In August I was in Florida – actually on my boat – and I got another phone call in that same very quiet, polite voice. "Mr Byrne," it said, "you're going to hear soon that Brian Epstein has met with an accident."'

(It was an eerie echo of the call, supposedly from the *Daily*

Express, to 24 Chapel Street when none of the six people there had let a word of Brian's death leak out, asking if it was true that he was 'terribly ill'.)

There was no reason to suspect Byrne of inventing his account; despite his straitened circumstances, he never asked any payment from me nor published a book himself. However, the dates don't line up. According to Brian's punctilious associate, Geoffrey Ellis, the Seltaeb lawsuit was settled in January 1967, but his death wasn't until six months later.

In December 1980, as I was putting the final touches to *Shout!*, John was assassinated by a demented fan, resulting in a global outpouring of grief and a second wave of Beatlemania that has continued to grow exponentially ever since.

My book thus had a horrible topicality, increased by its speculation that the manager who'd been so helplessly and hopelessly in love with John might himself have been murdered. Taking Nicky Byrne's testimony seriously got me accused of sensationalism in some quarters, but I could hardly have ignored it.

Far from sensationalising, *Shout!* didn't mention my discovery at the tail-end of my research that at the last weeks of Brian's life he'd written two suicide notes, or perhaps drafts of a single one, which he'd evidently decided not to use and his PA Joanne Newfield had found in his bedroom after his death.

When Queenie and Clive Epstein heard that I knew about the notes, I had both of them on the phone at once, begging me to leave it out of the book. I've never forgotten their voices down the line chorusing 'Please, Philip ... *please*, Philip.'

They were good people who'd already suffered grievously, so I agreed.

Later, I had to break it to them that Brian might have been

a victim of foul play. But that seemed to trouble them less than the thought of his even contemplating one of Judaism's great sins.

* * *

Brian's death remained a cold case for me during the years when I followed up *Shout!* with individual biographies of John, Paul, George and sundry other rock legends. It was briefly warmed over by my Jimi Hendrix book, which set out in full the deficiencies of Jimi's inquest by Westminster's indolent coroner, Gavin Thurston, assisted by the discredited pathologist Donald Teare, and caused me to reflect how equally inadequate Brian's had been at their hands.

My interest blazed up anew, however, in 2024, when I read my research associate Peter Trollope's notes of his revelatory encounter with Reggie Kray in Parkhurst prison during the mid-'80s. This ultimate insider in British organised crime seemingly knew for certain that Brian had been murdered, albeit not by his own 'Firm' ('It wasn't us') but, he'd hinted, by the American Mafia to which the Firm had been fraternally linked.

Kray's professional observation that 'it's easy to kill someone and make it look like an overdose' took my mind back to the elaborate arrangement of Brian's deathbed where he'd supposedly lain in a barbiturate stupor – the business correspondence, the *Yellow Submarine* script, the novel with his place marked, the chocolate digestive biscuits, all rather like theatrical props. And also to the inquest statement by police inspector George Howlett, never subsequently followed up, that 'some blood appeared to come from the nose and when I moved the body, more came out'.

All one can say is that if someone really had been stalking Brian with evil intent that August Bank Holiday weekend of 1967, they would have needed to be extraordinarily close behind him to be aware of his sudden departure from Kingsley Hill back to London, and extraordinarily cat-footed to have entered 24 Chapel Street, found their way to his bedroom, carried out their mission without noise and exited without detection.

Nor was the matter to end there. Sixteen months after Brian's death, his former lawyer David Jacobs was found hanging from a satin cord in his garage in genteel Hove. In recent weeks Jacobs had sought police protection and told a private detective he considered hiring, 'I'm in terrible trouble ... they're all after me.'

'They' were presumed to be his long-time clients the Kray Twins – hello again, Reggie – after he'd refused to act for them in the joint murder trial that would end with their getting life. But there was a much bigger 'they' with a much deeper-seated grudge: Jacobs had had sole charge of distributing Brian's non-Seltaeb merchandise licences so was directly responsible for the resultant chaos and cancellation of Beatles-themed goods worth $78 million. In the US, losing people much less than that could get you killed.

The inquest verdict was suicide, even though the evidence hardly pointed to the lawyer's having been suicidal. The day before his death he'd sent a young actress friend a postcard inviting her to lunch at Le Caprice restaurant in London the following week.

But why make away with him so long after Brian's death, if that was what happened? Was it a case of revenge being a dish best served cold?

* * *

Today John and Paul's modest childhood homes are National Trust properties; John has had Merseyside's former Speke airport named after him; George's tiny birthplace in Wavertree has been belatedly awarded an English Heritage blue plaque and Ringo's in Madryn Street is part of a redevelopment scheme wherein his name will doubtless be everywhere.

Yet Brian has no blue plaque in the city he glorified and glamorised beyond its wildest dreams; only a brown one, paid for by private donations, at his birthplace in Rodney Street. 197 Queens Drive, the house in which he grew up, and where so much ground-breaking Beatles business was transacted, remains in private ownership, unmarked save by the tour buses from the city centre that stop to look at it all year round.

Similarly in London, despite repeated applications by his old friend Geoffrey Ellis, English Heritage refused to grant 24 Chapel Street a blue plaque without ever giving a reason.

In 2014, Ellis found a potent ally in David Stark, the musician, PR and founder of the Songlink organisation who, like many in the business, was mystified by Brian's exclusion from a company now including John Lennon, Jimi Hendrix and Bob Marley.

Stark proposed the alternative of a plaque at Sutherland House, the office block in Argyll Street next to the London Palladium where NEMS Enterprises had once occupied the fifth floor. There the only permission needed was from the building's freeholders and was readily given so long as it didn't cost them anything.

The plaque was unveiled to mark what would have been

Brian's eightieth birthday in a ceremony attended by, among others, Ellis, Stark, Tony Bramwell, Bill Harry and songwriter Mitch Murray. Its position above a Five Guys hamburger restaurant is not inappropriate for someone generally agreed to have been 'the Fifth Beatle'.

Also in 2014, he was posthumously inducted into the Rock & Roll Hall of Fame – although with his numerous discoveries he'd effectively created a rival one of his own.

His proposer, Martin Lewis, had been a protégé of The Beatles' press officer, Derek Taylor, and gone on to co-create and produce the *Secret Policeman's Ball* series of benefit shows, albums and films for the human rights organisation Amnesty International.

Lewis orchestrated an international campaign on Brian's behalf with the support of George Martin, Nat Weiss, Geoffrey Ellis, the promoter Sid Bernstein and many others, while proselytising for him in the media, arranging the reissue of his 1964 autobiography, *A Cellarful of Noise*, and writing a new introduction for it.

Disappointingly, Lewis recalls, little support came from other pop impresarios who like Brian were Jewish and gay. 'They said words to the effect, "Look, he's dead . . . he can't help anyone in the business. So why should anyone waste time campaigning for him?"'

It took sixteen years for Lewis to get him into the RRHF – and then only in a half-hearted way. He was put into the non-performers section – by then renamed The Ahmet Ertegun Award, after the co-founder of Atlantic Records – together with the Rolling Stones' former manager, Andrew Oldham, his one-time hireling for NEMS' publicity department. 'Two bygone

British managers squeezed into one segment,' Lewis recalls with disgust, 'like a supermarket special.'

Normally, inductees had their own individual slots of around fifteen to twenty minutes with fulsome introductions and tributes on film but in the 2014 ceremony's five-and-a-half hours, Brian and Oldham were given five minutes between them – as Lewis notes, 'an entire three quarters of one per cent of the show's running-time allocated to the man who gave the world The Beatles'.

Almost as long in gestation was the statue of Brian finally unveiled in Whitechapel, Liverpool, near the site of the long-gone NEMS store, in 2022 around the fifty-fifth anniversary of his death. Cast in bronze, only a little more than life-size and a surprisingly good likeness, it could almost be the real Brian, heading resolutely for The Cavern on the most important day of his life.

His commitment to the stage – his abiding first love – was acknowledged by the renaming of a Liverpool theatre from the Neptune to the Epstein and complete refurbishment, including a 'Brian's Bar'. It reopened impressively in 2011 but over the years has faced declining audiences and recurrent threats to its funding by Liverpool Corporation and at the time of writing its future looks precarious. One can imagine how Brian would have hated that and longed to have a shot at turning it around.

Now his chief contribution to the theatre is the life-story that went so immeasurably far beyond it. He's been the subject of two well-received plays, Andrew Sherlock's *The Man Who Made The Beatles* with soap star Andrew Lancel in the name role and Tom Wright's *Please Please Me*, reflecting his latter role as a martyr-stroke-hero of the LGBTQ community. Such is his hold on the imagination of young actors that more will likely follow. He's centre-stage at last, if not quite in the way he always wanted.

Bringing that life-story to the cinema screen has been more problematic. As a result of *Shout!*, I was myself commissioned to write scripts about him by two different producers. The first project soon fell by the wayside but the second seemed a certainty as it already had Jude Law attached to play Brian. Sadly, financing the film proved so tortuous that Law grew too old for the role and it had to be abandoned.

In 2024 came the biopic *Midas Man*, a weird choice of title since Brian's golden touch tragically failed him in the end. It had a powerful central performance by Jacob Fortune-Lloyd but was sunk by its terrible script, stingy production-values and total lack of empathy for the period. Three different directors and a list of producers, assistant producers and associate producers almost as numerous as the cast irresistibly brought to mind the definition of a camel as 'a horse designed by a committee.'

All biopics bend facts and reshuffle events but this one simply left most of them out. Brian's epic moments with his boys – the madness of Beatlemania or the furore over John's 'more popular than Jesus' remark – consisted only of clunky monologues to camera by Fortune-Loyd with a background of stock news-footage.

Then in 2025 the Oscar-winning director Sir Sam Mendes began production of four biopics, each dealing with an individual Beatle. The top-tier playwrights Jez Butterworth, Peter Straughan and Jack Thorne were recruited to allow all four to be released at once, supposedly in 2028. The difference from other Beatles films, a largely sorry bunch, was that this one 'had the music'.

Brian was to be played by James Norton, one of the most acclaimed young actors of his generation both in the theatre and long-running television series like *Happy Valley* and *Grantchester*. Brian no doubt would have found it piquant that his alter-ego had been raised a Catholic, read theology at Cambridge (gaining first-class honours) but became a Buddhist and, like him, left the Royal Academy of Dramatic Art without graduating. Maybe smiled a little, too, over Norton's very obvious heterosexuality.

Brian had waited long years for someone like this, with range and insight enough to convey his every paradox: the self-invention and destruction, the lovability and lovelessness, the daring and the doubt.

Waited, one might say, at Liverpool's Beatles Story museum, just round the corner from a glass case containing effigies of his boys in their *Sgt. Pepper* satins. Arranged on a dressmaker's form is one of his dark blue cashmere and wool topcoats from Aquascutum which in its own right attracts thousands of sight-seers each year.

Brian would love that.

Acknowledgements

I have of course written about Brian Epstein before, in my Beatles biography, *Shout!*, and individual biographies of John Lennon, Paul McCartney and George Harrison. However, those earlier portraits dealt insufficiently with the anti-Semitism Brian always faced, which seemed to have dwindled in the years since his death but now is sickeningly on the rise again. His predicament as a gay man in a savagely homophobic world, I regret, was similarly understated.

This book is dedicated to Peter Trollope, a beyond-brilliant researcher for my music biographies since *John Lennon: The Life* despite recurrent bouts of ill-health, who tragically passed away in 2024. Peter's academic daughter, Thea, took his place, proving herself every bit as dedicated and tenacious as her dad.

I was lucky once more to have the generous help of Bill Harry, The Beatles' teenage friend and founder/editor of the iconic *Mersey Beat* newspaper. As well as fact-checking my manuscript, Bill provided photographs of Brian that had never previously been published. Grateful thanks also for their fact-checking to Alan Clayson and producer Martin Lewis, the latter a tireless advocate for Brian through the decades when his achievements were all but forgotten.

My sincerest gratitude to my wonderful and much-missed editor at Simon & Schuster, Suzanne Baboneau; to Ben Schafer at Hachette US and Sophia Akhtar at Simon & Schuster; to my agents, Fiona Petheram at PFD in London and Christopher Combemale at SLL in New York; to David Stark for the image of Brian's blue plaque in Argyll Street. And to Sue and Jessica, my everlasting love.

Philip Norman
London, 2026

Source notes

Prologue: Ronnie Kray's big idea

Peter Trollope archive. *The Profession of Violence: The Rise & Fall of the Kray Twins* by John Pearson (Weidenfeld & Nicolson, 1972). *Shout! The Beatles in their Generation* by Philip Norman.

1: 'Eppy'

Shout!, *John Lennon: The Life*, *Paul McCartney: The Biography* and *George Harrison: The Reluctant Beatle* by Philip Norman.

2: 'Help me, I am lost'

Peter Trollope archive. *Liverpool Echo*. Author interviews with Queenie Epstein, Clive Epstein, Joe Flannery and Malcolm Shifrin. *Shout!* by Philip Norman.

3: 'FORWARD, BRIAN'

Author interviews with Queenie Epstein, Clive Epstein, Joe Flannery, Malcolm Shifrin and Rex Makin. *Epstein* by Ray Coleman (Viking, 1989). *Shout!, John Lennon, Paul McCartney* and *George Harrison* by Philip Norman. *Alan Turing: The Enigma* by Andrew Hodges (Random House, 1992).

4: 'THE IMMACULATE DECEPTION'

Author interviews with Queenie Epstein, Clive Epstein, Joe Flannery and Joanna Dunham. *Epstein* by Ray Coleman. *The Love You Make: An Insider's Story of the Beatles* by Peter Brown and Steven Gaines (Macmillan, 1983). *I Should Have Known Better: The Beatles, Brian Epstein, Elton John and Me* by Geoffrey Ellis (Thorogood, 2004). *Shout!, John Lennon, Paul McCartney* and *George Harrison* by Philip Norman.

5: 'MISTER BRIAN AND MR X'

Author interviews with Clive Epstein, Joe Flannery, Peter Brown, Geoffrey Ellis, Larry Parnes and Vince Eager. *Epstein* by Ray Coleman. *Standing in the Wings: The Beatles, Brian Epstein and Me* by Joe Flannery with Mike Brocken (The History Press, 2013). *Shout!, John Lennon, Paul McCartney* and *George Harrison* by Philip Norman.

6: 'Right then, Brian – manage us'

Author interviews with Bill Harry, Peter Brown, Tony Sheridan, Bert Kaempfert and Bob Wooler. *Cavern Club, The Inside Story* by Debbie Greenberg (Jorvik Press, 2016). *Shout!, John Lennon, Paul McCartney* and *George Harrison* by Philip Norman.

7: I'll always take care of John'

Author interviews with Rex Makin, Bob Wooler, Allan Williams, Mona Best, Pete Best, Mimi Smith, Bert Kaempfert, Tony Barrow, Neil Aspinall and Dick Rowe. *Shout!, John Lennon, Paul McCartney* and *George Harrison* by Philip Norman.

8: 'They looked as if they'd been steam-cleaned'

Author interviews with Sam Leach, Brian Kelly, Frieda Kelly, Tony Bramwell, Ray McFall, Geoffrey Ellis, Pete Best, George Martin, Gerry Marsden and Joe Flannery. *Shout!, John Lennon, Paul McCartney* and *George Harrison* by Philip Norman.

9: 'The most hated man in Liverpool'

Author interviews with Horst Fascher, Astrid Kirchherr, Millie Sutcliffe, Pete Best, Mona Best, Cynthia Lennon, Joe Flannery, George Martin, Sam Leach and Little Richard. *Shout!, John Lennon, Paul McCartney* and *George Harrison* by Philip Norman.

10: 'Have you heard about the boys?'

Author interviews with Queenie Epstein, Clive Epstein, Tony Calder, Dick James, George Martin, Helen Shapiro, Frieda Kelly, Giorgio Gomelsky, Larry Parnes, Tony Bramwell, Andrew Oldham, Cynthia Lennon, Billy J. Kramer, Dot Rhone, Bob Wooler and Yoko Ono. *Shout!*, *John Lennon*, *Paul McCartney* and *George Harrison* by Philip Norman.

11: The Nemperor

Author interviews with George Martin, Bob Wooler, Cilla Black, Richard Lester, Walter Shenson, Lionel Bart, Sid Bernstein, Walter Hofer, Geoffrey Ellis, Edward Marke, Nicky Byrne, Lord Peregrine Eliot and Malcolm Evans. *Shout!*, *John Lennon*, *Paul McCartney* and *George Harrison* by Philip Norman.

12: 'No, not my boys!'

Author interviews with Brian Sommerville, Wendy Hanson, Cynthia Lennon, George Martin, Nicky Byrne, Lord Peregrine Eliot, Sid Bernstein and Mal Evans. *Shout!*, *John Lennon*, *Paul McCartney* and *George Harrison* by Philip Norman.

13: 'He was always locked in a cell'

Author interviews with Joe Flannery, Tony Bramwell, Robert Freeman, Brian Joyce, Walter Strach, Cilla Black, Gerry

Marsden, Billy J. Kramer, Pattie Boyd, Johnny Hutchinson, Bill Harry, Brian Matthew and Sandra Caron. *The Brian Epstein Story* by Deborah Geller (Faber & Faber, 2000) from BBC2 *Arena* documentary edited by Anthony Wall. *Shout!, John Lennon, Paul McCartney* and *George Harrison* by Philip Norman.

14: 'Mr Brian Epstein at Home'

Author interviews with Derek Taylor, Nicky Byrne, Lord Peregrine Eliot and Brian Matthew. *A Cellarful of Noise* by Brian Epstein (Souvenir Press, 1964). *The Brian Epstein Story* by Deborah Geller. *'Shout!, John Lennon, Paul McCartney* and *George Harrison* by Philip Norman.

15: 'Our MBE means Mr Brian Epstein'

Author interviews with Allen Klein, Derek Taylor, Tony Bramwell, Peter Brown, Geoffrey Ellis, Wendy Hanson, and Nat Weiss. Audio interview with Joanne Newfield by John Fielding of *Sunday Times. The Brian Epstein Story* by Deborah Geller. *Shout!, John Lennon, Paul McCartney* and *George Harrison* by Philip Norman.

16: 'I didn't know they let queers in here now'

Author interviews with Tony Barrow, Mal Evans, George Martin and Nat Weiss. *The Brian Epstein Story* by Deborah Geller. *Shout!, John Lennon, Paul McCartney* and *George Harrison* by Philip Norman.

17: 'That was the start of his depression'

Author interviews with Tony Barrow, Mal Evans, George Martin and Nat Weiss. *The Brian Epstein Story* by Deborah Geller. *Shout!*, *John Lennon*, *Paul McCartney* and *George Harrison* by Philip Norman.

18: 'Please bank my happiness'

Author interviews with Peter Brown, Geoffrey Ellis, Sid Bernstein, Nat Weiss, Sandra Caron, George Martin, Wendy Hanson, Nicky Byrne, Larry Parnes, Keith Richards and Peter Trollope archives. Audio interview with Joanne Newfield. *The Brian Epstein Story* by Deborah Geller. *Shout!*, *John Lennon*, *Paul McCartney* and *George Harrison* by Philip Norman.

19: 'Eppy is still together'

Author interviews with Peter Brown, George Martin, Nat Weiss, Walter Shenson, Derek Taylor, Joan Taylor, Brian Joyce and Cynthia Lennon. Audio interview with Joanne Newfield. *The Brian Epstein Story* by Deborah Geller. *Shout!*, *John Lennon*, *Paul McCartney* and *George Harrison* by Philip Norman.

20: 'Beware the Ides of March'

Author interviews with Peter Brown and Geoffrey Ellis. Audio interview with Joanne Newfield. *The Brian Epstein*

Story by Deborah Geller. *All You Need Is Love: The End of the Beatles* by Peter Brown and Steven Gaines (Monoray, 2024). *Shout!*, *John Lennon*, *Paul McCartney* and *George Harrison* by Philip Norman.

21: 'HIS LAST STARTLING WORDS'

Author interviews with Queenie Epstein, Clive Epstein, George Martin, Nat Weiss and Peter Brown. Audio interview with Joanne Newfield. Inquest reports from *The Times* and *Evening Standard*. *The Brian Epstein Story* by Deborah Geller. *Shout!*, *John Lennon*, *Paul McCartney* and *George Harrison* by Philip Norman.

22: 'IT'S EASY TO KILL SOMEONE AND MAKE IT LOOK LIKE AN OVERDOSE'

Author interviews with Queenie Epstein, Clive Epstein, Joe Flannery, Nicky Byrne, Martin Lewis and David Stark. Peter Trollope archive. Press reports of David Jacobs inquest.

INDEX

BE indicates Brian Epstein.